Moving Worlds

For Uma and Rosie

Moving Worlds

Edited by
TIM EDENSOR
and
MIJ KELLY

Polygon
EDINBURGH

© Tim Edensor and Mij Kelly

Polygon
22 George Square, Edinburgh

Set in Linotron Bembo
by Photoprint, Torquay, and
printed and bound in Great Britain by
Bell and Bain Limited
Glasgow

British Library Cataloguing
  in Publication Data
Moving worlds : personal recollections
  of twenty-one immigrants to Edinburgh.
1. Scotland.   Immigrants.   Social Life.
Biographies.   Collections
I. Edensor, Tim   II. Kelly, Mij
941.1082'0922
ISBN 0 7486 6002 X
      0 7486 6011 9 pbk

The Publisher acknowledges subsidy
from the Scottish Arts Council
towards the publication of this volume

Contents

Acknowledgements

First and foremost, we owe an enormous debt of gratitude to all those without whom *Moving Worlds* would have remained an unrealised idea – the interviewees. Whether or not their stories are represented here, they all gave freely of their time, put up with our phonecalls for more information and, in many cases, supplied us with photographs.

We must also extend our warmest thanks to Myra Martin, Esther Robertson, Nahid Aslam, Reza Azam, Gary Robertson, Vicki Hobson, Fiona O'Kane and, particularly, to Kate O'Brien, for their help and enthusiasm in adding to the collection of interviews.

We received help and advice from too many individuals and organisations to list here, but we would especially like to thank The Multicultural Education Centre, Roundabout International Centre, Neighbourhood English Teaching, Gregor Robertson, Mr Rabstaff, Sylvia Dimes and Alison Gunn.

Thanks are also due to Edinburgh District Council for providing us with a grant to buy cassettes; to Caroline Paton, Sheila Stringer, and Chris Wheeldon for typing up individual stories; and, most of all, to Rosemary Williams who transformed some 300 tattered pages of bad handwriting into a similar number of pages of immaculate typescript.

All royalties from the sale of this book go towards the Moving Worlds Fund which has been set up to provide financial support to other local multicultural projects.

Introduction

This book arose out of a discussion about the power of oral history to rescue the individual from the stereotype. The way in which people tell the story of their lives, how they have dealt with their experiences, how they look upon their past and face the future, seemed to be more emotionally involving than almost any fiction. Somebody pointed out that the stereotypes used to define immigrants in our society are particularly rigid and oppressive, and the *Moving Worlds* project was born. This book gives the lie to all those glib generalisations about immigrants, and it does so as directly and as potently as possible, through the experiences, personalities and words of its contributors.

Edinburgh is not generally regarded as a multicultural city. Nevertheless, it does contain a great cultural diversity and is a good example of those urban centres in the UK where the presence of ethnic minorities is overlooked. In contrast, areas of high ethnic population, and particularly areas of black protest, receive a great deal of (mostly adverse) media attention, which not only gives a false geography of immigration but also an incomplete picture of the experience of immigrants in the UK.

Despite the city's reputation for bourgeois insularity, Edinburgh folk have a long tradition of contact with peoples from other lands. Scotland's own turbulent history was the cause of mass emigration in the 19th and early 20th centuries. At the same time, because of political and economic pressures in their own countries, emigrés from Eastern Europe, Ireland and Italy were arriving in Edinburgh and Leith. The census records for 1891 (which are the most recent available) show a massive influx of Highlanders – especially Orcadians and Shetlanders – and Irish, and the beginnings of immigration from Europe. One tenement block in Commercial Street in Leith housed three Germans, two Swedes, one Norwegian, a Dane and an Italian.

The movement of people has been a constant throughout history and is not confined to the past three decades. As a result, Edinburgh

1

is home to long-established, as well as more recent, immigrant communities and boasts a wonderful diversity of cultures. We have tried to reflect this richness in the stories included here, which range from that of a Lithuanian man who came to Scotland in 1913 to that of a Vietnamese girl who arrived in 1980.

Something we had not anticipated, but which simply arose because we were interviewing people who had come to Edinburgh from abroad (as refugees, as workers for the 'Mother' country, dislocated through war, chance or economic forces) was the way their tales illuminated certain world events and trends, and highlighted the vital human details obscured in many historical accounts.

The drama and immediacy of the stories demanded that *Moving Worlds* be presented as a collection of narratives, in which we have tried to reflect the emphases and ideas of the storytellers with as little mediation as possible. But oral history has certain limitations and it is important that we outline our methods and approach.

Perhaps the first thing we ought to explain are the criteria behind our choice of interviewees. We were primarily interested in the economic and political factors that lie behind much immigration. We felt it was necessary to stress that as an imperial and economic power Britain has actively encouraged immigrant labour from colonies and former colonies, and also to show how political repression and upheavals elsewhere have forced emigrants and refugees to come to Britain.

So that was our starting point, but obviously the interviewing process has been informed and guided by the concerns of the participants. Something that quickly became clear was the salience of colour prejudice which dispelled the popular Scots myth that racism stops north of Gretna Green. Although it would be an oversimplification to pretend that all the black people we spoke to wanted to articulate their experiences and feelings about racism, or that discrimination is only directed at those immigrants who are black, as one respondent said, 'Your colour can't hide . . . the blacks . . . are obvious and you can tell there's a lot of them here. But there's really not a lot more than other immigrants'. That this colour factor has been reinforced by the state, particularly through its immigration policy, was spelt out by one interviewee: 'Every country has the right to control people coming in, but as soon as you legitimise the treatment of different groups differently, then you legitimise racism.' As a result, the crude equation that 'all immigrants are black' and 'all blacks are immigrants' prevails – although black people form less than 40% of immigrants to the UK. We are aware that the proportion of stories by black people included here belies this statistic, but we wanted to counterbalance the racism that creates stereotypes and muffles and distorts the voices of black people in this country.

Of the 70 interviews carried out on behalf of the *Moving Worlds* project only a fraction could be included here. The scope of the project meant that in our selection we have been able to include people from a wide range of political, cultural and religious backgrounds and could reflect a diversity of experience, whether determined by sex, age or class. Inevitably, though, there are some glaring omissions. Only a handful of the interviews were carried out by someone from the same community as the interviewee, and it is difficult to gauge how this affected the response we received. Nevertheless, most people were pleased to share their story with us. The world outside their community seldom shows interest in their heritage – a sad comment on the cultural insularity of British society. The problem of our only speaking English meant that certain groups of people were neglected. There were those, also, to whom we could not gain access because of cultural restraints. These are often the individuals who are most isolated and we hope that their experiences can be recorded by researchers more suitably equipped than ourselves.

As people's memories can be faulty we have attempted to check historical details and to provide further information where necessary in the notes. We tried not to be rigid in our approach to interviewing and although we had a series of set questions, we felt it was important to let the interviewee steer the course of the conversation. Undoubtedly people are selective in their recollection of the past, but rather than regarding this as a weakness in oral history, we see it as a strength, for it shows people defining and making sense of their lives, and no matter how painful or unpleasant their experience, this makes it impossible to perceive them as victims defeated by forces beyond their comprehension.

Nearly everyone we approached let us into their lives, if only for a few hours, and shared their history and ideas with us. We came away disarmed by their strength and individuality. These encounters broadened our field of vision and made us realise the potential for cultural exchange and enrichment in our society. As editors, our main aim has been to pass on this appreciation to the reader, and offer *Moving Worlds* as a tribute to all those who were interviewed.

MAX

'Scotland's Been no Bad to Me'

Max Mendick came to Edinburgh in 1913, after spending the
earlier part of his life in a small village in Lithuania. He was
the oldest person to be interviewed for this book.

I was born in 1897 in Lithuania, Russia, in a small village called
Komai. I'll give you an idea o' the size o' it if you like: when a
peasant with a horse and cart came into the village, by the time the
cart was in the village the horse's head was oot the other end! There
were several streets, with a market place in the centre and a church at
one end with a clock which very seldom worked. There were about
80 Jewish families and the rest were Catholics. There were two kinds
o' Jews, a wee bit different from each other. There were more o' us.
They lived on the other side o' the village. We had one synagogue
and they had another.

We had quite a big piece o' land for ourselves about the most land
that anyone had in the village, and we had a kind o' double house and
a big stable. My mother grew cucumbers on the land. The Lithuanian
government had no money to pay for imports so they made a law: if
you had a piece o' land you had to grow something on it or it would
be taken away from you. That's why she used to grow cucumbers.
See, my brother had a pony and cart. He'd load it up with cucumbers
and take it to a bigger town about 17 kilometres away. There was a
market there every Monday. When people asked him, 'What did you
get for your cucumbers?' he replied, 'If I'd had to hire a horse and cart
I would have been out o' pocket'. Everybody was poor. There were
only a few big towns that had banks. At that time, young children,
they died, a lot o' them. You see, there was no doctor. I mean, if
a woman had to have a caesarian birth she'd die. Same with illness:
they'd just lie on their bed and there'd be nothing much they could
do about it whether Jew or Gentile.

I went to the Hebrew school until I was 13 years o' age. Then I
would have gone to a higher class but my mother had no money to
pay for it, so I came oot. I helped my mother to start with. She was

a sort o' hawker. She went round the villages, to the peasants and the landowners, and she had a wee basket with needles and thread and a whole lot o' other things, all sorts, you know. She would sell them all about and they would pay her with tatties and corn and wheat and stuff like that. When I reached 14 years o' age, I went oot on my own. I used to go to a village and buy six dozen eggs or so from the women there, and skins from their husbands, from sheep and other animals, and bring them back in a big box. I would sell them to a wholesaler and he would gather up more skins and then take them to Riga, the nearest big town, to sell. Mind you, under the Tsar's law a Jew wasnae allowed to sell on the market in Riga. He would engage someone to sell for him and he would stand on the corner lookin' on.

There were, within a few miles, dozens o' villages close to one another with landowners and peasants. We got on well with the peasants and had no bother from them at all. But you see, Russia is a rural country. Even now, with 270 million people, only 70 million live in the big cities like Moscow, Leningrad, Kiev, Odessa. When I was there most o' the people were just small peasants. It's not like here where a farmer's got 1,000 acres. The biggest town in Lithuania was Kaunas, the capital. It had a population o' 90,000. In our village we got on very well with the Catholics. You see, the small villages had no problem with the Catholics. We'd have business with them, trade with them. Jewish boys and Catholic girls would speak together in my day, but before that the Jewish life and the Catholic life had been altogether separate. Very seldom would you get a Jewish boy marrying a Catholic girl or a Catholic boy marrying a Jewish girl. It maybe happened once in a hundred years.

Standin' in the village was a church, and on Sunday they used to go to church and then they used to come out and get drunk – nearly every house sold vodka. It was like a public house; you'd buy half a bottle o' vodka, sit down with your drink an' the proprietor gave you bread and herring. A Jew wasnae allowed to sell alcohol, but there was a police sergeant in our village and we used to give him a rouble or two now and again so he kept quiet. We used to have markets several times a year. People came from great distances, buyin' and sellin'. An' there was one Catholic, he lived in the very centre o' the market place, and he started sellin' vodka. Bein' a Catholic, he got a licence and he wasnae frightened; but people didnae go to him. I asked one o' the customers, 'How is it that when one o' your own kind has a pub and you can sit and drink there and nobody worries about it, you choose to go to the unlicensed Jewish house?' 'Aye', he said, 'If I get drunk in his pub he'll turn me out on to the street. If I get drunk in your house and the bottle's empty and I throw it through your window, you don't say anythin', do you? That's the difference!'

Now and again we found a Jew on the road, killed. I remember one Jew, travellin' to the next town with somethin' to sell, was killed. All that he had was three roubles on him and that was stolen. The police came and made enquiries but they said, 'We cannae find anybody'. That happened now and again, but it was nothing to worry about, really. But in the big towns, Odessa, Kiev, and in the Ukraine, they were tremendously anti-Jewish and it was very bad. But who created these pogroms? There were so many millions o' peasants and beggars who had no homes, no work, no nothin'. They'd gather in crowds and come into a town. If anyone touched anyone, one o' their own, they would kill Jews and burn their houses and rob whatever they could. It would maybe go on for several days and then the Tsar or police would send in the Cossacks to stop it. The rich Jews would help the poor to build up their lives again. When I lived there, most o' the pogroms had been stopped because the Tsar was always borrowin' money from Britain and America and they started complainin' about such pogroms.

My father had served in the Tsar's army before he got married. Then, in 1903, there were rumours about a war with Japan and he was called up for manoeuvres. If a man joined the army and went to war, his wife an' kids could starve as far as the authorities were concerned. They didnae pay you anythin' at all, no like here, apart from a few coppers to buy cigarettes. That was the Tsar's rule. My father wanted to get away from the rumours o' war and try to do better for himself. There was no future in Lithuania. So he decided to leave and come to Britain – not because o' anti-Semitism, but because he couldnae make a livin' there. There were plenty o' Jews in Russia who were rich under the Tsar. They didnae come here, but the poor came. And thousands and thousands o' peasants went to America. Some became miners and then went back home and bought farms. So anyway, my father had a brother in Leeds, who'd come here before him. He arrived in Leeds and they had a quarrel. They couldnae agree so my father came to Edinburgh. He hadnae seen any opportunities in Leeds and he'd heard that there were a lot o' folk from our village in Edinburgh. My father was one o' the Jews who didnae make a great success here. He sold cheap jewellery to the farmers. He had this jewellery box, and he used to gather up most o' his jewels in a lodging-house in Galashiels, and he'd travel to farms and sell watches to farmers. Most Jews did that kind o' thing, some would sell jewellery, some would sell slippers, some would sell drapery, some would sell pictures. He didnae do very well anyway.

Some Jews came here and didnae like it. I remember when I was a kid, an old Jew, who'd been to Edinburgh, came to our house and told my mother not to go there, and to get my father to come back to Lithuania. 'In Edinburgh', he said, 'you've got to wash stairs! If you don't send your kids to school, the police will come and take them away from you!' He was absolutely appalled. [laughs]. Anyway, my father used to send letters tellin' us to come here. But there couldnae have been a great deal o' love between my mother and my father. You see, he didnae have to send money to bring us here, because we had property there which could have been sold to get us here and a great deal more. But she didnae, my mother never left, and eventually in 1913 I and my older sister decided to come here. We had to report that it was OK here and then she'd come too with my younger brother and sister. We wrote and told them to come but then as soon as she sold oot and started plannin', war broke out in 1914. During the First World War the village was burnt down along with our house.[1] I remember in my little lifetime there I saw fires twice. If the wind was blowin' and the fire started in the middle, it would burn half the village down. If it started at the end o' the village and the wind was blowin' towards the town, it would burn the whole lot down, you see. There was no fire brigade or anythin' like that. It was awful, we just used to look on and watch it burnin'.

When I came to Edinburgh I found a lot o' Jews – from Russia, Lithuania, Latvia, Hungary, Bulgaria. They had a big community then – more than double what it is now. They're all dead now, o' course, except one, Berger, the fruiterer. He used to be a pal o' mine when we were young and he's about a year an' a half older than me. His family was over here before I arrived.

I learnt English. When I made mistakes people corrected me. I could have gone to night-school but I started goin' about with the girls. But I learnt to read. I used to go to the silent pictures and I learnt to read the writin' on the screen. The only thing is, I cannae write. I wouldnae be able to read your handwritin' but I can read print.

Compared with Lithuania it was good here, and I liked everythin'. In fact, when I went out into the street and I saw a policeman and he didnae bother me I couldnae believe it. Then I used to go dancin' and we used to be oot until two o'clock in the mornin' on Saturday night and we needn't go to work on Sunday. Yes, I thought this was a great place. I could never have imagined anythin' better than this.

My sister became a tailoress workin' for another Jewish woman who kept a tailor's shop. She took me to Weinstock Cabinet Makers in Balcarres Street where I got a job as apprentice cabinet-maker for 18 months. Somebody told me there was a cabinet-maker who'd started a small workshop in Rankeillor Street. I was 18 years o' age and I went to this man. He asked me what I earned. I was earnin' ten shillin's a week at Weinstock's but I said 15 shillin's. War had broken oot and workers were scarce so he gave me the job for 15 shillin's a week. We used to start at six in the mornin' and finish at six in the evenin'.

In 1916, Britain had a contract with the Tsar that all the people that had come to Great Britain should go back to Russia to join the army. And if they didnae want to they had to join the army here. I was called up in 1916. They had a registration officer in the police station in the High Street. 'Do you want to go and fight for your country?' I said, 'No'. They didnae even know that the Jews hated Russia. We werenae even Russian citizens in a way, we were second-class citizens. Under the Tsar we werenae allowed more than an acre o' land or to move into big towns. We had to stay in the village we were born in – that was our life. The only thing they did was to take us into the army. The officer said, 'Well do you want to join here?' I said, 'To tell you the truth I dinnae want to fight for any country, but if I have to fight I'll fight for Britain'. As it happened, they found me medically unfit for military service due to my eyesight.

In 1919 my father took a shock [stroke] and he died. He hadnae made much o' anythin'. I didnae hear anythin' from my mother from 1914 to 1919 and then I got the letter that told me the village had burned down. They had no money. As my mother had two younger kids, I had to support them, I had to send money to build another house. Well, I wasnae well off at that time, I had just started myself. I sent £50. Now £50 was five thousand roubles, a lot o' money at that time. You could buy ten times the amount o' goods as here for the same money. They built a small house. My brother wasnae workin', he was still young, and I started sendin' a pound or two oot every month. You see, I kept 'em goin'. And after the Revolution, when Britain an' America divided Russia, Riga was in Latvia and there was a frontier between Lithuania and Latvia, and our merchants couldnae sell goods in Riga. Nobody had any money, just an acre o' land. The Jews were especially poor because they had nowhere to sell.

After workin' in Rankeillor Street, I left and worked for a Pole in East Crosscauseway. I worked there for quite a few years as a cabinet maker, but when he retired I couldnae get a job. I bought some wood and made six wardrobes and I took them to Howie's, a big shop in Cockburn Street, and they accepted them. In 1928 I got a big workshop o' my own and became established. My eldest lad is from my first wife, she died after the Second World War. At first, the older boys used to follow me to the synagogue but later on, when I bought a shop in the High Street, I couldnae go. I've done pretty well. Scotland's been no bad to me. In the 70 years I've lived here, I cannae say anybody's said, 'Bloody Jew!' to me. I've made a lot o' good friends. Even now, I go down to the Meadows and I say 'Good Day' to a lot o' people and we talk.

I miss the peasants in Lithuania even though I was only young when I left. I remember in the beginning o' winter I went to a village and a peasant sold me a sable skin. I gave him two roubles for it and I went to a market we had every Wednesday. My mother told me to ask for four roubles for it. 'Laddie, what do you want for that skin?' 'Four roubles.' 'I'll give you three. You won't get any more, I know the right price!' So I sold it to him. I liked that sort o' thing, the bartering. And you know, I'll tell you somethin'. It doesnae matter to me now, but it's a funny thing: if Lithuania had become a free state, possible to live in, in freedom, I would have gone back. I still say that most o' the Russian people, Jewish and non-Jewish, would have gone back to Russia an' been part o' the Revolution – in fact, many did go back. They left because they wanted to better themselves and they went back because they thought that a Revolution was goin' to mean freedom for everybody, plenty for everybody. But when they started complainin', Stalin killed them off. There's no one to go back to.

When I returned to Lithuania in 1934 there was no big change. My village was still basically Jewish, although there was only one synagogue left, which had been burned down and rebuilt. My mother was still alive and I met one o' the peasants who'd got a big farm. He spoke to me in English. He'd been a miner in America for a few years and he'd made $3,000 which could buy a big estate in Lithuania. But when I went there in 1934, I said to my old pals, 'What the hell are you doin' here?' I said, 'England doesnae let you in, America doesnae let you in, but you can go to Africa. Pack up everythin' you've got and get to Africa!' I told my family and everybody there, 'You're between two fires: Germany on the one side and Russia on the other. There's goin' to be trouble. Get oot o' here if you can. Burn the bloody village!' 'God will help us' – that was their answer. But they could never dream – I mean who would dream? . . . Would you think that soldiers would come in from another country, take oot a crowd o' people, make them dig their own graves, put them in a row and shoot them down – men, women and children?[2]

When I enquired to the Red Cross and the Jewish organisations, they told me, 'Your people were shot. They didnae live long enough to be in a concentration camp'.

NOTES

1. During and shortly after the First World War, the Red, Polish and German armies vied for control of Lithuania. In 1918, however, Lithuania achieved independence. This lasted until the Molotov–Ribbentrop Pact of 28 September 1939, when Lithuania fell under Russian control.

2. During the Second World War, Lithuanians received brutal treatment at the hands of the Nazis. A total of 473,000 Lithuanians lost their lives, including 136,000 Lithuanian Jews who were killed in concentration camps.

LEI-PING

'Just Like a Newborn Baby'

Wong Lei-Ping was born in Hong Kong in 1955 and came to Britain in 1978. She now lives in Leith where she and her husband run a shop.

I have a big family: parents, two brothers and four sisters. We were all living together before we got married, but now my sister is in Australia, my brother is in Taiwan, my other sister is in Singapore, I'm in Britain and the others are still in Hong Kong.

Actually my parents came from China. My big brother was born in China, but they came to Hong Kong before I was born. Although they both came from rich families, they had lost everything because of the war between China and Japan. They don't talk much in their own language. Occasionally, I would hear them speak one or two sentences, but they spoke Cantonese to us all the time. In Hong Kong most people speak Cantonese; maybe the neighbours or the people upstairs or downstairs speak a different dialect, but most people understand Cantonese although they keep their own language to speak to their own family or their own people.

Here, like in Leith, every flat has three or four floors, but in Hong Kong nearly all the buildings are more than that! Maybe some of them have 20 floors. Most of them are very, very modern because there wasn't enough room for all the people, and all the old buildings were rebuilt. But except for being very crowded Hong Kong is quite a good place to stay in because the weather is good and everything is handy.

Because we lived in the city, with all the high buildings you felt very, very like a bird in a cage and when we were older sometimes we'd hire a boat and go out to the islands where there were not so many people. Some of the islands have no people living there at all because they are so isolated. I liked the islands. The air is so fresh there. In the city, neighbours are very close to you and every day you see them. If you need help, people often come because it's so crowded – and if you speak a bit louder they hear what's happening to you!

When I was born, my parents were not rich; in fact we were quite poor when I was a child. The first house I remember was only about 60 or 70 square feet for eight of us – my youngest sister wasn't born then. One room! Everything was in there. Can you imagine 60 or 70 square feet? Can you imagine eight people – two adults and six children staying in that room? All the kitchen things were in the corner and there were a lot of shelves from the floor to the ceiling! [laughs] We had two bunk beds and I think every one of us children slept on the floor under the bed at some time. It was good fun. We used to fight to sleep on the floor! You can imagine how crowded it was, specially as my parents were street traders and they kept some goods in the room.

And then when I was five, we got a bigger house, about double the size but still one room. At first we felt better but as we grew up it was not easy! My parents had a bigger business and more stuff so we stayed on the floor because there wasn't enough room for beds for nine people. Here it's quite cold; I wouldn't feel comfortable sleeping on the floor here. But in Hong Kong it's quite comfortable because the weather is hot and you feel nice and cool on the ground, you know.

When I was a child I didn't really go to school, I went to the children's centre. They're not actually schools, these places are for the parents who can't afford to pay for their children to go to school. Nowadays the system is different, but there used to be no free education. Parents had to pay, and parents who had seven children couldn't afford to send them all. For this children's centre my parents paid almost nothing. It was much cheaper but you'd have to miss a lesson if you didn't have the pens, pencils, paper that were needed. Twelve pence a month included everything and every day we had lunch and milk. We did some reading and some writing but not as much as in school; girls did knitting and sewing. And when you were ten you had to leave.

Not every family or every person has the same things happen, but I was brought up in a very traditional Chinese family where boys were more important than girls; they had the best things – like my brother who finished university 17 years ago. My parents really insist girls shouldn't have as much education as boys. My youngest sister has just finished university, but my parents had never agreed to her going and they still say, 'Girls shouldn't . . . because one day they will marry and they will have their own children. What happens? They stay in the house and look after children. So they waste their education'. They think a woman's place is in the kitchen.

But my sister and I don't agree with this. We have the same strong feeling. I never even finished primary school. I finished Primary 3 in the children's centre and then I went to Primary 4 in the public school, but I couldn't follow the other children, you know, because at the children's centre the level was quite a bit lower. And the first year I am in Primary 4 I cannae manage and at the end of the term I feel it's really, really difficult. The teachers felt I shouldn't go into Primary 5, but they gave me the chance to try. But it was really, really difficult and I stayed in Primary 5 the following year and then I left. I was thirteen. My older sister and I really regret that we missed that chance to get an education.

My parents were quite strict and we were not allowed to go and play outside with other children in the street. Usually we helped our parents because at that time they were street traders and all of us had to help, looking after the youngest and, you know, cooking meals, helping with housework.

At first they sold vegetables and fruit, but I think the main reason they gave that up is they had seven children, and every child would pick at the food! Then they changed to selling clothes or socks, or china or glasses. At first, I remember they had a wee push-cart, then they got a stall. And every day we all had to take goods down there and when we'd finish we just brought them back home.

When I was 13, I told my parents I was going to work in a factory, to get my own job, you know. Well I gave all the money to my mum and told her I was finished as a street trader because I didn't like it. It is not an easy job, especially for a child and I didn't want my parents to work as street traders all the time so they finished the street-traders life from that time. My father's retired now and my mother works full-time.

Because I'm quite small, I remember when I was looking for a job I looked like a nine-year-old girl – shy and nervous talking to other people. Fortunately, my sister worked in a textile factory and she was able to find a job for me. But because I knew nothing about factories and because I wasn't well educated and had no confidence I felt very, very nervous. When I started work, the supervisor told me I was to sew buttons on a shirt, and she told me what to do just once or twice, that's it. She thought I should be able to do it. But I couldnae work out how to use the machine and I was really frightened to ask in case I lost the job. Fortunately my sister worked in the same department, I could ask her. That made things much easier. We used to start at seven and finish at seven, and we had a one hour break. It was piece-work: if I made less I got less money, if I worked hard I got more

pay. In fact, putting a button on a shirt by machine is not a hard job.
It took about a month and then I got on fine. I had a chance to learn
how to make button holes – and I made button holes until I left the
factory a half-year later.

I was so happy when I went to work in a different factory because
people didn't look down on me as a learner and the supervisor was
different. For the first year I was there I got fixed pay and then the
factory changed its policy and paid us for what we did. In Hong
Kong there are some unions for some jobs but it's not like here.
When I worked in a factory we didn't join any union. Most of the
people I worked with preferred to be paid for what they did rather
than at a fixed rate because at least you know you can work harder
and get more pay. I think that's a better way to do it.

You know when you go to work some people can spend all their
wages for themselves, but in my family, my sisters and I gave all the
money to my parents because my brothers and my younger sisters
were still in education. We didn't mind because we felt it was our
responsibility to help the family. When we went to work everything
changed in the house; it was not like when we were children. When
I was about 16 we moved to a bigger house. We got two rooms and
about 400 square feet; we got television, fridge, telephone, everything. Although I had left school I felt quite sensible because I knew
it was hopeless for me to go to high school as my parents don't agree
that girls should have a higher education. And if I'd gone to school
my parents would have had more fees to pay. So I went to work
and my family got much better living conditions. At first we gave
them all our wages and later my mum gave us a little back. They
knew if we hadnae much money we couldnae go out often [laughs].
And they still insisted we had to save the money, put it in a money
bank. Occasionally we were allowed to take a little to buy a shirt or
a dress, and of course when we were a bit older naturally we asked
for a bit more.

When I was 19 or 20 I changed jobs. I became a sub-contractor
making buttonholes and buttons. I employed some people to work
for me so out of my wage I had to pay my employees. And I used to
work in three factories at the same time, you know. I didn't have to
stay in the factory. It didn't matter how many people I employed or
how early or how late I started; the main thing was, say they needed
these things done not later than tomorrow, I had to make sure it was
done. And sometimes I had to stay in the factory overnight to do it.

Every year in April and September there is a day for the ancestors.
People will go to the cemetery to see all the ancestors. They bring

flowers and some cake and something special for the people who are dead – something they used to like. Like my grandma, she's dead, but my father and his brothers still go every year because they believe she knows if they go or not. They give my grandma something traditional like long sticks of incense. We call them *hern*.

Chinese New Year is the most important day in Chinese society. There is a lot of traditional food, people sing, there's dragon dancing and many other things too. Married people give lucky money to people who are not married yet or to children. They put some money in a red pocket and give it to children, especially to those in their own family. If your sisters were not married yet, you'd give them the lucky money but if they were married you would stop. But my parents still give us lucky money because parents always think that you are children!

My husband and I, we met each other when I was a teenager in Hong Kong. Then he came to Britain for work and three and a half years later he came back and we got married. He has a cousin in Newcastle who has a restaurant and a carry-out, and his cousin said, 'We need a helper, why don't you come here to do something different for a bit of a change, see something different in Britain.' And because he was single at that time and he had only his father in Hong Kong (his mother, his sister and his brother are in China) he came.

When we got married I expected my husband to find a job in Hong Kong, you know, because I felt that for me it would be very difficult to move. All my family stayed together all the time! We never left each other, even for a day or two. I couldn't imagine leaving them and going away very, very far. But he suggested that I came here to see something different, to see if I liked it and we could go back if I didn't. In fact, because he'd been here three and a half years he was quite settled here. At that time I didn't want to leave my country because I had a big family, I had a good job, I had so many good friends, you know. So I came here for only one thing – to follow my husband. I left everything behind. I felt really terrible. And I didn't know much about Britain. I knew I'd got a house I could stay in and maybe if I got a chance I could find a job. I never thought there would be any problems [laughs] because my mind was very chaotic and there was no time to think. You can imagine if you were born there, you lived there, had friends and family there, all your life – 22 years! Before I came here I didn't think about what I would be in Britain – until the trouble came when I arrived in Heathrow airport and I discovered 'Oh I cannae speak the language!'

In fact, I'd got everything ready: marriage certificate, passport, visa, health certificate from the Hong Kong government. I didn't think I'd have a problem entering Britain. My husband had come back here first, and because Hong Kong is quite small and I didn't know about Britain, I thought, 'Well, I'll go to London and take an aeroplane to Newcastle' and I told my husband to meet me in Newcastle. I knew it would be expensive and time-consuming for him to come and meet me at Heathrow, and because I held two tickets, Hong Kong to London and London to Newcastle I thought it would be OK. Oh, but when I arrived in Heathrow airport the immigration officer asked me questions that I didn't understand, and the Chinese boy standing behind me tried to translate, to help. But the officer was not so pleased. He said, 'Not your business, go away!' And I sat there six hours. He just ignored me. It was very dreadful – during that time I felt very dreadful because I couldn't understand English. I didn't understand at a'. And because I hadn't wanted to leave Hong Kong, I was very angry about what the officer was doing. I was thinking, 'If I got a plane I could just go back now! Terrible Britain!' [laughs]

In the end I remembered I had a telephone number for my husband. The immigration officer didn't understand me and he never even tried to get anybody who could speak Chinese to help me, so I went straight to him and gave him my husband's phone number and I pointed at it. He contacted my husband and asked why he hadn't come to Heathrow. In the end he let me go past. And when I got out of the airport I thought, 'Oh where do I go to take a plane to Newcastle?' [laughs] All the luggage was stood there and I didn't know which airport or gate to go to for Newcastle. There were a lot of coaches and cars waiting outside and I pushed the trolley with all my luggage in round and round. I didn't know what to do! I had my husband's phone number but I didn't know the code from London to Newcastle, I tried and tried it but I couldnae contact him! And a coach driver saw me going round and round and he whistled at me lots of times. Every girl is the same; if a man whistles at you, you just ignore him. You don't look at him. But in the end I felt hopeless. And I went back to the man in the coach – I cannae speak English so I point to the aeroplane ticket, hopefully he will understand what I mean. He looks at the ticket and suddenly puts all my luggage in his coach! I said, 'My God. No! My luggage!' because I didn't know him and there was no one in the bus. I was so frightened. He took my luggage, took me away. What can I do? [laughs] At the time I had got to cry because no one understood what I was saying. And then he took me to a different part of the airport.

I still didn't know what was happening. He pointed and he asked me to come down and he took a trolley and put all my luggage in it and showed me the way to the information desk. And he asked at the information desk which flight went to Newcastle. The driver was so very, very helpful, otherwise I don't know what would have happened. That was the first time I felt 'Oh I don't know the language! I don't know how my new life will be here!' I was so tired, you know. It took such a long time and everything was happening the same day: left my family, left my country and took the plane. I cried for six hours because I missed my family and didn't know when I would go back to see them. The air hostess served food – 'No I don't want it! I don't want it!' I was still crying when I got here. It took a long time . . . fortunately it's over now.

So that's how I discovered I didn't know the language and people didn't understand when I spoke Chinese. How difficult to get a job; how difficult when something happened, or I was ill and had to see the doctor! When I wanted something I couldn't ask for it. When I went to the supermarket I always got the wrong thing because they had no Chinese working there and I just used my imagination and guessed by the packet.

I stayed in Newcastle just one month and then we both found jobs in a fish and chip shop in a small Scottish town. And I knew it was a chance for me because it was difficult to find a job if you can't speak the language. We moved north with all our things in the car. But unfortunately when we arrived we just went to the shop to have a cup of tea and when we came out the car had been stolen. Everything was in there! At that time I'd come from Hong Kong just one month and I felt very bad. It was 11th November 1978; I remember that date very well because then I knew I had nothing at a'. Even my handbag was in the car. We had no house, no clothes, I just had what I was wearing. You can imagine!

Fortunately the boss was very kind. We stayed in his house and the next morning he gave us some money and took us to the shop to buy toothpaste, slippers, a towel. He's a good man and helped us to settle down for a month in his house and then we moved to staff accommodation. Four days later the Glasgow police phoned us and they'd arrested four boys but they'd got very few of our things back. They said these boys had followed us by car for ages because our car was full of stuff.

Our new boss was so good because he gave us the chance to learn and he taught us what things cost. At first I couldn't manage at a' and he was very patient. He said, 'Take your time: that's fish and chips,

that's vinegar'. because I didn't know anything at a'. Salt, vinegar
and sauce, I always mixed them up and even when I went to sleep
I was always dreaming about my job: 'This is sauce, this is vinegar'
[laughs] – always! But it wasn't a hard job; it was quite easy. As soon
as I learnt what things were called I felt much better.

I faced people at night working in a fish and chip shop and
Chinese carry-out and I felt very, very strange because I'd never faced
people like that in Hong Kong. They were drunk. Although in the
morning they were gentlemen and ladies, at night it was completely
different you know! And all the violence, nearly a fight every day in
the shop!

When we were working there, the Scottish lady who worked with
us didn't like to call me Lei-Ping or Mrs Wong. She said, 'That's
strange. You should have an English name'. But I said, 'That's the
name my mummy gave me. I love it!' And all the time she tried to
call me some English name but I never answered because I got angry
about it. Your name is your name, you know. If British people go to
Hong Kong or China it's not necessary to have another name. I don't
need an English name at a'. People call me Lei-Ping. At first they feel
strange, but I think as soon as they start it will become easy. But my
husband, he's not very strong about that. The lady called him Peter
all the time and he answered. And Peter started from there.

I started to go to college because we lived in such a small village
with not many foreigners, not many people to understand what I
said. There's no English class there so we set out for Stevenson
College every morning about quarter to eight. But every day we
didn't close the shop till 12 midnight and then we had to finish the
washing up, have supper, and go home about half past one. And
every morning at half past six I had to get up to make breakfast
and then we'd drive to Edinburgh, 25 miles away. I didn't mind
but my husband was not really happy about getting up that early.
We couldnae concentrate in the class because we hadn't got enough
sleep; we were not ready for thinking. We found the classes difficult;
we couldnae manage. And then my husband stopped going. Well, as
he stopped I couldnae come because I couldnae drive at that time.

When I really started to learn English was one and a half years
later, when I was expecting my son. We'd moved into rooms in a
house and I started to learn English with a home tutor who came
to my house once a week. Each day after she left I read for six or
seven hours a day. I was studying for myself. Looking up in the
dictionary what words meant. And gradually I understood more
and more.

At the time I was expecting my baby, and even going to hospital for check-ups, I didn't know what people were saying. That's why I had a very strong feeling to learn. I *must* learn the language because if anything happened to me or the child I knew how dreadful the situation would be if I couldnae speak English because my husband couldnae speak much. I sometimes imagine if I cannae call the doctor or something and it really pushed me, pushed me very hard to learn English.

Later I started at Falkirk College. Of course, the college had to charge something. I said, 'I have no job', and the teacher said, 'You have to have something to prove you are unemployed'. When I was a child in Hong Kong there was no such thing as unemployment benefit and also it was easy to get a job – maybe it wasn't a job you liked or the pay didn't satisfy you, but always the chance to get a job was easy. And I think in Chinese society there's always a very strong feeling – 'Don't ask other people for help.' Like here, I had no job but I didn't go to claim unemployment benefit because I was ashamed to. Also Chinese people in Britain often don't speak English. We don't know much about Britain, and when we have a problem we are ashamed to ask people for help and the problem is never sorted out. So when I first went to the college I didn't know anything about unemployment benefit, that if you have an unemployment card you have certain rights – you don't have to pay for education or medicine. If you can't ask how can you know? Just like a newborn baby, but a big one! [laughs] If I had a problem I would just sit – 'Oh my God' – you don't know how to sort it out. It was very dreadful for the first few years.

My little boy's name is Chung-Leung. Chung-Leung is a Chinese name because when he was born I still didn't know about English names and I thought I'd give him a Chinese name because he is Chinese. People say he is Scottish because he was born in Scotland, but for me it doesn't matter what passport you hold, or where you're born: he's Chinese.

Together we speak half and half. Because [laughs] I can't speak much English, he teaches me English and I teach him Chinese. But I can't expect him to understand Chinese very well because that's impossible here, but I try as much as I can. Every day I teach him Chinese and he writes one page of Chinese and I read him a story. In fact, I give him harder homework than school. Also during the school term he goes to Chinese class on Saturday at Drummond High School. And sometimes we get videos of Chinese films. I think that is very helpful. He'll sit there and watch them three or four times and suddenly he'll speak a whole sentence in Chinese! I'm surprised and I say, 'Who taught you that?' He says, 'The video!'

We've been in Edinburgh about four and a half years. We came because we bought a shop here. Usually I work in the shop. We don't have much social life here, though, because with working and studying there's really no time and sometimes I have to bring home the paperwork like VAT and book-keeping. For most people it's quite complicated enough, but for me it takes ages to understand and work out. That's why I haven't got much time to meet other Chinese. But it makes no difference to me whether people are Chinese or British or come from other countries. I meet people naturally. I don't insist on going only to meet my country people.

Maybe one day we might go back to China or Hong Kong. In fact, there's not much difference after 1997 between China or Hong Kong, you know. But we'll just wait and see; we won't decide yet. You know people are quite funny. If you left this country you'd miss it and maybe after several years you'd want to come home, because whether you like where you are or not, your country's your own country. And except for being crowded, Hong Kong is quite good. You don't have to face pressures like racism or being a second-class citizen. That's easier you know. But especially because I was born there. If you went there you might like it or you might not, but because I stayed there 22 years – that's not a short time – I cannae forget it.

ABDUL

Ninety Days to Leave

Abdul was born in Uganda. He came to Edinburgh in 1972.

My parents were born in Africa; my Mum in Kenya and Dad in Uganda. It was my grandparents who came from India. My grandfather came from Bombay in 1920 when he was about ten years of age. There were a lot of people who had already come to build the railway. When my grandfather's family arrived in Uganda they decided to stay in a place called Masaka where they knew some friends. They started working for other people and slowly got into their own businesses. East Africa was under British rule at the time, so everyone was a British subject. But when Uganda became independent in 1962 one had to renounce one's British citizenship.

I was raised in a small town in Western Uganda. The area was known as 'Mountains of the Moon'. There's Mount Rwenzori behind it which is very picturesque. The town was small, maybe about the size of Kirkcaldy. In that area there are a lot of tea plantations, and we had a thriving business and a couple of industries. Our factory was in the National Park so at weekends we used to go and stay there. At night we could hear elephants roaming outside and we had a speedboat which we used to take on Lake Victoria. We were brought up with a silver spoon, and had people to work for us. I never had to do any washing-up till I came to this country! But, this lifestyle had not come easily, for my parents had struggled – they used to work 14 to 16 hours a day to build the business up to what it was when we left.

The town was multiracial. Most of the businesses in the centre of the town were run by Asians, and the Africans used to stay mainly on the outskirts, on the plantations – although in the ten years after Independence there were a lot of changes, with the Africans coming into the town and opening businesses of their own. I had more African friends than Asian or European friends. We used to go pheasant shooting with our catapults in a big gang. I am aware of more racial conflict in this country, which is supposed to be more civilised. All the servants were African but Africans had servants too. The schools we went to were mixed, no segregation of colour, race or creed. The formal language was English but we also spoke Swahili – but, see, in Uganda every district has its own language. Where we lived it was Lutoro. The Asian community was not homogeneous either, it mainly comprised Muslims, Hindus and Sikhs. One has to compromise because one can't stay in this world if one says 'because I am of a certain religion I am a better person' – you can't say that. If you believe in something it is up to you, it is personal.

When Idi Amin came to power in 1971 there was political tension and tribal conflict. Obote was from the Achol tribe, and Idi Amin was from Northern Uganda, from the Kakwa tribe (West Nile). Obote wanted to 'Africanise' in a different way. He nationalised a lot of things, then Idi Amin denationalised everything. I suppose some blame must be placed on the world powers because they wanted a foothold in Third World countries and whenever somebody new comes to power they compete to win that ruler over. So these guys get greedy: they're not running the country, they're too busy seeing who they can get the money from. The world powers definitely influenced Uganda. At first, Amin was pro-British and Britain was the first country to accept him as President. But it's politics, you see: whatever Britain says outwardly it doesn't always conform to it in practice. Like afterwards, when they were condemning Amin, at the back door there were planeloads of whisky going to Uganda.

Anyway after a year's honeymoon [laughs] things started getting bad. Uganda used to have a surplus of funds, it was the most stable economy in Africa, and then the bomb dropped. One morning we woke up and we read in the papers that Idi Amin had a dream and he said that in his dream all the 'foreigners' were sabotaging the economy of the country, and therefore had to be expelled. He was giving them 90 days' notice to leave. Everybody thought it would just cool down and go away. We didn't bother because we thought of ourselves as Ugandans and never twigged. But after about a month things started getting worse, people started disappearing, they were getting harassed, and so we went to get our passports and status verified in Kampala. Everyone of foreign descent had to queue – we had to sleep in queues at night. And then we were told we were no longer Ugandan citizens and they took the passports away. That was it. The only thing left for us was to go to the British High Commission to get back our old nationality. I think we were treated worst in the British High Commission: every time you had some document missing you were thrown out, and you were treated like common dirt. The thing was, outside people were getting shot and disappearing and everyone was frightened. And at the same time a lot of people started getting stateless, through technicalities, as we did.

What happened then, was the Canadians moved in and they started taking some refugees. The UN brought them in, you see. The Canadians were far better, they treated us like human beings. But the British were terrible. When we came here we really got good treatment, once we had landed that is, but over there . . . it was like the two faces, Jekyll and Hyde. We didn't want to go to either country, we wanted to stay put, but it just got worse. So we said, 'At least let's sort out where we're going'. The Canadians told us it was better to get the British passport because we could give other people a chance to go to Canada. Finally, we got our passports.

The Asians were not politically motivated, they did not want to be involved in politics, they just wanted to help build the country's economy. The Africans were making good progress but you can't expect everything to happen overnight. Like, after we left, all the factories were run by the soldiers who had no experience. You can't pick someone off the street and tell him to run a factory, there's no way. Nobody really knows why Amin did this. Maybe he just lost his head.

When Idi Amin came to power, he established an army barracks in our town. We used to get a lot of soldiers buying stuff from our electrical shop, and one afternoon a soldier walked in and said, 'Right I want this . . .' He bargained for the price and asked for a receipt. And then this guy went outside, brought in six more soldiers with machine guns and said, 'If it works properly, we'll come and pay you'. I mean, there's no way you're going to argue with them. So we thought we'd just close the store down. This was in the middle of the 90-day period, so they knew they could get away with it. Even the police were frightened of them; there was no order. And people were frightened at night, they would sleep with the lights on; they would sleep in other peoples' houses and move around each night because a lot of people started disappearing. The local Africans were just as frightened of the soldiers as we were, they were getting the same treatment as us, but I suppose because we had the goods and the money we were an easier and more tempting target than the Africans.

I was 15 when I left Uganda. When we finally decided that we had to get out of the country there were only about ten days left. We took our own car and we hired a taxi to take our stuff from our town to Kampala. We had left our documents in Kampala just in case, on the way, somebody took them and tore them up. And at the first check-point, just three miles out of our town, we were stopped by the army. My father had an old pass and managed to get through the check-point with my mother, aunt and cousin. He had phoned the District Commissioner in the morning to ask if we needed passes but had been told, 'No, no, it's OK'. So we didn't think we needed one. But they stopped our car with myself, my uncle and my younger brother who was only nine at the time, because we didn't have any passes. They said, 'Where are you going?' and we said, 'We are leaving the country. We are going to Kampala to fly out'. So they checked our stuff and took us to the barracks. I've never been so scared in my life.

We were put in an officer's room with all our bags on the floor and all the soldiers were going through them. They said, 'I like this. Can I take it?' And you dare not refuse. So half of the stuff disappeared in a few minutes and they started saying, 'Where has your father put the money?' The watches were out, the cameras were out. And then we were all taken into different rooms, you see. My younger brother had a book in his pocket and when they found it they took him to the officer. It was an address book and the soldier thought he had found something. The officer asked him, 'What is this?' My brother said, 'This is an address book and if you put your name and address there, when I go to the UK I'll send you a postcard'. My brother was very scared but he just said this. And then the officer said 'Oh, right, you are my friend. Leave him alone!' It could easily have been the other way round. They could have kept him or even shot him for being so outspoken. We were all frightened because none of us knew what was happening to the other.

Now, in the meantime, my dad went ahead to a very small village and he was trying to find out what had happened to us. Most of the villagers knew us because of our shop. So he parked the car there and asked them to look after my mother, my aunt and my cousin. He walked three miles to the District Commissioner's Office and he found out that we were in the barracks. My dad said to him, 'You'll need to come with me,' but he said 'I'm not coming'. So he phoned the Chief of Police, but he was frightened too. The District Commissioner eventually phoned the barracks and they told him they were trying to find out where we'd put the money. That morning, my dad had put some money in the bank and he had a receipt with him, so he could show that the money, rather than going out of the country, was in the bank. Well, the soldiers said, 'Send him along, we want to question him as well'. So the District Commissioner said, 'You go there and we'll follow to make sure that you get out'. So he came along and after half-an-hour we were released. We'd been there two-and-a-half hours but if felt as if it was years.

On the way to Kampala there were about 16 check-points and at every check-point we had the hassle of opening bags. At one of the check-points a soldier was drunk and he nearly hit me with a stick. But we finally reached Kampala.

The day before, my older brother had nearly been arrested. He'd just posted a parcel at the Post Office – that was the only way you could get clothes and things out of the country – and when he and his friend were coming back, they were talking, and a couple of soldiers said, 'You were talking against the President. Come on, to the barracks!' and they had to bribe their way out, they had to bargain, you see. That was the only way out. If you thought, 'Oh, I'm going to complain, on principle,' it wouldn't work. Giving money was the only way out. I think a lot of Asians survived because of money. If my brother hadn't had money he would probably have been dead. The consolation is that at least you're all alive and well. Money is here today and tomorrow it's gone. But at least your health is still there.

We didn't know what the reception here was going to be like because of the treatment we'd got in Kampala. We were half-scared, anxious. The only picture I had was from all these Charles Dickens novels – the dark streets of London, lamps – all that. But when we came here we were very well treated. We were taken to Westmoreland RAF Camp in Kent, near Maidstone, and we went to a local school there. We sat our 'O' grades again, and we passed them. The standard of education was the same as in Uganda.

The camps had dormitories, but they were all partitioned off for the families. We were all Ugandan-Asians, a few hundred of us. At least we had a warm bed and the food was OK. My parents didn't want to stay in the camp because all their lives they'd been giving things to charity. Dad, who was a member of the Town Council, helped to start a nursery school and a lot of projects for the community. And then all of a sudden we were in a situation where we were receiving, where we had to queue for food and he wasn't keen on that.

In the meantime, a close relative of ours had come to Edinburgh from Uganda, and in Edinburgh the housing waiting-list was shorter than down south. My Dad came and had a look and said, 'Well, if we have to start life anywhere in Britain, it may as well be in Edinburgh'. We were only in the camp two or three months, although lots of people stayed longer, from six months to a year.

We used to get the Supplementary Allowance and when we came here, the Social Services got us some furniture for our house – at least we had a start, whether it was old or new. You can only build on a start. Edinburgh is a beautiful city and it is my home now. When we went to school everyone was great. We fitted in well.

Slowly and gradually, we got accustomed to staying here. The thing is, we didn't find a lot of difference in the way of life here. See, we were brought up in a culture that was a combination of both the East and the West, so we didn't have too much difficulty in adapting to staying in Britain. If we had come directly from the East, it would have been more difficult. I think the majority of Ugandan-Asians found jobs and adjusted easily, more easily than any other Asian immigrants coming to this country. I feel sorry for some of the other refugees who can't speak the language and who have a different way of life. They are far worse off than we are.

A lot of people had told us in Uganda that when you go to Britain you will find the people friendly and helpful. Over there we were led to believe that in Britain certain things don't happen. That there was a different norm: for instance, people could walk the streets safely. When I was in Kampala, in my school hostel we used to have a Superintendent, who came from London, called 'H.H.' – we used to call him 'His Highness' – and he used to tell us stories about Britain, about how you can live here and you don't have to use locks. The first week we were in Edinburgh we were robbed! But when I went to East Africa sometime back I was talking to some Africans, and they still have this impression that in Britain nobody lies, nobody deceives you.

When you come here you think that people are educated. But there is a lot of ignorance and illiteracy and the people are not prepared to understand what people from other countries are really like. I'm sure that if they did understand they would change their opinions about a lot of things. There are a lot of different Asian people here, you know, and people generalise – you get a lot of people saying, 'Pakis'. It's got to the stage where even I would say, 'Go to the Paki shop round the corner'. Because at school it's part of your growing and it affects you like that. But when we were in Uganda we never found this thing, especially not at school, which is where you educate your mind and where you don't need these things thrown at you. When a person is born in this country he or she is British. But you still find people trying to categorise you. If you see me here, you think

– with a racial bias – 'Oh, he is from India.' But if you see another European in Australia you would say they were Australian. People categorise you. They always mention 'West Indian' or 'West Indian origin'. Maybe nobody does it consciously and maybe nobody means it, but it happens. I guess it's human nature.

I've never been to India. My parents have never been to India because our roots were cut off. I don't know anybody there and I would still consider Uganda my home, but I wouldn't like to go back now. At the moment there's no law, inflation is running at 1000% and there is just no future there. But if it was not like that then I would certainly consider it.

Broken Promises

Haipha George and Nasra Affara were born in 1911 and 1919 respectively. They were brought up as Christians in a Palestine that was under British mandate. The creation of the state of Israel changed the course of their lives.

Haipha Palestine was part of the Turkish Empire until the British came in 1920, and then everything changed.[1] Suddenly there were Americans and English everywhere. I was in Jerusalem at the time, an innocent child – it's good not to know anything [laughs]. But I don't have very pleasant memories because my parents died and I was brought up by my uncle. He was a good man but my aunt was the opposite, you see. She had five daughters of her own and why should she end up with another two? I and my brother went there. But Mr Semple, the head of the college, took two of us as well, 'cause my father was his assistant and friend, and when boys at the school couldn't pay my father had tried to help them. So Mr Semple said, 'This fellow tried to teach other people and to pay for them, so why shouldn't I take two of his children?' He was a good man.

Nasra Apart from a plantation of tobacco, my father owned a small fruit orchard and grew vegetables. That was his main living to start with. We were not rich but we were comfortable; most of the people owned their land. That was important. Some of them lived off the land and some of them owned shops where they sold their produce.

I can still picture our big orchard and my two brothers and I used to sleep there in the summer time in the open. I don't know what has happened to the orchard now. Of course, the Zionists have taken most of the good arable land from the people.

When I was nine, I went to a Christian Missionary Society School in Nazareth but then we sold our home and our land and we went to live near Jerusalem because my father got a job working with the British and Foreign Bible Society. He stayed in that job for the rest of his life. When this job came along, the first thing he wanted to give us was a good education. There was the chance of my two brothers going to Schneller's, a German school in Jerusalem. It was one of the best schools, then, for boys and this is really what made my father sell his land. Marout, my older brother, was very clever at school. He was awarded a scholarship to go to Germany. He had just finished school when the war came in 1939, and he couldn't go. And because this was a German school it closed.

If you went to Jerusalem you could find almost every denomination under the sun. They all wanted a spot in the Holy Land. So we really had a variety of schools. There was the CMS schools, the German schools, French schools – you name it, it was there.

We never learnt our own history in school. Never once! We spoke English and Arabic, we learnt French, Spanish and English history. To be quite frank, we were not so interested in it. But I never knew anything about my own homeland, nothing about our own culture or our own history. I was absolutely ignorant about it. Of course, we got the scriptures – this was daily – and the Old Testament was drilled into us like anything. Well, we were Christian Arabs and there were some Muslim Arab girls too in the school, and they also had to learn the scriptures. The missionaries in those days literally believed in the Old Testament word for word: 'This is the Promised Land and the Jews will come back.' They not only predicted, they *helped* the creation of the state of Israel – through the belief, which is wrong, that the Old Testament was still to be fulfilled.

But it finished when Christ came. He fulfilled all these prophecies. In fact, the Prophets in the Old Testament, if we read them properly, prophesy Christ and what he was to do (nothing about the land; he never mentioned the return of the Jews to their land or anything about the Promised Land). So we Palestinians, especially the Christians, feel the West and particularly America, especially the Fundamentalist Christians, were to blame for what happened.

I think there was a lot of hypocrisy out there. Some missionaries felt superior to the people there. They preached Christ down the peoples' throats as if they were savages. The missionaries always preached down to you. They were up there, you were down here.

OK, you were preached to about Christ, but your real needs were not met. I'm sorry, that's the truth and many of us resented it – even we Christian Arabs resented it. And we felt that because of Britain's mandate, they had power over us.

At first, I was naive because I didn't know my own culture. I respected them and looked on them as superior. That's how I thought: they knew better. And because I was ignorant of my

past and of what my people had done, I didn't see the British
as oppressors. But the Arabs felt very bitter about the way the
British had broken their promise to the Arab people. In the First
World War we were promised independence if we helped the Allies
to kick out the Turks.[2] The Arabs did help and even before the dust
had fallen, Palestine was broken and divided between the French and
British. And to add to that, they promised that they would give the
Jews a home in Palestine – not a *state*, a *home*. Lord Balfour, he was
the one. And right from the beginning, they'd made it seem that the
Jews were already there, that we were the minority already and that
they were the majority. They were only 7% of the people in the land
whilst we were 93%; we owned almost 92% of the land.

At that time we lived very happily with the Jews. My father went
round selling them the Bible and discussing the Bible with them.
And he had many friends amongst them. I would emphasise that the
relationship between Jews and Arabs, whether Christian or Moslem,
was excellent. I suppose we Christians felt a little more secure to
have a Christian government there, like the British, and to have the
different Missions. But the Moslems felt threatened; they felt that
their religion was threatened although they were strong enough not
to let it penetrate. No Moslem would dare to become a Christian. If
he became a Christian he was disowned by all his people; his life was
threatened. The British encouraged this sort of thing. Their policy
was all the time divide and rule. They only interfered when things
became obvious.

So really Britain was not there for the good of the people but
because it was strategically an important area for them. So we Arabs
felt terribly hurt and stabbed in the back.

Finally, when Hitler came on the scene, the gates were opened
for Jewish immigration to Palestine and they started flooding in (by
that time America was encouraging this). They were fleeing to all
different parts of the world from the persecution in Germany. *But*
when the Jews were really in need of support and wanted to go to
Europe and America – no – you wouldn't allow it! I remember when
I was still a young girl, in my teens, all we used to hear was that a
lot of Jews were coming into our country because Europe wouldn't
have them. They were offered other homes like Uganda and somewhere in America, but somehow it never materialised.[3] So they had
no place other than Palestine. Even from the last century, and after
the First World War, the Zionist movement won the collaboration of
the British government and laid the foundations for the colonisation
of Palestine.

It was not until I became older and the troubles began that my father started to tell me about all this. When I left school at the age of 16 and went to train as a nurse, things were beginning, politically, to become tense between Arabs and Jews. Just after I left school in 1936 we had the big strike in Palestine and then we started to question it.[4] My father told us all about it. He was very, very bitter and very strong. The riots started and the strikes, the Arabs protesting – 'Stop immigration'.

I remember I was in Ramallah near Jerusalem and there was bombing, heavy fighting in the towns, ambushing, convoys of cars – Jewish convoys were always protected by British armoured cars.[5] And there was a curfew that went on day after day. The people were allowed out for a couple of hours to buy their food, fetch what they wanted and hurry back home. And when things were getting very bad, for instance when a British officer was killed, the curfew was immediately imposed and the town surrounded by troops and – 'Everybody out' – women and children to the churches and mosques and the men to the town square. And, of course, there was always a traitor or informer who would be behind in a car and when the men were paraded in front of the soldiers (it was almost military occupation then) he would just tap on the window and point out those who he thought were guilty or were involved in the fighting. And these men would be sent to prison without any trial. Some of my father's cousins were put in prison for several months, and also some of our friends who were innocent, completely innocent, and had never held a gun.

My family were not involved personally in the fighting, but many of the fighters would come and ask for shelter and food. We helped them. It was really tight-knit and the whole community wanted to help. We didn't dare not help in the end – if you didn't, your life was threatened by your own people. Of course, if you did help then your life was threatened by the government. So if you helped, you helped secretly, although everybody was under suspicion then: the mandate of the day didn't trust any of the Arabs.

Haipha As a child I loved everybody really. We didn't think, 'This is a Jew' or so on. We loved them all. My uncle taught English in a Jewish school and he was loved a great deal. He was a man of the Church. He used to preach in Arabic and German, and also knew French and Hebrew. The Rabbi was his greatest friend.

And then all of a sudden we started to understand about the troubles. We used to help the Jews; they used to run and hide in our house during the riots. We never thought they were a danger to us.

And when they came in greater numbers and started to own shops we all wanted to buy from them. They'd greet you very nicely and they lowered the prices whereas the Arab is serious when he is selling something. And when I was training as a nurse I loved the Jewish nurses very much. One of them knew – she was political and I felt that she was sad for me. She liked me so much and I didn't know what was going to happen, see. But bit by bit they started to set up shops and the British collected all the arms from the Arabs and all was given to the Jews.

I still didn't know enough. I was so stupid and not interested in politics at this time. But they made us open our eyes and see their treachery.

We never killed the English people there, the Zionists did that – and the British were on *their* side! In Jerusalem I remember they found two British soldiers hanged from the trees, by the Zionists, to make them hurry and leave.[6] I opened my eyes then. I cried. And there was a Moslem doctor in the operating room who said, 'Why are you crying? Be ashamed of yourself that you should cry for those who gave away your country'.

My sister used to work as a private secretary to the Attorney General. His name was Sir William Trustcott. And because it was too dangerous in the area they worked, they moved the office to the YMCA. But my sister had classmates in King David's Hotel, also working as secretaries, and sometimes they'd go and drink coffee with her. One day they set off after coffee, two beautiful girls – one of them was to be married in two weeks, and the other one said, 'I have an appointment. I want to make my hair look nice for my boyfriend', you know how young people talk. And my sister said, 'Bye bye. Thanks for the coffee'. She crossed the road to the Y and the King David was blasted.[7] Sixty English people died there. After five days they called her because they knew she was a friend and she had to go and identify them. The stench of death was horrible. She went there and just found the head of one friend, and then the body of the one that was going to get married. After ten days of living with that she wrote me a letter about what had happened. And I thought, 'If I had to do this I would go mad. How is my sister carrying on? How?' And then I heard she had a nervous breakdown. She never recovered.

The Zionists were doing all these things to the English people who gave them land and helped them. Then we started to know where we stood and how we had been deceived.

Nasra The Jewish side was well armed and organised. They were like a government within a government. And yet every Tuesday in

Acre some of our young men were hung for just having a gun. So many, many hundreds of our men were hung. But we had no other way. Nobody was listening to us. We were losing our land, our country.

And this continued until the breakout of the war in 1939 when Britain stopped immigration. And you know why? Because they didn't want trouble on their hands; they were too busy with the war. Then near the end of the war the Zionists and the British were working together; the Irgun – Begin's lot – were preparing to take power.[8] But when in 1945 things were starting to erupt again between us and the Zionists, Britain was exhausted from the war, and in terrible debt to America. And America was dictating what should happen. They demanded that 100,000 Jews enter Palestine immediately. Britain just couldn't cope any more. They sent I don't know how many commissions to make peace, and every time someone important came the Zionists assassinated them. Count Bernadotte was one. He said, 'The Arabs have been badly treated. It is unjust', and he tried to make peace. No – they assassinated him.[9]

Finally, the United Nations decided that they would divide Palestine. At the voting America put pressure on all the different nations and everybody who had a loan was under pressure, even threatened. And they voted for the State of Israel and hell broke loose in Palestine.[10] By that time I had married. I met my husband in one of the mission hospitals in the East. He was a missionary of the Church of Scotland, from Aden – Dr Ahmed Affara. We met in Palestine, in a mission hospital in Hebron where I was a staff nurse.

Anyway, by the end of the war I was with my husband in Aden, which was a British colony then. All my relations were still in Palestine and of course I was in touch the whole time, so we knew what was going on. And directly after the war, Zionists came to Aden and spoke to all the Jews there, asking them to emigrate to Palestine, while the British were still there. Riots broke out again in Palestine and fighting became very intense. The Zionists were fighting the British more than ever because they wanted to put the pressure on them to leave, and the Arab countries were threatening to intervene. In Aden itself, there was fighting and looting and burning of Jewish houses, Jewish shops and synagogues. So the British had to intervene and they surrounded all the Jewish areas and deported them at their own request by plane at night to Britain because most of the Jews from Aden refused to go to Palestine, to the new State of Israel. My husband's best patients were Jews. They were very happy in Aden. They owned good shops and actually lived very happily, very happily with the Arabs there. Because of the State of Israel the Jews in other Arab countries suffered an awful lot.

As I said, when the State of Israel was created, hell broke loose. I had a sister in Haifa, my eldest sister, Meriam. She had six children and she had great hopes for them. They had a lovely two-storey house and a booming business and then because of this terrible fighting (the Jews were winning in the north) my sister left. She didn't leave of her own free will, nobody did. Who would leave their home just like that? She had to leave at the point of a gun.[11] Her husband was afraid for his life because they were shooting men on sight. So he dressed as a woman and put my sister and the family on a lorry going to Jerusalem. They left their home, their business, everything. They've never seen it since. They went back to our father in Ramallah, near Jerusalem. She just came with her children and stood at the door. At that time my father had three tents in the garden for the refugees that were fleeing, so she stayed with my father until she could organise something. I remember sending them a sum to start them off – everybody in the family gave them a little money. First of all they were given a tent by the people who were helping the refugees and they lived in it for two or three months. And then her husband joined her. He had had to go around Palestine to avoid places where there was fighting. Then they made a decision: not to start a home in Palestine. They went over to Jordan and they've been there ever since. It was the best decision they could have made. It took them a long, long time to settle down and they lost the most important things: the education of their children and everything they had possessed since they were young. They were one family out of the three-quarters of a million Palestinians who had the same misfortune.

Now when the whole of Galilee and the whole of the north, was taken by the Zionists, there were a lot of people still in the villages. Why should they leave? It was their home. And a terrible thing happened in a village near Jerusalem, Dir Yassin. The Irgun (Menachem Begin was their leader) went in and they slaughtered every man, women and child – 250 of them. And that put terror in the hearts of the villagers.[12] Then Allon, who is still a member of the Israeli government today, said to the Jewish leaders, 'Speak to all the Arab heads of the villages and tell them, "I want to give you some advice because I am afraid for you. I advise you to leave. Leave for a short time. Otherwise it's going to be terrible: what happened in Dir Yassin will happen to you. Why don't you go for a week or two and then come back?" ' And one village after another, they left in terror.

And as they say, some of the Zionist leaders, the whole of that area was 'cleaned' of the Arabs.

Haipha We used to move from one house to another because my husband was a government official. We stayed in Nablus for eleven years. In 1948 we were still in Nablus and my family had to fly out of Jerusalem. My brother worked at a government office there and everybody told him, 'Leave, it's going to be worse'. He had about 7p in his pocket. He went to Lebanon. He was lucky, he found work, but I was deprived of his company.

I wanted to live in Jerusalem. I looked for a house but they told me, 'Better not go to Jerusalem', so I chose Ramallah. I put my three daughters in a Quaker school there. Then I saw how people suffered everywhere. All around – refugees. I volunteered for the Red Cross and I could see the miseries: the tents used to fall on them at night; they had nothing – all their belongings were taken from them by the Zionists. And the Red Cross tried to help with these things, but some of them didn't want to be helped. They wanted their country, they didn't want charity. But how could I be politically involved? I had a family. You have to care for your children and stand apart, suffering inside. But I've seen miseries all around.

Nasra In 1948 we came to Britain for a visit. Things were cooling down in Palestine and we had to make a decision. Our eldest daughter was nearly five and we said, 'Where are we going to educate them?' Aden wasn't such a great place for education, especially for girls at that time. Middle East? – Palestine was out. We knew there was going to be more war. We couldn't see ourselves in any of the Middle Eastern countries. And when I came here I liked it and we said, OK, it would be Scotland.

First of all we had some roots because of my husband's education. He took his medical degree here and he had a strong association with the Church as a missionary. When I came here for holidays in 1948 and again in 1952 I spoke at the General Assembly of the Church of Scotland, to the women, and we spoke at many Sunday schools, churches, guilds and so on. So I felt we were accepted and had friends and could live here.

We came in 1955 and at that time we had four children and I was expecting the fifth. We bought a house in Greenbank, up in Morningside, and settled our children in school. One of our neighbours was a lady of 87, a Queen's nurse from Inverness. We'd moved in, and I'll not forget this, this old lady came and she said, 'Do you need anything, dear?' I said, 'No, thank you very much'. I told her my name and introduced all my children and, 'Oh my', she said, 'You've got so many bairns!' I didn't know what 'bairns' meant! And then, when my husband left (to go as a missionary to Aden), that night I put the children to bed and of course, I broke down and started crying. It dawned on me that I was alone for the first time in my life with all of these children. And the bell rang. Now who was it? Tears come to my eyes even now – the old lady. She came in and she hugged me and I cried in her lap. I mean it was so lovely!

But without my husband I was really lonely. I knew I had a lot of friends but I felt that I just couldn't go to them whenever I liked. It was different in our country, you could call at anybody's, you know. Somehow I was afraid, I didn't want to intrude. I didn't have my husband with me and my children were all very young. The youngest was just a year and a half. But I tell you what – I was such a busy person with having my family, getting them ready for school and doing all the chores, and then I was called upon so often to speak to different churches that this kept me going. I was always involved and the Church was good to us. I think because of my husband we really had a good reception. I was one of the lucky. I was very happy in Greenbank. And every Sunday the treat was to go and watch television at Auntie Miss McClay, the old lady of 87, and the children helped her a lot, doing shopping, doing anything. She became like a granny for them and when my baby arrived she used to come and take the other one, who was two and a half then, out every single day while I fed and bathed my baby. So I was a very lucky person.

I must say, once or twice, one of my daughters felt prejudice at school, because of, you know, our colour. My children are neither white, nor dark, you know. They're in between. And once, I think one of the other children called her, 'Blackie' or 'Darkie' or something and she came home crying. 'Oh', I said, 'They go and sit in the sun to make themselves your colour. You tell them, "You can't get this colour naturally" '. That was the end of that.

After ten years we moved to Nile Grove, and I don't know why I never took any notice of it at the time, but one lady came and she said, 'Do you think you will be happy in this street?' It did not strike a note in me that there was some resentment. It dawned on me three years later when more immigrants were coming. I don't know if you've heard about Mary Kennedy House. The YWCA started it as a house for students who came overseas. But the problems of prejudice against people from overseas and about colour was beginning to become really quite evident in all parts of Edinburgh. And the first people who saw this danger were the YWCA. I was on a number of committees like the British Council and the YWCA, and we invited families from overseas to our homes, to the centres. And when the Mary Kennedy House for students and their wives was started, you know, the whole street in Nile Grove wouldn't allow it. And then I knew why that women had asked me that question. Why? – It may lower the standard of their street. It may bring down the price of their homes. It may do this, it may do that – prejudice!

It took us three years to fight this and meantime the house stood empty, dry rot started and it cost double what we intended. Finally, they allowed it to open and we had people, the pick of their countries – doctors, lawyers – coming to do advanced studies. They were highly educated, respected people and the local people were overcome by how lovely they were. They started inviting them into their homes and they would come into the House. But it didn't happen overnight.

We were fighting prejudice. Many people refused to let their homes to black people and all this took a long time to combat: speaking to churches, especially to guilds, and telling them about the background. 'Why do you send missionaries?' I used to ask them. 'What for? Why do you go out there to be missionaries when you have people coming here to your country and you haven't got the grace of Christ even to welcome them into your homes?' And little by little, after years of hard work, things started to become better and I think the people in the churches now do understand. I wouldn't say the prejudice has completely gone. No, there is still quite a lot of prejudice.

For the first few years I felt that I mustn't make a permanent stay here: 'I'm not here for good, I'm just here to educate my children and then go.' I wasn't settled, I didn't feel at home. I had a lot of friends but it wasn't home. My children felt the same, especially the second eldest. She cried the whole time, she cried bitterly. 'I want to go back to Aden. I don't like it here.' I used to feel so lonely and I suggested to my husband one year, when he was back on holiday, that I go with him to South Arabia. 'We'll put the children in boarding schools. I need to escape. I'll come back and help you there.' He said, 'Oh, no, we are both sacrificing. I know it is not easy on you, I realise that, and neither is it easy on me to be by myself there and come back once every two years.' We talked this over with close friends and they were with me because they knew that both of us made an impact on the church in Aden, more so than when he was by himself. I wanted to go back there with my husband but at the same time my heart was with my family here. He didn't give in. Had he said yes, I would have gone back with him like a shot.

I felt that longing to go back to where I belonged. I've been here 31 years, that's a long time and I'm in my sixties now and until I was approaching sixty I was still wanting to go back, but more to Palestine than to Aden. But now I see Palestine as it is: it's not Palestine, it's not my home. In my heart it is my home but it has changed so much, and my children have grown, they're established here, they've got children. So I became tied. And another thing: my youngest son died at the age of eighteen months, suddenly in his sleep, and after that I felt, 'I can't go now. How can I go and leave him here?' And then my husband died here. He is buried beside my son. So I have established roots here and I find it hard – all these things put together.

Now my granddaughter, Nadia, she's seventeen, and six weeks ago a Zionist women came to her school and gave a lecture on Zionism and *kibbutzim* in Israel. She was saying so much untruth about the land – that it had been empty. Since when? I've never known it as such. Nadia knows all the history about Palestine and she was so upset that she walked out in the middle of the lecture. And then the teacher next day asked her why. She came to me quite upset. I said, 'Nadia, do you feel you did the right thing?' She said, 'Yes granny'. I said, 'I'm proud of you, that you had the courage to do that, but you should go and speak to your Mum and Dad and see what they say'. Her Dad knows everything about the Palestinian question. He's the secretary of our Palestine Action Group in Edinburgh. And she told him what happened. He told her, 'I'm proud of you, but you sit down and write a letter to the teacher explaining your point of view'. So she did. The teacher read her letter and the next day he said, 'I think you were right to do what you felt was right. And we should know more about this situation.'

All my sons-in-law know the situation. All my daughters know it very well. When somebody asks them, they say, 'We are Palestinian and our mother is Palestinian'. They look upon themselves as Arab Palestinians. I have not indoctrinated them in any way but the whole situation has taught them.

Haipha I came to Edinburgh because daughter number one married an American-Arab but when her husband died she came here. My second daughter married Nasra's husband's cousin, a doctor who had studied medicine here. He came to our country and asked for her hand, so I told her, 'Go!' I used to be in love with Scotland. The third of my daughters, the youngest, didn't want to go to college and her sister in Edinburgh advised her to come here and be a nurse. So she came here; she finished her nursing and then she couldn't go back to her country. They wouldn't allow her. She was longing to see Jerusalem and Ramallah. I was in Ramallah. My husband had died and I was all alone and I was terrified with the bombings and the troubles. So I said the best thing to do was to sell my house and go to my daughters. I came over in 1975.

When I first came to Edinburgh I had something wrong with my tooth and I went to the dental technician. He asked me 'Where do you come from?' So I said, 'From Jerusalem'. I didn't want to mention Palestine because I didn't like to hear it even. And when I said Jerusalem (they all believe that Jerusalem is a Jewish place completely) he said, 'Oh Jerusalem! You know we were always on your side. We went as soldiers there. Do you remember us with our red caps on?' I said, 'No, I was away from Jerusalem by the time you were there'. He said, 'Yes, the orders were that we had to go to every house, every Arab house, and see if there were arms there and we used to give them to you. And even when they started to kill British people, the rule was that even if they killed your brother you were not allowed to raise a gun against a Jew'. And he said, 'This happened to my best friend: when he turned his back, a Zionist shot him'. And I stood there and I told him, 'I'm sorry to hear this and I'm sorry to disappoint you - I'm an Arab, a Palestinian Arab. I'm not Jewish'. He was shocked. He turned away so quickly.

Nasra People have a different idea about the Arabs. It's because of the propaganda and the media. Every time there was a war coming on they whipped up such propaganda. In peoples' minds the Arab has become a terrorist no matter what he is. And when we used to tell them we were Palestinian Arabs they treated us differently.

Haipha I didn't like it here at all. I still don't like it. You know, our life there was much easier – you could get home-helps, the groceries came to the door, I had a nice warm house. You know we have got nine months of the sun, and in winter even, it comes out and you can wash and do anything. The weather was a great asset. And then I left my friends – I miss them so. And I find it difficult to carry paraffin to the house and all those heating bills coming in. I can't cope with life. All that I get, I pay for repairs and bills. And you never have money for yourself. And how you live uncomfortably, with the aches in your body due to the cold! And who would listen? And who would care? Nobody. How can I love it?

And the neighbours. Because we had dogs we had to live on the outskirts of the city so as not to disturb people and I always wished to live in a house like this – 'Oh lucky people who live close together like that'. I never thought about the noise, coming in drunk at night, screaming and talking at the top of their voices. And as they come in, whatever they have, it's just thrown down and we have to sweep for them. No, it's not as I wished it to be. I thought this was a cultured country. And faeces on the street everywhere – I used to feel sick. So how can I love it? I'm not rich enough to stay out and enjoy the good things, so mostly I'm in the house and there hardly passed a day without hearing bad news. Innocent people being killed, just shot, here and there. And then you can't leave the house door open. What is this freedom when your door has to be locked all the time?

I was trained at the Scottish hospital in Tiberias. The Scottish people behaved differently there; the older generation was different, quite different. They really were Christians. But here I don't feel the Christian spirit at all. They call themselves Christians but they are not in the true sense. Money and power – this is all they care for. But the Scots in Palestine were very good, they were missionaries, you see, and they acted as missionaries. The doctor used to be on duty day and night, and with an empty pocket. He just served others. And with the third class who had no money to pay, free treatment, he was better than with the private patients. I don't see this any more. I long to see such people as that.

No, no, I can't go back because what do you call it when they tell you to take off all your clothes and search you? They take off your shoes and X-ray them and all this – could you put up with it? They don't trust us, you see, although they are the attackers. I will not go back. They don't allow us to go back. They don't allow anybody to go back. Even government officials who were away, when they returned they were finished, there was no home, nothing!

The British Nation

By now Britishers are known to every nation
The best politicians in God's creation
In every land they make a penetration
Whether by agreement or by invasion
In their country there is cooperation
But elsewhere they cause complication
In every town and every station
They pay big sums on each occasion
Kings and ministers bow to the temptation
They go far in their imagination
And scheme ahead for each generation
There can't be better in organisation

Riots under their administration
Never failed . . . and no hesitation
In every trouble they are the foundation
Crimes are committed by their instigation
And on others they throw the accusation
For Arabs they discouraged education
Unity and civilisation
In short, what's certified about the British nation
Leave aside their intrigue and discrimination
Is – sending all to hell with the best recommendation.

Haipha, May, 1948

Nasra Today we have seen the fruits of the wrongs done to our people which have resulted in extreme bitterness and hatred on both sides. But in spite of all the wrongs done to the Palestinians, they are still ready to talk about peace – which is our desire. The *intifada* (uprising) is all about deciding for ourselves and achieving peace through self-determination.

NOTES

1. In 1918 the population of Palestine numbered 644,000 Arabs and 56,000 Jews. The First Zionist Congress, held in Basle in 1897, had drawn up a programme to create a home for the Jewish people in Palestine and in November 1917 the British government (which had no legal authority over Palestine at that time) issued the Balfour Declaration, promising the Zionist movement 'the establishment in Palestine of a National Home for the Jewish people'. When the Turkish Empire collapsed after the First World War, the League of Nations approved a British mandate over Palestine which incorporated the Balfour Declaration and included provisions to facilitate Jewish immigration.

2. By 1916 the British Government had promised self-determination to Palestine and other Arab countries in return for support in the First World War.

3. In 1903 the British Government had offered an area of 6,000 square miles in the highlands of Uganda for the repopulation of European Jews. However, the Zionist Congress of 1905 rejected any colonisation outside Palestine and its neighbouring countries.

4. The anger of Palestinians flared into countrywide demonstrations in April 1920, May 1921 and August 1929. Between 1936 and 1939 an all-out revolution developed which was preceded by a six-month general strike paralysing the economic life of the country.

5. British attitudes towards the Zionists fluctuated between open support and collaboration with them and attempts to frustrate their activities in Palestine.

6. In July 1947 Irgun kidnapped and hanged two British sergeants in retaliation for the execution of three of their members.

7. The King David Hotel in Jerusalem was bombed by Irgun on 22 July 1946. Ninety-one people were killed and 46 injured.

8. Menachem Begin was commander of the militant Irgun Zuai Leumi from 1943 to 1948, after which he moved on to form the Herut 'Freedom Party'.

9. Count Bernadotte was a mediator for the UN. In 1948 he was assassinated by Zionists because he favoured the return of the Palestinian refugees to their villages.

10. The state of Israel was proclaimed on 14 May 1948, on the basis of the 1947 resolution of the General Assembly of the UN. Under the resolution, Palestine was to be divided into two independent states – Arab and Jewish. During the ensuing Arab-Israeli War of 1948-49, Israel captured much of the territory set aside for the Arab state.

11. The formation of the state of Israel and the subsequent Arab-Israeli War led to the expulsion of nearly a million Arabs from the territory of Israel and the invaded Arab territories. Israel ignored the UN resolution of 11 December 1948 on the rights of refugees.

12. In April 1948 Irgun attacked the Arab village of Dir Yassin, killing 254 people.

LAL

'Go West Young Man'

Lal Khatri was born in 1907 in Mahatpur in the Punjab, in
British India. He came to Britain in 1929. He is a lifelong
member of the Labour Party and has been very active in
the Fabian Society as well as being the vice-president of the
Inter-Faith Association Council.

There was British Rule in the Punjab but very little contact with
any British. The British were employed in the civil service, mostly
in administration, and the others were soldiers. You wouldn't see
them unless they came out for shooting and hunting, and all that
nonsense. I only met one British gentleman in my area while he
was enjoying his vacation trying to shoot. He lifted up his rifle to
shoot this peacock and fortunately for him I told him, 'Don't do that
because they'll lynch you here if you shoot a peacock'. He was very
grateful and we parted friendly. I come from quite a loving family
with thirteen brothers and sisters, and I was a bit more pampered
than any other boy could be because I was the first boy in the family
after three sisters. We had a more cohesive family than you find here
now. You've arranged homes for the old people.

There was no trouble when I was a child, none whatever. They
were really good people, good living people who cared for each other. Every man of your father's generation was 'Uncle' irrespective of
who he was. And any lady of your mother's generation was, 'Auntie', see, whether Moslem or Hindu. Hindus, Moslems, Sikhs, they
lived like brother and sister. We had no police station, no policemen,
and yet everyone in the village was a policeman. If anybody was
doing damage to anyone's property, somebody else would take it
in hand.

My grandfather had a shop and my father carried it on. They were
agents for the farmers. My father's job was to find the merchant to
buy whatever was in season – chillies, grains, cotton – and fix the
price between the farmer and the trader, you see.

43

There was a certain amount of free education for the farmers because they paid Land Tax and under British Rule you were well considered if you paid the tax, but when I went to school my father paid for my education. It was a Hindu education and we went to school when we were six. We'd muster in the morning, the whole five classes and the teacher and the head, and we sang, 'God Save the King'. That was the start to the day, 'God Save the King'. Then we went to boarding school six miles away from the village and I was there until 1924 when I matriculated.

I left school and helped my father with his business for four or five years. Well, father wanted me to carry on my education but I left school – the Independence movement was very much in ascendancy at that time. Just about four years before I left school, Gandhi had taken the reins as leader of the movement. The movement became very prominent and it didn't matter where you were, you knew the stories even though there was very little press. I couldn't help but get involved. You paid your membership which was a penny a month. I didn't make any speeches or anything like that, but I'd go to hear prominent speakers. 1919 was the decisive year when the British ruling authorities reneged on their promise of Independence to India after the war was over. India had given men and money – everything – to the Raj so that they could win their war against Germany, on the understanding that when the war was over, political priority would be given to Indian Independence or Home Rule. But in 1919, instead of fulfilling their promise, the British passed a Bill called the Rowland Act: assembly of more than two was illegal irrespective of what you were doing. Two or three neighbours couldn't even discuss their needs with my father.

1919 was also the year that there was a massacre of unarmed people in a park in Amritsar. There was only one exit and a General Dyer placed the machine guns and started shooting because they'd held a meeting which was illegal under this Rowland Act. Also, gradually the quota of Indian goods which could be sold became less and less. Then Gandhi launched the Boycott of British Goods Campaign across the country. That's when you saw all the bonfires of Manchester-made cotton and people started buying the homespun linens. The boycott of all British things and the English language was just as important as burning the clothing – so I wasn't going to speak English any more!

I saw Gandhi before he took up the leadership of the Independence Movement. He travelled the country and held meetings in different places. And, of course, Gandhi made his vow that he was going to see as many people of his country as he could and his conveyance was by foot. I think he was a good man and did everything that he could have done. As a matter of fact, when I came to Britain, the political parties here couldn't believe that Gandhi was acting without any ulterior motive. They couldn't trust him – there couldn't be a leader that had no ulterior motive. Although the movement I supported opposed British rule, that did not mean that we opposed the British people – as a matter of fact it was partly due to the British people in the shape of the British Labour Party that we finally gained our Independence.

I was helping my father in the shop and then I suddenly decided to have a trip abroad. As things stood, Indians were not welcome in any country in the world other than Britain. Australia was closed and America closed their borders to immigration in 1912 and you couldn't go. I mean, you couldn't even put in an application that could be turned down. So I decided to come to Britain, and I got my passport and came here in 1929. I came by boat and my father paid my fare. I thought I would make money here but I landed in the Depression.

We stayed with an Indian chap in London for two nights and then on Sunday morning a man came from Edinburgh to London, and fortunately for us he had a return ticket. It was a Day Excursion from Edinburgh but he wasn't going back so he gave me and another chap the ticket. The two of us wanted to come here. One place was as good as another. So that free ticket brought us to Edinburgh and the fellow gave us an address to go to in South Clerk Street. Right enough, the lady took us in there and then.

The job situation was terrible in 1929 and the welfare and social security benefits were not the same as you experience today. The depression is bad now, the only difference is that now the unemployed are better catered for because the Labour Movement always fought for the underdog. A lot of people don't believe in welfare but I do. The weakest link of the community should be supported by the strongest.

When I arrived the differences were very glaring. People could die of starvation in India and when I came here I saw people playing football with half-loaves, kicking them to each other. And you could see then, as you see nowadays, fish and chips half-eaten, lying on the street. And that kind of thing went against my grain, coming from a country where they were glad to have food. In India when you were poor it was your neighbours who bore the brunt. They and your relatives saw that you were kept alive irrespective of whether

you were a Hindu, Moslem or anything. The next glaring difference
I found was that I had no vote in my own country, but when I came
here I found that I got the vote without even applying for it. Under
the same rule! British Rule here, British Rule there! And yet the
British tell you that they have done wonders for the colonies which
is not true.

Och, I felt homesick, but you soon get over that because you
have no means to get back. Nature gives you strength to bear the
burden, as the saying goes. At that time there was no community of
Indians other than university Indians, and they were not the ordinary
working-class people of India. Working Indians would have been
about ten at the most in Edinburgh and Leith. There were a few
immigrants already settled in Leith even before I came; West Indian
sailors mostly.

Anyhow, looking for a job was hopeless, hopeless, and the only
thing a friend could advise me was, 'If you get a pedlar's licence
from the police and you buy some stuff and sell it, then that will
give you some income to live on if you are lucky'. I managed to get
the licence and it was very good from then onwards. Things were
hard but I could always get enough money to buy bread and pay
for my room and all that sort of thing. We sold all sorts – shirts,
dresses and blouses. I sold what I had with me and took orders for
anybody wanting anything, all on my own account, of course. The
prices were quite reasonable but lots of people had no money. Even
one eleven-pence-ha'penny article took two or three visits for some
customers to pay for. Some people banged the door in front of you,
didn't even give you a chance to say what it was, and others would
open it and suddenly realise that they could do with an overall or a
girl's dress. Oh, some of those people became friends through that,
and others, of course, had no time for you at all.

But coming to Leith, you saw the difference between people –
because people in Edinburgh and the surrounding countryside didn't
think twice about shutting the door in your face. But not in Leith,
whether they could afford to buy or not. Well the thing is, Leith
has an affinity with people of all lands, being a port. Leith people
emigrated to other places and that had a direct effect on the families
here: 'How'd we take it if our people there were in the same boat as
this chap?' So I think from a natural human understanding point of
view, in these days, Leith people were superior to Edinburgh people. They had no racial prejudice as such simply because they had
somebody away from home. This was my deduction – they could
not bear their son or husband or father being ill-treated in New

Zealand, Canada or Australia or even India, for that matter, and they had respect for everybody as human beings. They were good people who never did you out of a penny. The people gathered together who were unemployed during the day. They would chat to you and they would remember the 1914-1918 war – how they saw the Indians in the trenches and how they were attached to such-and-such a regiment. And some of these boys served with the army in India. They knew a few words of Indian and that gave you a kind of uplift, that somebody knew a few words of your language.

In 1937 the call came from the government, from Anthony Eden, to learn First Aid and to be in the Home Guard. My wife and I had both already attended classes for First Aid and were members of the Thistle Section of the St Andrew's Ambulance Association, so we joined the Air-Raid Precautions and the Rescue Service as volunteers. Because we knew what we were doing, they used us to train people. Later, when the ARP and Rescue Services had been amalgamated into Civil Defence, I got a full-time paid job with their First-Aid unit.

I have come across a lot of incidents of prejudice, more institutionalised prejudice than personal prejudice. Although most people did everything really to avoid discriminating against you, the Royal Air Force and the Royal Army Corps had no compunction. During the war they had no hesitation in letting you know that you were not needed because of your colour or country of origin. 'That's the Rule Book', the sergeant in charge of recruiting people would tell you, 'I can tackle every and any Tom, Dick or Harry of European descent . . . but not Indian descent'. I was a British subject, but he kindly advised me on both occasions I went to see him, to go to India: 'Young men are needed there'. I even said, 'Why not enlist me here and send me to India, I'm not bothered'.

I was told that Rowntrees had taken Duncan's Chocolate Works over and that they needed some men. I went for a medical there and got the job. It was in 1944, and although the war wasn't over until 1945, the danger of any bombardment was lessened and I wasn't needed by the Civil Defence. So I was working in Duncan's until 1947. In 1947 there was a severe winter, so much so that the railway-line points froze and the supplies of chocolate ingredients weren't arriving. They could not really run three shifts so they wanted to knock off one shift and, as it happened, I was along with the shift being discharged. They said there was no racial prejudice but the company rules were 'Last come, first go.' In my case it didn't work out like that. The people who'd started six months before stayed in

the job and I'd been there for two and a half years. I asked the fore-
man what was the rule and he told me. I said, 'It doesn't work out
in my case'. – 'Oh that's management's prerogative.'

Luckily a neighbour of mine worked in an engineering shop in
Brown Brothers and I got a job there. I was with Brown Brothers
from 1947 to 1972.

Most immigrants, when they first came here, came to Leith.
The idea was you couldn't rent a house in Edinburgh and in certain
cases you couldn't even buy in Edinburgh because the agent didn't
entertain you. If you were black you didn't get any further than the
agents. These immigrants started in the same kind of job I started
in, in 1929 when I first came, because they couldn't get jobs other
than on the buses and not everybody could drive a bus. Some got
driver's jobs, some got conductor's jobs. They could do any amount
of long hours and that made the money, and coming from India and
Pakistan, saving was in their nature, so when they had enough to
open their shop they didn't hesitate. As the money grew, they got
their own houses, and practically every one in Leith at present is a
house owner, a shop owner and finished with factory work.

In 1975, my wife and I went to India, and when we came back after
three months, the National Front had shown its ugly head in Leith.
They even went to the Sikh temple in Mill Lane and daubed graffiti
right across the wall. It has been on the increase ever since. Where
Indian people lived, the neighbours started to complain, 'Not racial
discrimination or anything against them . . .' but they couldn't stand
'. . . the smell of their cooking, the curry'. That was always their
excuse. Occasionally, we have got windows broken here. Prejudice
started as it became harder to obtain work. The country didn't need
the labour because their own people were unemployed. They didn't
appreciate Indian or Pakistani or West Indian workers; but to the boss
Indian, Pakistani and West Indian workers were really more depend-
able than their own indigenous population for turning up to work.

We have a Sikh temple here in Mill Lane. We also have a Hindu
Mandir. We haven't got premises yet but we meet in Leith Community Centre once a month. I go to that, the Sikh temple, and I go to
the Unitarian church as well on Sunday morning. Some of us are of
the opinion that there should be a sharing of faiths in the community
irrespective of what religion you follow. There is a common ground
for us to fight for: the betterment of the community. And we should
forget the past. Religions are not to divide, religions are to unite.

I live alone – that's the saddest part of my life. There is nobody
to surround me here. My brothers and sisters want me to go back

to India but I don't know. I haven't made up my mind yet. Aye, I've lived longer here than I've lived there but then again there they do everything for me. Here I have to do it for myself, that's the only difference. We'll see. We don't know what the future will hold.

MELROSE

The Myth of the Mother Country

Melrose was born in 1936, in St Elizabeth, Jamaica. When she was nine her family moved to Kingston and in 1956 she came to London to train as a nurse. Now a district nurse, she has five children and lives in Edinburgh. We interviewed her in Spring, 1987.

My family were fairly what you would call middle class. In Kingston we had our own family house that the grandparents stayed in. It was the extended family system where in the one big grounds there's three houses. My grandparents stayed in one, my aunt and her husband and family stayed in one, and another aunt and her husband in one. But then along the road, just about maybe a couple of chains, there's another plot of land, and another aunt lived there, and cousins lived at the back. So we were close; the whole area had a lot of relatives living within close proximity.

This arrangement was common among Jamaicans. Even when my parents moved away and lived outside, maybe a bus ride from my grandparents, we were there most of the time. And if we weren't there one weekend my grandmother would be most offended. It was more or less you had to be there, you know. That was the family seat as such [laughs]. You turned up.

It was good because my grandparents were really very nice, you know, very easy going old people and because there were so many cousins and aunties there weren't any restrictions on you as such. You plied each day between the various relatives. They had a shop and a bar and what we call a 'cold supper shop', you know, like you would say a café – but there weren't any seats. They sold groceries as well within the same framework, and at the back they did their own baking. Although my father worked outside, the rest of the family worked within the business.

We had a lot of the usual childish games, skipping, and 'peevers' as you call it over here. It was quite safe to go down to the beach and have beach parties. We joined the Brownies and Guides, and the church. We had to go to the church, and Youth Fellowship. There was lots of dancing and plenty of friends getting together.

Part of the schooling is fee-paying, and part is non fee-paying. Books were your own concern, even in the public school, except for jotters. You maybe got two jotters every six months, it's called free issue, but the rest of that was your parents' responsibility. There was no Child Allowance, no Family Allowance, no National Health Service, but medical aid was free.

Anyway, to talk about the school: you could go as far as Junior Cambridge, Senior Cambridge. I did the domestic science course and left just before I did my Junior Cambridge. There was a group of us (we were meant to be doing our exams) and we'd got magazines and we were sitting round the classroom and we were filling in forms. Just filling them in, because they said, 'Your country needs you'; 'Your Mother Country needs you'. I mean we always sort of looked upon Britain as the mother country. It was instilled in us in schools. I think it was just curiosity really, because we thought nothing more of it. But in return we got all these forms back, application forms. And we filled them up again. Unknown to my parents I just kept filling in these and sending them back and getting all the requirements like X-rays. Because the students were waiting a year or two to get into the hospitals at home, I thought, 'Well it'll be another three years before they get round to accepting me, and by that time I'll have got into one here or I'll have gone to teachers' college'. And the next thing was I heard that I had to start classes in London in January! Then I had to tell my parents. And they had about maybe four weeks, five weeks to get me here.

As usual, the family all got together and had a discussion. My father wasn't very pleased because he didn't think any of his children should leave the house before they were 21. And the usual caring – how they feel the family's got to stay together.

Then eventually they decided that OK, if that's what I really wanted . . . I left there when I was 19. Went to a hospital called Eastern Memorial Hospital, East End of London, where they spoke a different language completely from me because they were Cockneys and if you wanted butter you ended up with water.

There were quite a lot of Jamaican girls going to various hospitals and we came over by boat. Before I got here we stopped in Paris and that was the first time I'd seen snow. And then we came over here. And my first experience was these great brick walls and doors slamming, because we weren't used to doors being shut like that.

It was quite cold because it was January – oh praise be, January! And they showed me my room and there was a heater to be plugged in. No one told me that if I shut my door and did not have my key I couldn't get back in, so of course I was in my pyjamas and decided to run to the toilet and just slammed the door because I was never used to these Yale locks. And I came back and couldn't understand why the door wouldn't open. And I met a French girl who was a student in the same year as me, her name was Claudine, and she ran down for the master key because she had more insight into this sort of thing coming from France, and explained always to keep my keys with me and showed me how to put the snib on. But nobody had bothered to tell us that, and it seemed like a little thing but it was big.

And then when I went for meals they just didn't ever seem to put salt in the food. It was basic – potatoes, brussels sprouts, roast beef, and the first time I got rice in the hospital home (it was their attempt at cooking rice and I was so pleased they'd cooked it), the grains were hard, it was swimmin' in the water. If you mentioned rice their limit was rice pudding, you know.

I came as a student nurse. We did not have auxiliaries and so when you started, you started at the bottom and you were trained as a student nurse from day one. And you started with the bed pans and you got graduated to the flowers [laughs] and you eventually worked your way up.

For me, I have been pretty lucky, pretty fortunate in choice of hospital, general situation. There was some degree of prejudice but because of the hospital I was in, which was mostly run by Chinese, Irish, West Indians, a few Spanish girls and a very few English girls, you found that although there were slight prejudices against each other there wasn't the massive prejudice.

When I came over here I was so free I didn't know what to do with myself. Whereas I had always been accustomed to the structured life, to turning to my mum and saying, 'Well, right, I'm going to such and such a place', and she'd say, 'Well, don't be back any later than . . .', now I could be later. And for some reason I didn't want to be. It took me the good part of maybe six or seven months before I ever wanted to be any later than the usual time I got back at home. But everybody was in the same situation. We all had to live in up to the 3rd year, so you made your own entertainment by chasing about the corridors making noises [laughs], going out to parties, making your own parties. We had to be in for 10.30, and we could always find ways of not coming in if we decided we didn't want to. We decided that we weren't at home, why should we have to come in at 10.30?

We had very, very little money. It would be about £4 something per month. It wasn't a wage as such because we lived in and we got all our meals so to speak. I know by the time I was doing my midwifery I was getting about £4 10/- a week which was really good money you know, very good money.

I met my husband because he was a cousin of a Jamaican girl that I was quite friendly with. I had only come here for three years and then at the end of that I met my husband; I didn't ever think I would stay this long. He'd been over here about two years longer than me. He worked for a Scottish firm, hence the travelling northwards. We went from London to Birmingham to Nottingham, Manchester, Scunthorpe – because his firm would send him to various places. And then we decided by the time we started having the children that we had to settle for somewhere and it had to be Edinburgh. I just loved Edinburgh. I came up here for holidays and decided it was so lovely – of all the places I'd been this was where I would like to live.

Looking back now, I didn't give the lack of a black community here much thought. I didn't even feel that I wouldn't be welcome. I just thought, 'Well, this is where I want to stay, and it's too bad, they've got me! I'm making it home and I'll give it the best stab I've got'.

Well, we bought our house in Kingsknowe and that'll be 24 years in March that we're there. And I came up with two young children, one was two, the other was six weeks old (that's Claudine, named after my French friend). And the children just grew up there and met other children and it's funny because they were really quite happy and I don't think any of these children that they grew up with for a long time ever bothered them. If they called them names, it hadn't anything to do with colour, it was just names that any child would call another child. I think now my children are growing up with a little bit more of this prejudice being rammed home and I think it's mostly through things being highlighted in the media.

We used to be the only black family in the area and I found my neighbours were really nice. I found one neighbour very curious. She used to ask stupid little questions. Oh she would say to her daughter, 'Look, they've got white nappies'. Well, the daughter would come and say to me 'Mum thinks you should have black nappies'. 'Oh, I see, poor mum. Just say to mum, Mrs Duff has never ever seen a black nappy in her life, but if your mum has one that she would like to show her she would be pleased to see it.' Maybe I'm a bit stuffy, but I just felt because of her stupid remarks, that I was more intelligent than her and there was no reason for me to climb down to her level. There was no reason I was going to lower my standards to match her stupidity, so if she wanted to be close to me her mentality would have to rise a little bit, which it eventually did. Well, we became quite good friends because the children became quite good friends. She was about the only one that we found a little bit prejudiced. Like, she would ask the next-door neighbour how she felt about having a black person beside her. And I remember my neighbour saying that, 'If all the whites who lived beside me were as good as her, this place would be a better world'. And I thought that was really, really nice. So we all stayed very good friends. The first Hogmanay we spent here they wouldn't let us sleep. We just shut our door because we thought 'Nobody'll bother'. But they just about knocked the door down. We had to open the door and let everybody in. And they always liked my husband to first-foot them because he was tall, dark and, they say, handsome as well! They liked that, you know; they thought he brought them good luck.

I carried on nursing in between having babies, and I did day duty, night duty, became day sister at Astley Ainslie, did staff nurse work at Bruntsfield, sister's post at Longmore – just worked my way up. Went on the district nurse's course and I've been a district nurse ever since. I've done a family planning course (after I had five children of course [laughs]), practical work, teacher's course and now I'm doing a counselling course.

I wouldn't say I have achieved much financially but I think I've achieved a lot for my self-satisfaction. The things that are important to me are the home, the family, that I've got a career and that I've got my health and think the wealth might eventually follow [laughs]. I think what happened was, I looked on Britain as a challenge. I think I'm that kind of person, that if I make a decision, I make the best of it.

My sister came over when she was 14 to stay with me. She's now a nurse, married to a Scotsman who is a history teacher. And my mother came over. She came over for six weeks' holiday, then went back to Jamaica to have a look again and decided she wanted to come back, and she's been here now, what, 17 years. My brother stays in Canada and my other sister was away in New York at the time, so Mum felt she was going to stay where there were two children.

I miss the Jamaican sunshine, but I don't think I'm the kind of person that pines for something or pines for somewhere, providing I can hear from the family and I know all is well. And I think once my mother was over here that was more or less it.

The basic thing about most people who came when I came was: they saw it as a challenge, and they came because the British at that time were asking for people to come. Well, we had Enoch Powell or his agents in the West Indies sayin', 'Your country needs you'.[1] You wouldn't believe it! But maybe that's why the guilt is with him all along. I think after the war, they needed all the hospitals and railways to be manned. I mean, the hospital I went to first was almost like a League of Nations. At that time it was a matter of you come and you work and you earn and you go home and you sleep and wake up and earn. There were the few who could pull themselves out from that and went back and carried on into further education or just improved their lifestyle. But most couldn't do that.

And a lot of people who stayed, what they did was they stayed in a community, so therefore you get the black areas building up. But that is natural because if you go to Canada you will find there's a part – maybe British Columbia or somewhere like that – where practically a whole area is maybe full of Scots people, because they've gone there and they know a friend and so they stay. And this is how you're getting the communities. You know, your colour can't hide. There are communities where you find a collection of maybe Polish or Irish, and it's not so obvious until they either speak or when they have their days. But for blacks, the Chinese, they are an obvious race and you can tell there's a lot of them here. But there's really not a lot more than other immigrants.

At school we had to learn these songs which imply that Britain is the mother country. Everyone that came over in the early years saw Britain as a mother country, and I don't think it really occurred to us that Britain wasn't going to act like a mother country until we came over and saw people's attitudes and realised that they weren't special as we'd thought. Because we thought, oh, you know, this is going to be something special. And one of the things that got me was that people had homes without bathrooms. And their attitudes too: people we thought were civilised, supposedly civilised people. A lot of things they did to their own people didn't seem as civilised as we would imagine because we couldn't have done it. You know, like I'd nurse people who'd maybe say, 'Oh, I haven't seen my son for 20 years', and they're dying. And you'd say, 'Well, where is your son?' only to find that the son is about a stone's throw away. And you think, 'Well how can they be just a bus ride away for 20 years without contact?' I mean, we just didn't feel we could do that. On the whole, we were brought up to honour the parents. So although this country is part of the parental thing that's been instilled in us, gradually we realised. It sort of drifted away. And as more people came in and wrote to people back home, then the myth of the mother country started dying away. And then you feel, well if we are partly your children what the heck you doin' treating us like that, because we wouldn't treat our children like that. And gradually it begins to dawn.

BERNIE

A Life Foretold

Bernie was born in India in 1915. In 1945 he married and
settled in Edinburgh. He has four children and ten grandchild-
ren. At the age of 72 he works part-time driving a mini-bus
for pensioners and disabled children.

My great grandfather was a British ex-Army Major. He married
my great grandmother – she was from a convent. See, there's an
awful lot of girls from the convents in India who were converted
from Hinduism to Christianity. And at one time the British soldiers
intending to settle in India, which I believe they were encouraged to
do, used to marry girls from the convents, you know. So we all
derived from the army; from the army going to India and the soldiers
intermarrying with the girls there.

I was born in 1915 in Secunderabad, in the state of Hyderabad, ken,
southern India. And I lost my mother when I was three years old.
Now what happened, she had already lost two sons at birth before I
arrived on the scene. I was an instrument baby, which caused my disability. The next baby she had cost both her and the baby their lives.
I'd have loved to have known my mother. I remember her funeral.
I can remember a long carriage with six white horses with black
plumes: the hearse that carried her to her last resting place. That's all
that I can remember about her. She was a school teacher and had a BA
degree. Her maiden name incidentally was Scottish, she was Dorothy
Johnson. When my mother died, my dad was determined he wasn't
going to put me in a home. He had two sisters in Bombay who were
younger than him. The older of the two, ken, was a nursing sister in
a hospital, and the younger was an office clerk, but she was engaged
to be married. So he wrote to the eldest of the two – would she bring
me up? She agreed to right away although she'd only seen me once as
a baby. So my Dad packed up and he came to Bombay, got a job as
an engineer on one of the ships running up the coast there, and my
aunt Sarah took me over completely.

57

Of course, my Dad was paying her and it was just marvellous living with her. Across the road from us was St Peter's school. It was a High Church of England school and its church was at the end of the road, where they rang the Angelus every morning and night. And that struck me, you know, as really funny. I was only about three and a half, and I'd never heard that before.

But in the house my aunt had a picture. It was of a field in England, somewhere in the country, with the farmer and his wife bowing in prayer and a church in the distance. And it was called 'The Angelus'. That's how I got to know what the Angelus really meant.

My aunt's house was in a long, long building: she had the first house in it. There was a stair going up the side of the house to the first floor where we lived. You walked on to the balcony and you had your front door there. And at the top of the stair you had a trap-door, and at night you lowered it so nobody could get into the house. And she also had - oh she had two lovely dogs. They were both bloodhounds, you know; they called them Gypsy and Trixie and they were bigger than me when I first went there. Anyway, the interesting thing was, right at the back of the house this hill rose up. It was called Mazagon Hill. They later changed it to Bundawarda and there is actually a waterworks beneath it. And I mean it *was* a hill. It was some height. A railway ran along the far side of it – the suburban electric railway, and the lower end of it had a garden and swings and a bandstand and everything. Now, on this hill was a higher level on the far end on which grew three tall palm trees – we call them *palmyra* trees in India. I used to admire them. And there was a big marble sundial put there by a Parsi businessman. From there you could see the whole of Bombay and the whole of the docks.

So anyway, I used to go up there every day with my ayah until I grew older and started to go to the kindergarten. Of course, the first thing was, my aunt got an ayah in to look after me. She had worked as an orderly in the hospital with my aunt. She lived with us and because she was a Jewess, there were certain times, like Christmas, if we were going to have chicken, she used to get it killed by her own priests so she could join in the meal. Anyway, that woman stayed with us for years.

India is a vegetarian country and I never saw a butcher's shop until I came to Great Britain and saw meat hanging in the window. You're not allowed to do that in India. The Mohammedans have their own butchers, but they have to have a special licence and are not allowed to have it on the main streets where everybody can see it. The Mohammedans lived amongst themselves and the Hindus lived amongst themselves: they never lived in the same place. In our block of flats, there were about eight families, all Portuguese or Anglo-Indian. The house where my aunt lived was on Belvedere Road.

I started my education at four and a half. St Peter's across the road from us was a primary school, but attached to it was the All Saints Mission. They had Indian girls there learning to be nuns. And they made all sorts of things using these wee beads with black tips on them. We call them Devil's eyes; they used to make necklaces of them, and all the girls wore them. Anyway, the All Saints Mission had a kindergarten. There were about twelve of us in the class. We all paid our fees to the mission itself. And the teacher there was a Portuguese woman: her name was Mrs De Souza and she was an awfy nice woman. So I was there until I was able to go to the primary. Now we were Catholic, and St Peter's school was High Church of England, but it made no difference to us – Protestant or Catholic in India, nobody bothered. When I was at St Peter's I was told by the headmaster, ken, the rector, that if I wanted to go to the Catholic church I was welcome to. But I didn't because although my aunt was a staunch Catholic and my dad the same, they said, 'If you're going to a Protestant school, just go to their church, it makes no difference.' I was at St Peter's primary for quite a few years and it was during that time that I first decided to come to Scotland in a rather roundabout way.

It was a Christmas party to which children invite their parents and friends. I was a really good singer (I've no got the same voice now). By this time Mrs De Souza had been made headmistress of St Peter's and she always knew I had a good voice, so I was picked to sing the verses of a Scottish song and the children had to, ken, join in the chorus. And the song was – what was it now? –

> Sweet and low,
> Sweet and low,
> Wind of the western seas . . .

Now, you know how you get stagefright – well funnily enough I never had stagefright. I didn't even know there were people in the hall, 'cause when I was singing that song my mind got carried – I was away up in the north of Scotland somewhere and I could hear the chorus the children were singing. I still can't explain it to this day. That's when I decided I must go there! I didn't want to visit any other place in the world, but Scotland – yes!

Anyway I went to that school until I was seven, when my aunt married and had to give up the house. Well my dad took it over, actually, but I had to leave St Peter's and go to a convent school where I was living in. It was run by the Sisters of Jesus and Mary. Mind you, it was a girls' school, but they took boys in up to nine. So I went there until I was nine, then I got transferred to St Mary's High School which was a Catholic school. The school was all Anglo-Indians, Eurasians and some British children. We never spoke the Indian language – I spoke English since ever I was born. And it was run by the Jesuit priests, you know; it was a fee-paying school. Eurasians are – like I talk about the French Indians or the German Indians, we call them Eurasians. But Anglo-Indians were particularly British, and we always prided ourselves on that fact although we always mixed together. I had a few Indians friends, but they were few and far between. And I had a lot of Portuguese friends. They were from Mormugao (now Margao) mostly, which was a Portuguese state in India. And there were some French from Div and Daman and various other places where the French had colonies. We all got on well. At our school there was only one Indian teacher and he was the drawing master.

So I was there until I was 15 anyway. I'm disabled in my right hand. It's about an inch and a half shorter than my left and I can't raise it above my shoulder. Anyway, the curriculum for the new boys coming in was that every Saturday morning you had to go in the boxing ring, regardless of who you were. I could hit like hell, but I couldn't stop anybody hitting me because I can't lift my hand higher than my shoulder. I have this disability but oddly I never really played on it, you know, and anyway I got hammered because I couldn't save myself.

My education was all based on the English culture. I was born of mixed culture with Indian blood but I never knew the Indian culture. You did Preliminary, then Junior Cambridge, then Senior Cambridge and that's what we were taught. I wanted to study the Indian language, or even French, but no, they didn't let you; you had to study Latin, which annoyed me at the time. So I can't write the Indian language although, before I left, I'd learned to speak six or seven different dialects.

I was always afraid of the Indian culture. I'll put it to you this way: at St Mary's our dormitory was right on the top floor. Now I used to lie awake at night and the Indians would maybe be celebrating a wedding or some other festival and you used to hear the drums goin' on. I used to be shaking in my shoes, I was so frightened. And I'd lie for hours hoping and praying they would stop. I don't know what it was that affected me that way. We had our own school band an' all, but that was mainly classical music. The Indian music frightened me.

The funny thing was, we could get on with the Mohammedans but the Hindus we found hard to get on with because they had a culture all of their own. I was frightened to go into a Hindu temple and I remember one thing – and I couldn't sleep all night because of it – was if a priest from a temple died, they used to sit him up in a palanquin, dress him up and walk through the streets with him on their shoulders. And if you saw the sight! Mind you, it is only a human being that's dead, but these were things that frightened me. And I don't know if being a Catholic affected me in that respect.

And another thing that puzzled me in India was this: you know they're talking about South Africa and apartheid. Well India is the last country to be critical. In my time, the untouchables were absolutely cast away. An untouchable had to live on his own, he couldn't mix with the others, especially the Brahmins, the high caste. The outcasts or the Dades, as they called them, were not allowed to mix with any-body except their own people. I was more sorry for the untouchables than I was for other poor people in India; I mean it was a country of beggars and you could see leprosy round about you on the street.

I mind the time the Prince of Wales came to India, ken, later the Duke of Windsor, and there were riots all over. And my dad and my uncle were given guns to go out and help the police quell the riots. They were actually armed, ken, because the Prince of Wales was to go on parade in Queen Street. And my aunt had to go to the police station to help with the injured and wounded 'cause she was a nurse. We got trapped in a tramcar. They smashed all the windows and we all ducked under the seats, you know. The tramdriver just put it on full throttle and we drove through. God knows if he killed anybody or not.

School days were great. I'll say this about the Jesuit priests, I admired them. You never got two minutes to yourself to get into trouble. You either had to be in the choir (which I was in) or in the band, the boy scouts or the cadets. They always had you occupied. You never got a chance to waste your time. My only waste of time was trying to study Latin. It used to drive me up the wall.

There were Indian schools, state schools, that all the Indian laddies went to, ken. There was one just where my aunt lived. Once, I was home for the holidays, I didn't want to go back to the boarding school and my dad said, 'What are you going to do? You've got to go back, there is no other place for you'. I said, 'I'll try the Indian school here'. I was there for half a day because of all the writing, I couldn't read it. And the master of the school, ken, he just laughed at me. I was lost completely because I had never learnt to read and write the language. I tried it once or twice on my own but I was no good at it.

The struggle for Indian Independence was going on all the time I was there. We were aware of it, and as Anglo-Indians we were worried because we knew (well I was too young to understand – I began to understand it later) that sometime or other we would have to decide whether we were going to be Indians or leave the country. See, they were going to give us that option. But at that age you don't worry about these things. You never think you've got to make your own living some day.

So anyway, while I was at St Mary's my dad's ship got sold to an Indian state – Bhavnagar State – on the Kathiawar peninsula. There were two sister ships actually; they both got sold to the same state, and because they were diesel ships and diesel engineers were few and far between in India, my dad was asked if he would like to go with them and get employed by this Indian state, by the Maharajah. He was offered a good job as a state official, as chief engineer, so he moved there. I was still in the boarding school and I used to go up in my holidays and visit him. It was about two days and a night's run down the coast. The only thing was, I knew myself, that if I went there we were going to be isolated from our own community. As an Indian state, there were Hindus and Mohammedans but no other Anglo-Indians, except my dad and his second engineer.

There was one thing about this state, they had a great engineering workshop. I'd seen it so I knew what it was like. When we got there, my dad was determined that I would to go university and I was just as determined that I wouldn't. I wanted to serve my time as an engineer. My dad objected; he said to me, 'You can't be an engineer, you've got a bad hand'. I've always had difficulty putting on my jacket, you know. Even now I'm stuck trying to get my jacket on and off. Yet I can use it for engineering. Anyway, I said to my dad, 'Look, I want to serve my time as an engineer. You've got influence here. You could get me a job in the workshop', 'Oh no', he said, 'I won't do that. No way am I going to use my influence to get you anywhere other than a university'. So that left me a problem.

At the time there was a dredger being constructed there, under the supervision of Mr Brown, from Glasgow. He had a wee office and a wee clerk because his company was under contract to the Indian state to direct the building of this dredger. I thought I would go and see him as he was friendly with the port officer, Mr Johnson. So was my dad, they all used to drink together. So I went down to Mr Brown one day and I said to him, 'Can you get me started in the workshop?' He says, 'I know your father. Why can't he speak for you?' I never told him about my hand, I just said, 'All my dad wants me to do is to go to university and I don't want to go'. He said 'Well, come back in the afternoon and I'll speak to Mr Johnson'. When I went back he said, 'Right you've got to start on Monday in the workshop'. I was six years an apprentice over there, 'cause to go to sea you had to do five years' engineering and one year's electrical work before you were allowed to go on a ship.

I was quite friendly with the youngest daughter of the medical officer of the Indian state who was Portuguese. She used to play polo sometimes and I used to go and watch. She got to speak to the Maharajah – his name was Krishna Kumar Singhji. He had his own troops. India hadn't got Home Rule at that time, it was still British, and these wee Maharajahs were set up by the British government and could have all their own armies and troops. And they maintained them pretty well.

In this state in particular, if you happened to be coming home from work after ten o'clock at night you'd be stopped. The first time it happened to me I got the fright of my life. This sepoy stepped out of the shadows with a gun and he challenged me, 'Halt. Who goes there?' But it meant that you could walk the streets at night in safety.

Now in that state, in the workshop where I served my time, there were only Mohammedans and Hindus. And what surprised me was that they were such good tradesmen, you know, they were craftsmen. Being brought up in a school with other Anglo-Indian boys, I had never thought that Indians were as smart as that! But when I went to the workshop they taught me all I know as an engineer. One of the mechanics used to do all the cars, and the others used to work on ships and boats. And the turners were really smart men. And the blacksmiths – they had a funny way of working; they always sat on their haunches on the ground with an anvil in front of them. They done everything sitting down. They were smart men, there's no doubt about it.

Most of the Indian families didn't have toilets inside the house. There was no such thing as a flushing system there. It was all these tins, you know. The end wall of the house was your toilet and outside was a trap door where the untouchable would come with his cart and empty everything.

But most of the poorer classes didn't have anything at all. And this was another thing that was really odd to me. When I cycled down from my house to my work, they had two huge fields: one field for men and one for women. They were what was called the coolie caste, slightly above the untouchables.

Another thing about this state: they built their houses with wooden frames and they used cow pats to line the walls. And they used this for cooking as well, by drying it into wee, flat cakes which they'd burn. Everything was based on that, their homes and their cooking, and sometimes you'd see the women going along the roads, picking it up and putting it in a basket to take home to dry.

A lot of women worked at the port, unloading barges. All of the goods came from Britain and because they couldn't read, they were all marked with different colours. One day I was going into the workshop and there was a crowd of them sitting in the boatyard where the lifeboats were hung up. I walked past and after a while one of the boys came up to me and said, 'You shouldn't have done that!' And I said, 'Done what?' He said, 'You walked past those women whilst they were getting their meal and because your shadow fell on them they could not eat their meal'. I couldn't believe it! Just your shadow going over them! Later on I asked them, and they told me that it was because of their religion, especially because they were vegetarians and I ate meat.

You know, there's something here – mind I was telling you it was a Mr Brown that started me in my apprenticeship? Well, there was an Indian coolie woman working there loading ships, and she had a baby to Mr Brown. So that baby was an Anglo-Indian in other words, but God knows what he will be working as – a coolie or something. Mr Brown would just go away and leave them, you see. That's the kind of thing that happened and it's one reason why Anglo-Indians were looked down on by many of the English.

What I liked most about it was the colourfulness of the place. On certain feast days the women would come down to the docks. They covered themselves from the waist down but otherwise they just went into the water and nobody seemed to bother. Over here, people would stare and say, 'Fancy her going topless!' But nobody bothered there, they didn't bother and neither did we.

Right across the road from the house we lived in there was a Brahmin priest. He was a high caste priest and he wasn't supposed to come to our house because we had, ken, one of the untouchables coming to clean our toilets. But at night time, after dark, he used to come in and have a drink with my dad and nobody saw him! I'll tell you another thing: all around me were drugs, what they call ganja. And we had a coachman, we had our own carriage, and this coachman was always on drugs and he used to drink methylated spirits as well. But, mind you, despite the fact that I was surrounded by this, I wasn't interested. To this day I have only seen opium once and that was up at Surgeons Hall.

There was an Anglo-Indian boy who was on the railway, named Charlie, and he told me to come to the railway sports ground. I could join in the games there, you see, because they played cricket and hockey. So every night when I finished work I used to get on my bike and cycle to join them in their games. They were all Indian boys except Charlie. He was a fireman on the railway, but because he was an Anglo-Indian – and this was a monopoly that we had at that time – he got a higher wage than his driver, who was an Indian.

Something that was really very, very interesting but was also unbelievable happened at this stage of my life. I'd be about 16 or 17 at the time, and it was when my stepsister was born. One of the Hindu clerks in my dad's office said, 'Get the priest in from the temple and he will come to your house and give you a horoscope'. So my dad said, 'Oh well, I've got nothing against it. Fair enough!' Well, the priest or guru duly arrived. But they won't talk to the women; it's only the men they'll speak to. So when he came, my dad said, 'You talk to him in the living room and I'll go and bring the baby down' – because my stepmother, being a woman, couldn't come down. While he was upstairs bringing my sister down the man was talking to me. And he said, 'Do you mind if I look at your hand?' He looked at my hand then he felt my head and asked about my time of birth. He said to me, 'You'll be leaving India for good'. And he said, 'When you are about 24 you'll be in danger of losing your life and if you come through that you'll live to a good old age'. So I'm hoping the second bit's right! Anyway, after he'd seen my sister and left, I sat with my dad and told him what he'd said and we just laughed about it because, to tell you the truth, we lived just as you live here. My dad had a good job, he had good money, although it cost him all his money to keep us going because we had a carriage. The three servants were paid by the state. So I said, 'I don't believe I will ever leave India'. And I forgot all about this incident completely.

I got through my apprenticeship without any trouble. I used to swing a big hammer, and everything that everyone else did, I did. And I wouldn't let my disability beat me, even though at times it gave me bother.

When after six years I finished my time, I decided, 'Well, I have to get a job'. But I knew I couldn't work in the state because it was all Indian firms there and they wouldn't give me a start. When I gave them my name, they knew immediately I wasn't an Indian and there was no way they were going to help me out. So the only firms I was employed by in India were American or British firms like Ford, the Metal Box Company and Courtaulds, all in Bombay where I decided to go and live with my aunt.

I wasn't long there when I got a job with the Ford Motor Company on the assembly line. But when the orders ran down I got paid off. Then I went to another firm, the Metal Box Company of India with my friends, Charlie Walmsley and his brother Horace. They were Anglo-Indian but totally different from me – blue-eyed and blonde.

After that, I got a job at Courtaulds, which was the best firm ever I worked for in India. We made rayon material mainly for saris. Every evening after work, Mr Barnes the weaving master used to instruct us, give us all the know-how. And once a week we went to technical college. Courtaulds only employed Anglo-Indians and what they called domiciled Europeans, ken, boys of mixed parentage or English people whose sons were living in India. But they had six technicians, highly-skilled men, who were Indian, and they were all charge hands or foremen.

Then the Indians boycotted the firm because there were only six Indians employed there. They said they wanted the mill opened to Indian labour and to do away with the Anglo-Indian monopoly – our wages were pretty high, higher than any other mill because we were Anglo-Indians. So Mr Barnes sent for us one day and said, 'You may have heard they have boycotted our showroom. So we are going to close down and open to Indian labour. What you all do is up to you, because the wages are going to be halved'. See, where there was one of us they were going to employ two men, so naturally we all left. This would be about 1937–1938.

The Anglo-Indians got a bad name in India. I'll tell you why: they wouldn't work for low wages. The Indian would work maybe for a pound a week whilst we wouldn't work for less than a fiver. Well, I'm talking about in comparison. The Anglo-Indians wouldn't work as cheap labour and this is what was held against them. And for that reason there were an awful lot of boys walking the streets and getting a bad name for themselves.

Most of the railway staff in Bombay were Anglo-Indians – guards, drivers and the rest. I don't know if the British government had an agreement that certain jobs had to go to Anglo-Indians. In my time, there were dances held in the guards' and drivers' building, customs dances (the customs officers were all Anglo-Indian), and police dances (the police were all Anglo-Indian). And every Christmas they had big Christmas trees and parties. They held them in big tents and took collections from everybody for presents for the bairns.

It was the English colonials who were really prejudiced. I came across a boy in the Navy establishment once, a young naval officer, and he was lucky he didn't get a doing, 'cause when I went for a job he had the cheek to say to me, 'Where did you get your name from?' you know, in a rude manner. See, they came out with the idea, 'We're going to subjugate the country. We're the bosses, we'll do what we like'. They'd hardly been in India two minutes and they're telling you what to do. They were very, very rude people. And I found that mostly among the English colonials. Not so much amongst the Scots and Irish, who accepted you for what you were and took you depending on your own manners. I knew many Scots and we got on well.

There was one particular thing, I remember an Indian friend of mine pointed it out to me. As you can see, I didn't like the English colonials, and there was a reason for that. I'm not talking about soldiers – I'm talking about the big-business men and managers with big heads who came to India. (Previous to them it used to be the old colonels – I suppose my great-grandfather was one too!) Anyway, there was a picture house called the Pathé cinema and half-way through the picture you got a break and everyone used to go out and sit in this big open-air restaurant with their ice-creams or drinks. Now there were a lot of soldiers from Colaba barracks close by, and the business men would never sit amongst them or sit with them. My friend remarked, 'How do you expect them to treat us any better when they treat their own people in the same bad manner?' He was right and it was very odd seeing it happen.

Well, what happened in the meantime, my dad's ship was sold back to a firm in Bombay and when he brought the ship to Bombay he told me an engineer from Calcutta, Mr Aldridge, was taking over as Chief Engineer. My dad was going back to the state because his job was assured, you know.

The ship needed a trial run first, down the coast, and I sailed as Second Engineer. After the trip, Mr Aldridge (he belonged to the Bank Line, that's Andrew Weir's of Glasgow) asked me if I'd stay on. By this time it was an old ship, and I knew I'd have a lot of work on her, but I knew those engines inside out so I said, 'Yes'.

On the first trip the engine started well but soon it began to heat up
so the only thing we could do was to shut off the fuel before it blew
up. There was no water circulating through to cool it because the
Third Engineer hadn't cut out the water slots in the cylinder head
and there was panic-stations at the time because the ship's owners
were aboard. Anyway, these boys blamed me. They said, 'Well you
were in charge'. I lost my head and I said, 'Look you can keep your
job, I'm going'. So I packed it up and went home.

That evening, when I was in the house Mr Aldridge turned up
and said, 'I've packed up an' all. I was annoyed with them giving you
your books, you had nothing to do with what happened. I don't like
the firm anyway. If you come to Calcutta I'll try and get you started
with Andrew Weir's as an engineer. Come and stay with my family
until such time as I get you a job.'

When I got to Calcutta he was away on a ship. Calcutta was
a totally different place to Bombay. See I always compare them to
Edinburgh and Glasgow, because Bombay was more of a commercial city whereas Calcutta was more of an industrial city.

The Bengali people were very hostile to Anglo-Indians. I tried
for jobs but I couldn't get started because they were mostly Indian
firms. I tramped the streets for about a month. My dad was sending
me money to pay Mrs Aldridge for my keep but it was basic, you
know. I couldn't buy a cigarette and I was running down on shoe
leather, walkin' all over. One day, Mrs Aldridge had friends visiting.
They were Irish, business people who had tea estates in Ceylon,
and one of them suggested I go to a certain firm and see the
manager. They told me that he usually helped Anglo-Indian boys to
go to sea.

This is the interesting bit about it – I had no bus fare or tram fare
so I walks down to the firm the next morning and when I got to
the office there's an Anglo-Indian girl as secretary and she said, 'The
boss is away on holiday, won't be back for a month. But if you tell
me what you want I might be able to help you'. I said, 'I'm trying
to get away to sea as an engineer'. 'Oh,' she said, 'Well I'll tell you
what he tells other boys that come here. Go down to the Seamans'
Institute and ask for the minister, (this name I'll never forget) Padré
Jenkins, and tell him you're from this office, and he might be able to
help you.'

So I thought I may as well try that as nothing. I had to walk to
the Seamans' Institute because I never had any bus fare and it was five
or six miles away and pouring with rain. So I got to the Seamans'
Institute. It was quite a big building, with an archway and drive in

front, you know. And inside the archway was a taxi waiting. With it raining, the taxi driver had his windows up, so I knocked on the window and this English boy opened it, and before I could open my mouth – you know, it takes me back, it makes me feel sad about it – he said to me, 'Are you the engineer that we sent for?' I said, 'What?' He repeated, 'Are you the engineer?' I said 'No, but that's just what I'm looking for'. I grabbed my papers, I shows them to him and said, 'That's the job I'm after! I've come to see Padré Jenkins'. 'Well', he said, 'He'll be in and a', but if you're wanting an engineer's job jump in the taxi and I'll take you to the ship'.

So I never saw Padré Jenkins. To this day, I don't know who he was or what he was. I couldn't believe that it was happening to me, you know! So I went down to the ship and was introduced to the skipper and he said, 'Do you want to start as fourth engineer?' I said, 'Of course I do, that's what I'm here for!' 'Well', he said, 'I'd better sign you on before the shipping office closes because we're sailing at midnight'. It is so hard to believe these things happen, and here I was tramping the streets with no cigarettes, nothing.

Anyway, I got to the shipping office – it was 7 June 1939, the war was imminent. And the shipping master, he was a Mohammedan, he said to me, 'Have you any relations in England?' I said, 'No' and he said, 'Well how do you expect to live when you get there?' I said, 'That's my business. All your business is, is to sign me on'. He said, 'You haven't even got a passport'. But the skipper said, 'Well look, I'll take the responsibility for that. I'll sign a clause in the articles that if he wants to come back to India, we'll pay his fare back. We need an engineer and we want him to sign on'. Of course, with me having a bad hand, this was helping me tremendously because I didn't need to go through a medical. All this time I'd been dodging medicals, you see.

Now, as we came out of the shipping office, the skipper said to me, 'There's things you'll need like warm clothes, have you got any money on you?' I said, 'No, not a cent'. So he said, 'I'll tell you what . . .' and he gave me £20 in rupees, ken, the Indian money. I couldn't believe he was going to give me the money on trust! My wages were only £13 a month – £13 a month! And he said, 'Well there's £20, get all these things that you need and try to be on the ship at 11 'cause we're sailing at 12.' And he just went off in the taxi and I went back to tell Mrs Aldridge that I'd got a job. I'd been getting friendly with this lassie, Brenda, ken, her sister's daughter – and her sister didn't like it because they were Irish, and with me being an Anglo-Indian she wasnae too keen on it, although because I never had a job you couldn't blame her. So anyway, I went down and said 'Cheerio' to Brenda and she said, 'Write to us', and all the rest of it, you know.

I left India, that was in 1939. I've never been back since – but I'll get there!

That night when I got back to the ship as the fourth engineer, I couldn't believe it. We sailed at 12 midnight. And my watch was from 8 till 12 and when I came off watch, I sat in my cabin and I thought about this. I mean, it couldn't sink in that I was actually leaving India and I thought about what the fortune teller had said to me and it was so strange.

We went to Cochin and we were there for the day. That was the last I saw of India. We went to South Africa for bunkers – when they talk about bunkers they mean coaling a ship. Well we were going to the States but we had to get coal halfway across 'cause we'd run out otherwise.

Do you mind I was telling you about Mazagon Hill and the three trees on it? When I joined the Merchant Navy some of the firemen asked where I came from and I telt them. One said, 'Oh was that the big hill we used to see coming into the docks?' I said, 'Yes, right behind'. He said, 'Those three trees were a navigation point for ships coming into Bombay docks because they were so high up they could be seen for miles and miles . . .' It was called Three-Tree Hill.

And another very significant thing: I mean my dad was married three times. When he lost my mother he swore he wouldn't marry for five years and he didn't. And his second wife was a Gladys Sims, which was also a Scottish name, but she died in childbirth. And then he married a Stella McCoy – they were getting more and more Scottish, you see. And she died in childbirth. Oddly enough they all died in childbirth. And as I told you, Mr Brown started me, he was a Scotsman. My dad's superintending engineers in the firm he worked for before he went to the native state, were a Mr Ritchie and a Mr Muir. They were all Scotsmen – and I liked every one of them that I met. But the English colonials were the worst people you could come across. We just couldn't put up with them: they couldn't put up with us. That was the English colonial. The English I met later weren't the same 'cause when I joined the ship the Chief Engineer was from Liverpool; he was a totally different Englishman from the ones you met in India. I couldn't believe it. He was a working man, you understand. An English working man. So was the Second Engineer, from South Shields, and the Third Engineer, from Sunderland. The crew were all English and they were all working men, and they had a different attitude from the colonials in India.

Whilst we were in the States, war broke out, and when eventually we docked in Cardiff I had a problem, a very, very serious problem, because, as I told you, I'd left India without a passport or anything. At that time you didn't need a passport because India was British, but you had to have something to identify you. Of course, I had nothing, nothing to say where I was born or where I had come from or whatever. So anyway, after they had gone through everyone else the immigration sent for me into the saloon. And, of course, the questioning started: 'Where were you born?' – you know, the usual. And I told him that I was born in India of Anglo-Indian parentage but he said, 'Well, we've no identity at all for you. Now there's a war on, you could be a German or anybody'. I said, 'Do I look like one?' He said, 'No, we understand that and we know why you joined the ship, but you can't go ashore'. I said, 'You must be kidding! I've been over a year on this ship. I want to go to the pictures; I want to go and buy clothes; I want to do all sorts of things'. 'Well', he said, 'if you go ashore, report to the police and always report when you come back'. I said, 'I refuse to do that because I'm no a criminal. I'm no going anywhere near the police. If they want me they can take me now!' So he said, 'You're setting us a problem. I tell you what. We'll give you what they call a special passenger landing permit. Carry that with you at all times, ken, when you're ashore'. So I agreed to do that and it lasted me until the second year of the war when they gave out identity cards. After that I was in the clear.

We'd been across the ocean two or three times before I came to Leith in 1941. We'd been to Liverpool, to London, and Cardiff . . . and I was so looking forward to coming to Leith because I knew it was Scotland, you see. I told you about when I was seven years old and I had this dream about coming to Scotland. I thought the sky would be a different colour, you know; I thought everything would be so different; I never thought that grass was green over here. I had a totally different image of what Britain or Scotland would be like. And then when I came here I found that people still had to work to earn their living.

I remember the very first day that I arrived at Leith. I was ill at the time and I had to go to the Royal Infirmary in Edinburgh. Now, apart from the ship's company, I'd never been amongst a group of people who were all English, or all Scots, ken. It was always a mix. First thing I was stuck in an ambulance so I never set foot on the ground. And I must tell you, at that time I was very, very shy. Unless

I knew somebody I wouldn't speak to them. I don't know why, it was just something that I was brought up with. Like, I never swore until I joined the Merchant Navy and the Chief Engineer pulled me up for it. He said, 'Listen, don't tell the fireman "Please do this and please do that" they won't listen to you'. He said, 'Tell them to bloody well get on with it. That's the only way they'll listen to you because they may be British but they speak a different language from you or me'. In fact, we weren't allowed to mix with the ship's crew ashore. We could mix with them on board, but not ashore. If you were an officer you had to maintain that status. I got into trouble once or twice for that.

Now the only visitor that came to see me in hospital was one of the ship's engineers. I could understand it because you still do your eight-hour shift throughout the day on the ship. And I'm lying there in bed. I didn't know anybody. Now, next to me was an elderly man who came from Uphall, and whenever I heard his visitors coming I used to cover my head with my blanket and just lie there. So one day I'm lying there and the old man has visitors in – I think it was his wife and son. Next thing, somebody was poking at the blanket, so of course I came out. the woman spoke to me, she said, 'Why are you hiding under there?' 'Well,' I said, 'I feel uncomfortable. Everybody has got visitors and I haven't any'. 'Oh.' she said, 'You don't have to hide. It's all right. Just speak to everybody, forget about it'. And, I mean, I couldn't understand much of what she was saying. She spoke broad Scots, ken, and I didn't understand what the old man was saying at all, 'cause he spoke more broad than she did! So the next time they came in I wasn't in my bed. I went away to the dining-room and read a book. And when she was going out, she walked into the dining-room with her two lassies and said, 'There you are, hiding yourself away! You shouldn't run away. I left something for you, anyway'. Ken, she'd left me some fruit an' that. And of course the old man gave me a row for running away. So anyway, he says to me, 'Look, whenever you're out of here come up to my house at Uphall'. At that time there was no Livingston, just a station and a village. It was all countryside. So I said, 'OK, I'll do that'.

Well, I was so shy in those days I wouldn't even ask anybody where the toilet was. So this day, I got a bus out there and the lassie, Emily, met me and we went down to the house. I was dying for the toilet and I wouldn't ask them where it was. Eventually, I got the bus back to Edinburgh and by this time, I was fit to burst. So, mind the old Caledonian station, I walked in there and do you think I could find a toilet? – I just went round the back somewhere and, oh what a relief!

When I first got my Merchant Navy Passbook, one thing annoyed me, it annoyed me terribly. When I got it, under 'Complexion' it had 'Coloured'. I'd never heard that word before until I came here. And I questioned them, I says, 'What do you mean, coloured? Do you mean brown, black, white? What do you mean?' 'Oh', he says, 'I'm afraid that's what we have here. You'll have to accept it, ken'. 'My eyes are brown,' I said, 'But they should be "coloured" as well, instead of "brown" '. I had a bit of an argument about that, but it's still in my Merchant Navy Discharge Book. But that's one word that still annoys me to this day. Why don't they state a person's real colour, whether green, white, yellow, black, or what have you? But I must say this, in England I've found more discrimination. I have never come across it in Scotland. Never. Admitted, I've got friends, they might call me a black so-and-so and I'll call them something back but it's never done out of animosity. I've an awful lot of friends and nobody has ever been rude to me in the respect that they were trying to insult me. But I did get that in England, when I worked in Manchester. It was done in a sort of underhand way. But over here everybody's open, nobody bothers. And I love Edinburgh, I would never leave it.

Now, when I came in danger of losing my life, as the guru foretold, was in 1942. I'd been back and forward, and I was on this ship going to America. And in 1942, we left there to go to North Africa; we were carrying Canadian beer and food for the troops. And I think we were about two days off the coast of America, and it was about 2 o'clock in the morning when the ship got torpedoed, you see. And I can't swim. Even though I'd been at sea, with my Dad an' a', I never could swim. So I was terrified. The skipper had details of the men who could swim and the men who couldn't, so my position was in the lifeboat before it hit the water, to release the guy ropes – because if I'd have gone in the water I'd never had survived.

Oddly enough, when the ship went down it broke its back and the lanyard tightened and the whistle was blowing like anything. So anyway, we got sunk that night. There were three lifeboats. Now, the next morning the sea was getting rough, and the first boat, which I think had only five men in it, got picked up by an American coast-guard plane. Well, they said they could only pick up the first lifeboat because they didn't have room for everyone else.

Well, what they do when a ship sinks, they tie the lifeboats, one to the other, so they don't separate. We had water tanks, but no food in the lifeboats because somebody had slipped up. To prevent the stores being stolen when the ship is in port, they don't stock it up until they get to sea. It should have been stocked up then, but it wasn't. There were just a few biscuits and some condensed milk.

When the sea got really rough, we had to cut the other boat loose, because one would have sunk the other. We were rationed a wee teaspoonful of condensed milk mixed with water to make it last, and then you had these hard biscuits, and you got two bars of chocolate, ken, Cadbury's milk chocolate every day. And this went on: we were sitting in this lifeboat wondering when we'd get picked up because we expected the coastguard plane to come back, but for eleven days we never saw another thing. The boat was only meant to hold eight people but we had eleven in it.

It's an experience that you tend to forget through time but, oddly enough, I remember when I was in the lifeboat, all I was thinking of was Waverley Station. I don't know why that was going through my mind: 'Will I ever see that place again?' Because I didn't know Edinburgh that well then.

We used to put up an awning when it got warm to keep us from the sun, and on the eleventh day somebody says, 'Oh here's a plane!' And we wouldn't believe him because you reach a stage when you're well past caring. So we ignored the boy that was shouting at the plane. We thought he was just starting to imagine things. Anyway, there were two planes and they came over. I think one was a Sunderland Flyingboat and the other was an American Martin Flyingboat. We ended up in America, in Florida, and from there we went to New York where we heard that the other lifeboat had been picked up by a South American cargo boat. So we were all saved.

Well, that was the first time my life was actually saved. I gave it a lot of thought, because who expected that? I mean, we knew there was a war on, we knew things like that could happen and I'd had one or two narrow escapes before then. But that was the closest shave. Now, how can anybody tell whether it was coincidence? The guru must have known what he was talking about because he said it. So after escaping that, I'm hoping to live to 100!

It was whilst I was in digs that I met my wife. I lived in Madeira Street, Leith. My wife had lost her mother and she was in digs there with her father and her sister – so that's how we happened to meet. The first job I got ashore was with Henry Robb's. When my son was born, I said to my wife, 'I want to see him growing up. I'm no wanting to go away to sea again.' Anyway, I got my first job at Henry Robb's and from there I went to the Roperie in Leith. I

worked with Miller's London Road Foundry, with Bertrams Sci-
ennes. I worked on the buses, I worked with Burntisland Shipyard, I
worked in a laundry driving a van. I've done everything, you know.
I used to like changing over. I could remember every job I've done.
Anyway, I eventually finished up at Duraflex Industries – that's
where I retired from.

But I loved old Leith, you know, when the old Kirkgate was there.
Ken, I miss all that. There was the old Gaiety in Leith, the theatre,
and right opposite there was a shop where they sold lights and liver
and all sorts. Old Leith was really a marvellous place till they took
it all to bits. Ah, but Edinburgh's all changed. It used to be a great
place and I was sorry to see the changes.

I've never had regrets of being in Scotland. I never will regret it.
And I never want to go to India again, except to visit Bombay. My
father died in India. I never saw him again after 1939. I've lost trace
of my two half-sisters. I've lost trace of all of them. I still write to
my cousins in London – that's my aunt's children, ken, the one that
brought me up. They were the monied side of the family, ken, with
the doctors and that. My dad was the working class of the family.
They came here before India got Independence, so I never ever found
out how the Anglo-Indians were affected by it.

But I enjoyed my time in India – I wouldn't have enjoyed it had I
stayed, that I do know. But I enjoyed my childhood because it was
great. I mean, you were pampered, you had servants and och, it was
a good life. But as I grew older, and as I was in my secondary school,
I always had one worry in the back of my mind, and it always stayed
with me – my hand and my colour. See, if I had been in India today,
God knows what I'd have been doing because I'd never have stood
a chance. It's a funny situation, you know, once you leave a country
and you realise that you're glad you left it. I wouldn't go to live in
India, not now, unless I was highly technically qualified, otherwise
I wouldn't stand a chance. If you got below a certain standard that
was you trampled on.

How I made up my mind to come to Scotland was purely through
a song, and my mind being carried away. It's a very odd feeling when
you think about it. I mean, I wasn't an actor, I was singing on the
stage, just for the school, and yet I wasn't on that stage. I've been
with my wife up to the Isle of Skye and all over, and somewhere
round about Loch Lomond there's things that I've seen that I'd seen
before, and yet I'd never been there. You get experiences like that and
you wonder, 'How did it come about?' It was a matter of seconds.
If I had been a few seconds later, that taxi would have moved away

and I would never have got here. That's why I think about the man who foretold all this. It seems so hard to believe, you know. I mean my Dad had an idea he would never see me again when I left home – 'Oh,' I said, 'You're talking nonsense. I'll only be sailing from Calcutta to South Africa and back.' I never dreamed I'd be leaving for good. And I never saw him again.

JOE

Coming Out Alive

Joe was born on 11 March 1915 in the village of Porzow which was then in Poland but has since been absorbed into the USSR. He would like his story to be read as a tribute to the bravery and sacrifice of the Polish people during the Second World War.

We were a big family, four sisters and two brothers. My father was working for the railway as a joiner and at that time mother didn't work. When I went to school I was seven years old and I believe it was about then that my father got a house in Zdolbunov, the town where he was working, and we all moved. There was a big railway station with a big railway repair shop, and father worked there as a joiner. Where we'd lived previously it was three kilometres to the shop so it was much better in the town. And because my father was working with the railway we got a railway house – electricity and running water, inside toilet, and all these things which we hadn't had in the village. But my father died in 1924 when I was only nine years old. Father was only 52 when he died of a heart attack. Mother didn't get a pension from the railway, because Father didn't work long enough, and we had to leave that railway house. We went to a smaller house which was not as comfortable. My mother was a tailoress; she and my oldest sisters started to work in the house, making dresses mostly, for women and children.

When I left high school I must have been about 19. Everybody was called to the army who was 21, but I volunteered early. There was a system that if you had so many qualifications you had to go to the army only for a year, and then you were in the reserve rank. So eventually I got the rank of second lieutenant in the reserve. After I left the army I worked first in a state-run bank and insurance company. I was two years with them and, when I was about 23 years old, I went to work as a frontier guard. Now that was a very good

job because the Frontier Guard were under the Ministry of Internal
Affairs and had been organised like the army. So, although I was a
civilian, I started there in the rank of officer as I had had the rank
of officer in the army. It was a good job. I was working on the East
Prussian frontier near a town called Lomza. On the west was Germany, on the east was Prussia, and in between was what they called
the Danzig corridor through which the Poles had access to the sea.
That was given to Poland after 1918 by the Versailles Treaty, and it
was something Hitler was always objecting to.

In about March 1939 they called all of us who'd been in the Frontier
Guard to the army. That was part of mobilisation against the threat
that Germany could start the war.

Where I was in north Poland, directly on the East Prussian frontier,
when we heard the German tanks start moving it must have been
about six o'clock in the morning on the first of September 1939. We
were not surprised. Well, we knew enough about what was happening in Germany because we had a lot of contact with the people living
in East Prussia – there were a lot of Polish people living there. We
knew they'd start, although nobody knew the day. But when planes
started flying, and bombing, and tanks came in, we had to retreat.
We retreated roughly about 50 kilometres. There were some sporadic
fights, battles, but we'd been overpowered. They mostly came with
tanks, whereas we didn't have tanks you see. Our tanks were in the
west of Poland where the longest border was between Poland and
Germany.

Well it must have been on about the fifth of September I was
wounded during one of these small battles and taken prisoner. I was
in a German-controlled hospital run by Polish staff and I managed to
escape on the evening of the 19th of September. Already the Russians
had come and occupied Poland from the east, because Russia had a
secret agreement with Germany to partition Poland again; the eastern part, up to the River Bug, went to Russia, and the western part
to Germany.[1] The Russians came on the 17th of September. When
I escaped from hospital I knew they already had the eastern part of
Poland, where I was from.

I didn't go home. I went to Warsaw; I had an aunt there. But I
didn't realise how badly damaged Warsaw already was. To Warsaw
from where I was in hospital must have been about 200 kilometres,
but trains were running. There were a lot of people travelling in
different directions. I believe they would have taken me prisoner
of war if I had been in uniform, but I was in civilian dress,
you see.

The Germans were everywhere. All Polish army activity had stopped by that time – it wasn't any longer than two, three weeks and everything stopped. We knew of course that on the 12th September Great Britain had declared war on Germany. But by that time we knew that they couldn't come directly and start helping us. It was too far away. Only, we always thought that Great Britain and France had been more prepared for the war.

I was in Warsaw for probably about a week, just sleeping in the park, anywhere I could. Then I decided to go back east to where my mother was staying. I managed to get the train. It took me about five days, to get to the east end of Poland. When I came, the Russians were there. That was already about the middle of October. My mother and sisters all were alive, but we didn't know what had happened to my brother. He was in the regular army. And one of my brothers-in-law, he was a police inspector, and as soon as the Russians came in they took him. They arrested all the police force. And another brother-in-law was taken prisoner of war by Germany, but at that time we didn't know it. We knew after, when he wrote a letter.

I was living in my mother's house, and one day at the end of November 1939, the Russian secret police came and they arrested me, and put me in prison about 12 miles from where my mother stayed. I was interrogated. They always suspected that you had been working against them; right away they told me that I was a counter-revolutionary – probably because I had a brother-in-law who was fighting when Poland was at war with Soviet Russia in 1918 to 1920. And they were telling me that I had another brother-in-law who was a police inspector – that he was an 'enemy of the people' as they used to say.

They took me off to another prison in a town called Oriel. That was a big town in Russia. And in the middle of February 1940 they moved me again. There were about 40 to 60 prisoners in one cattle wagon. It was terrible because sometimes you could only stand, and we were about a week in that train. They took us to a prison in Charkow, in Ukraine. And usually when they took you from one prison to another, they started interrogation from the very beginning and sometimes something from your previous interrogation wasn't the same – and they'd start accusing you: 'You're lying'. Then eventually, must have been about March 1940, they took me to prison in Lubianka in Moscow. Well that was the worst of it. They would often beat you and kick you. We'd be starving and so they could do anything they wanted.

Well, of course at that time I was young; I was a little cocky, and although I could speak Russian I refused to; I wanted an interpreter. That made it worse for me. Sometimes I was correcting the interpreter. Well I was in very bad conditions; there were some things they put you through – isolation, eh, solitary confinement. And the worst was food. They didn't feed you at all, days and days sometimes. Then they suddenly brought you two or three salted herrings, and after that you wanted something to drink and they didn't give you the water. Just to get something out of you. The trouble was you never knew what to tell them. You didn't feel guilty of anything! They tortured us often – my toenails have been torn off. First smashed with the hammer and after torn off. So long ago, forty eight years, and I still have nightmares!

Well, they knew the Polish people were against them. What they always wanted to know was the name of the organisation that you worked for. They already, at that time, were saying that we had organised the underground army before they came in, and actually there was something in that. But I hadn't had time to be in some sort of active duty with this organisation – they'd taken me to prison very early. They arrested all the people that they call intelligentsia – all the teachers, reserve army officers, clerks from some banks and other offices. Just to take away all the people that could lead. And I was in Lubianka probably about to the end of 1940. Then one day they called me up and they told me that I was sentenced by the 'people's jury' (it was three people, like three judges). I was 'an enemy of the people'. I was sentenced to 25 years in forced labour camps. Well you just knew that you would get that anyway.

You could appeal against the people's jury. I appealed but I never got any answer. They took us all one day, again in a cattle train, and they took us by the Trans-Siberian railway by Irkutsk, almost to Vladivostok. We were in that train about three weeks. Oh, that was the winter; that was about February 1941. A lot of people died of course. People were dying in the railway wagons, and they used to stop the transport between the stations and tell you to take the dead people out. We used to bury them in the snow – just cover them with snow.

And after, they put us on some barges, and we went again about three, four, days. Eventually, after we left the barges we walked for about a week chained to each other. They didn't have a lot of guards. They didn't need them. Nobody even tried to escape because we were so far away. The distances – that's what people here sometimes didn't realise – the distances in Russia. The camp was in a wilderness,

a forest. The district is Kolyma. That's the most north-eastern part
of Russia, not far away from Kamchatka and Sakhalin. The distance
to the nearest railway station was about 400 miles.

When we came into the camp we started working in a big
forest cutting the trees down. And in the end I took ill there. My
right arm started to swell because whilst I was in Lubianka, during
interrogation one of the officers swore at me. And I swore back at
him in Russian and the two guards held me and he hit me with a big
chair and broke my shoulder bone, here. I was in hospital for about
a week, but interrogation started again and again. But when I came
eventually to that forced labour camp, under those bad conditions
my arm started swelling.

In that camp there must have been about 3000 people working;
they had a hospital. They took me to hospital because my illness was
visible. You could see my arm was all swollen. And one day the three
doctors come in and after they examined me they were talking and
talking about me, and at night time one of the doctors came back. He
was a Jew from Kiev, and he told me at that time that although I was
a prisoner, they would be asking me to sign some paper agreeing to
let them amputate my arm. He said to me, 'I rather think that when
they put your bones together in prison hospital they did it the wrong
way, and that's why it's swelling'. And he said to me, 'Don't agree to
amputation'. And when they came the next day I told them, 'I don't
agree', and one of the doctors said to me, 'Then you'll die because
gangrene will come up'. I said, 'Well, I don't expect to work here
25 years; I'll just die early'. And they gave me some injection and
the swelling came down a little. Then they decided to transfer me
to a light-duty job. Twenty of us walked to the barges. Then by
barges we came back to Vladivostok, and by train they brought us
back again through Siberia behind the Ural mountains, near (well
I'm saying near, but it was about 500 kilometres away) Sverdlovsk.
Sverdlovsk was a town on the eastern part of the Urals that we used
to call Ekatirenburg – where the Tsar and his family were executed
by the Bolsheviks in 1917. And in that new camp where we came in,
the light duty was loading railway sleepers on to wagons. That was
light duty!

Well, I was there until the war broke out between Germany
and Russia. That was June 1941. A lot of Polish people had always
thought that there would be a war between Russia and Germany.
We were always hoping that when that war started we would be
liberated. And as a matter of fact that's what happened because about
September, they told us in the labour camp that due to an agreement

between Churchill, Roosevelt and Stalin, all Poles were being liberated. They called that a 'General Amnesty' – but we didn't feel that
we had done anything wrong to be granted an amnesty.[2]

They gave us all these civilian clothes and told us we could go
and join the Polish Army which was being formed in Russia. Of
course we didn't know where. They sent us to work first on one
of these collective farms near the river Volga, east of Stalingrad.
There were about six of us, and apart from us you couldn't see any
men at all, all men being in the army. I was driving the tractor on
the farm. We'd been there probably till the end of November 1941
and I wrote a letter to the Polish Embassy in Moscow asking them
where to join the army. Eventually I got a letter back saying that we
had to go to a place called Buzuluk, the headquarters of the Polish
Army. It was quite a way from Stalingrad. But first we came into
a town called Kuybyshev; it was a big town on the river Volga,
north of Stalingrad. There was a Polish Embassy there because when
Ger-many started bombing Moscow the Russians transferred all the
foreign embassies down to Kuybyshev, away from the bombing.
Then I joined the Polish army in Buzuluk.

They transferred all the Polish army camps down south to Kazakh-
stan, then through the Himalayan mountains toward Afghanistan.
And then I believe it was March '42 when they transferred us to
Persia. We went through the Caspian Sea from the town called
Krasnovodsk to Pahlevii in Persia. And there were a lot of Polish
civilians you see, because the Russians had this system that when
they arrested somebody they deported all the family; they didn't
put them in prison but they deported them and they called it 'free
work' that they gave them. But my mother, two of my sisters, and
three children of one sister, they'd all been deported to Vologda,
somewhere halfway between Arkhangel'sk and Moscow. It wasn't
actually a labour camp, they stayed in a village and did forestry
work. (My other two sisters had been in territory that Germany
took over; they weren't taken by the Russians.) Even my mother
worked. At that time she must have been well over sixty five, and she
was working. And after, when the Polish Army was formed in the
south of Russia, they allowed these families to go down to the south
to join their husbands or sons. Of course as the Polish Embassy was
in Russia, they started helping them. But in the transportation from
Vologda down to the south my mother died. My sister told me they
just buried her somewhere near the railway. Somewhere in friendly
Russia! We in the Polish Army in Palestine knew that after training,
the time would come when we would be fighting Germans, who at

that time occupied North Africa. I was in a few camps in Palestine, Syria and Iraq. Then I volunteered for the Air Force and came here to Great Britain in 1943 to join the RAF. I went through all the initial training here and in Canada. I came back in 1944 and joined the crews and started flying operations over Germany. Well, the war finished eventually. I came out alive although not exactly unscarred. I was twice wounded but I'm not bitter about it. In war, any soldier must be prepared for that. But starvation, beating, tortures – all 'friendly persuasions' – never could be wiped from my memory. How can one forget that a million and a half Polish people died after being deported to Siberia. Not the army, not the soldiers: innocent women, children and old men!

When the Polish Army was organised in Palestine, under British care, all the soldiers' families had been settled in the civilian camps in Kenya. Two of my sisters, two nieces and a nephew were in Kenya all through the war years because I'd been in the British army. Meanwhile my sisters who'd been left in Poland had both been working. In a lot of places the Polish people worked in the offices. They knew the Polish language; they had to work. Well, after the war, my two sisters in Poland found my other two sisters in Kenya through the Red Cross, and they brought them back to Poland I believe in 1945 or '46. Well, they're all living now in the west of Poland because Zdolbunov is now in the Ukraine. After the war finished in 1945 it had already been decided that some part of Poland would stay in Russia – that was all in the Yalta Agreement, you see. And it was after the Yalta Agreement that the bitterness started against Great Britain and against America: that Churchill and Roosevelt had agreed with Stalin to the partition of Poland again and gave half of Poland to Russia.[3] We knew that the agreement allowed Poland to take some territory to the west of the former Polish border with Germany. Of course all these territories that we got after the war had always been Polish, only the Treaty of Versailles after the First World War had not given them to Poland. What we were given was only what had previously belonged to us.

I've been to Poland many times since 1960. I like to go there to see family and friends. However, in 1962 I wrote to the Soviet Embassy in London that I was now a British citizen and that I would like to visit Zdolbunov for two or three days, to see the places where I was born, where I was working, where I spent my youth. They answered me that the places I wanted to go are not on the tourist list.

When the war finished I was transferred to Scotland to the transport company in Crieff, and then to Polmont. At that time the army was helping farmers and we'd been transporting Italian prisoners of war to work on the farms. Eventually, the British government organised some sort of resettlement corps for all the Polish people who didn't want to go back to Poland. That was a two-year programme agreed by the Polish and British governments. We were still kept under army rule, under army pay, but we had a lot of courses giving us a chance to learn a trade. And later quite a few Polish soldiers went to work in the coal mines. I didn't go to the mines, I started working as an electrician's mate with ICI in England. But before that, in November 1946 I got married. My wife was from a Scottish family, a miner's family. Well I'd decided that I didn't want to go back to Poland. We were all afraid because the Russians knew that we knew what had been going on over there in their places. So when I decided to stay here I married, and first we stayed for about two years in the house of my mother-in-law. I was working in England and coming home when I could. Then, my wife got a prefab house, and I came back here. At first I was driving a lorry for a contractor, then got a job as a production control clerk with the TCC factory in Bathgate. I was working there for about five years, and then got a better job with the American diesel manufacturers Cummins. Of course when I went there I realised that I was already too old for any promotions because younger people were coming in, educated technically more than I was. I was working with that Cummins Diesel Company about 24 years, then when I came to the age of retirement, I retired.

NOTES

1. This was the Molotov-Ribbentrop Pact of 28 September 1939.

2. There was a Polish government in exile in London but Russia encouraged the formation of the pro-Soviet Lublin Committee who eventually formed the post-war Polish Government. With the annulment of the provisions of the Nazi-Soviet Pact, Polish internees joined the Polish forces assembling in Russia.

3. The Yalta and Potsdam agreements settled the question of Poland's western and eastern frontiers. Although Poland received nearly 40,000 square miles at Germany's expense, she lost 69,000 square miles to the USSR.

Illustrations

Nasra Affara in Aden.

Nasra Affara at 21.

On the quayside, relatives wave Melrose off on her way to England.

Melrose at 19 in London.

Bernie Eugene's brothers and sisters.

Bernie Eugene as a boy.

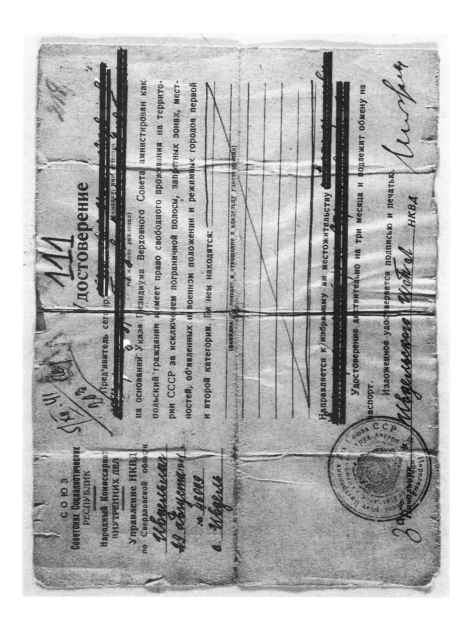

Joe Benjinski's release papers from the Siberian labour camp.

Baldev Singh with Pappinder in 1969.

Sophia Lavranou with her *moulari,* working in the family's olive grove in 1958.

Sophia Lavranou with her father, sister Nikki and cousin Dimitri in 1947. Her father is unshaven and Dimitri wears a hat as a sign of mourning for Sophia's cousin killed in the Civil War.

Myriam in Germany.

The letter from Myriam to her parents. The reply on the back was the last she ever heard from them.

Trevor Larmond (right) with his brother in
1948.

Shaheen on her wedding day.

Mr P.C. CHATHATY

Sunil Chatterjee's father: '. . . a body-builder and a keen sportsman'.

Sunil Chatterjee as a baby.

Sunil Chatterjee on Calton Hill.

Jose Emilio (far right) with other members of the Navy band in which he played during his Chilean National Service.

Lidia Capaldi's father, Mr Notarianni, and staff outside his hairdressing shop at 64 Elm Row in 1923.

Toni Capaldi (centre) with his mother and father and two sisters, Gina and Resta in 1920.

The model castle still stands amongst the remains of the camp at Lockerbie.

Jaroslav Bobak (far right) with fellow Ukrainians at the Rimini P.O.W. camp after the war.

Jaroslav Bobak and his wife on the day they were parted forever, 18th July 1944.

Jaroslav's matriculation photograph, March 1944.

Lal Khatri on holiday at Roker, Wearside in 1952.

Lal Khatri as a member of the ARP during the Second World War.

This photo of Lal Khatri (centre) with friends was taken in Leith Street Photographic Studio in 1931.

BALDEV

Goin' Roond the Doors

Baldev Singh came to Edinburgh in 1958. He and his wife, who was born and raised in Glasgow, are members of Leith's Sikh community. They have four children and run a grocery shop.

I was born in Lahore, in Pakistan, in 1947. That was the year Pakistan and India were partitioned and when they divided we all had to shift and go to India. People had to take everythin' they needed to wherever their relatives were. For the safety of their own people and kids they left everything behind. People fought amongst themselves when the British left India. I can remember when I was young, travellin' through villages, ken, just like ghost towns. The houses were empty and we were told, 'Take your pick. Wherever you want to move in, just move in.' Moslems went in fear o' their own lives in case they got killed stayin' amongst Hindus. Some of them stayed behind but most of them went to Pakistan, and from Pakistan most Sikhs came to India. When I was about two or three years old, I went to Amritsar and then we went to New Delhi where I was brought up until I was nine years old. It was a hard life for my family when they moved to Delhi. They had to start from scratch.

My memory of the house we moved into in Delhi was that there were just four boards around it, like half-finished. Each individual just had enough room to sit. There'd be six or seven steps up to the door and there'd by mud lying all around it – it was hellish, oh! And the land nearby: the grass would be three feet high and there were snakes, lizards, squirrels, mongooses and plenty of monkeys there. The monkeys used to take food out o' your hands. They werenae tame but if they got a chance they'd come and grab what you were eatin' and they were away!

Livin' was different in India. You didnae have the traffic or the roads the same as here, and in our streets we would just run aboot playin', naebody bothered. It was a different life altogether. The village was only two or three miles to the city centre and it was just fields, no tarred roads, no transport or nothin'. We used to walk or we used to go on these bullock carts.

The school, now that's a story itself, the schools here and the schools in New Delhi, well it's a totally different thing altogether. We used to sit on the floor, maybe forty kids in the one class, and the teacher sat on a square table in front o' you with a cane beside him. Discipline is one thing, but it was too strict. You'd no' learn much. I used to skip school, play marbles and other things, and if my mother found out, I used to get a helluva bashin'. In the end she got wise to me and she used to take me to the school herself.

When we moved from the village to Delhi, a year or two later, my father came to Britain. My mother's mother brought him here 'cause most o' my mother's relatives were here and wanted to bring him over. My grandad had travelled around South Africa. From there he came here, in 1938 just before the war, and after a while he got my grandmother here. They stayed in Glasgow first and my grandfather came to Edinburgh as a door-to-door salesman. Then he got a place to live here. He used to sell shirts, ties, hankies, blouses, things like that.

They all did that when they first came here, all the people who emigrated, and even today, they've got shops, wholesale, 'cause they used to do that in India. Back home some used to do farming but most used to go roond the doors or set up a wee shop like a stall and just sit there sellin' things. They couldnae speak English properly to go and get a job anywhere – fillin' in forms or speakin' in factories. But as the years went by they started to get the jobs. Well, first, Pakistani people started getting jobs in the factories then we just followed. But 90% o' Sikhs went roond the doors sellin' with a suitcase, took orders and delivered the stuff. It's freedom to them, you see. Naebody but themselves, naebody tellin' them what to do. They used to go whenever they felt like it and when they'd done enough they used to come home. Business was good here, it was a new place. In India the life would have been hard for my dad as a salesman, ken.

Although it is hard for anybody when they first come to a new place, or start a new job, the British then were more friendly in their attitudes towards oor people. They hadnae seen many coloured or turbanned people in this country and when they saw one of us they all used to be surprised, and they wanted to see what he sellt or how he spoke or what he could tell them.

In India we were poor. We were poor in a lot o' ways: moneywise, clotheswise, living quarters, you name it. My father used to send money every month. What he sent wasnae much, like, but it done us. There was only myself at the time and we had four uncles, three aunties and my grandad and grandmother and great granny living with us. I was young and I didnae know where Scotland or Britain was, I just knew my father was away somewhere. After he'd been here for six years we came across.

It was the first time I'd ever been on a boat – fantastic! We thought it was a different world. It took us 20 days to come across – 20 days of luxury. We used to see things we'd never seen before – the sea and the size o' the boat! First time we'd ever sat at the table and had a meal, we didnae know what to do or how to start – ken, everythin' was laid out. The food was that much, you never seen that much in your life!

Myself, my mother, my mother's two uncles, my father's two uncles and his cousin – aboot seven of us – came here. They were goin' to Manchester and we were comin' to Edinburgh. I didnae even know the place existed when I came across on the boat. We werenae taught nothin' about Britain. We didnae know where Britain was. I was nine years old when I came here and my grandparents didnae want us to come. They didnae want my father to stay here or us to come. We came here in March 1957 and I can still remember when we got to Southampton – the snow. I'd never seen snow before in my life. And it was that cold. My hands were numb and I was greetin'. Honest to God, I was cryin'!

The train from Southampton to Edinburgh was another experience – I'd never been on a train in India either. And in Edinburgh – the traffic and the taxis and the snow . . . There used to be trams here when we first came. It was great! The street lightin' an' the people walkin' aboot saying nothin' to anybody – ken, everybody minded their own business.

We stayed in number 12 Springfield Street. My grandmother was the landlady, she had the flat, and it was just the one room we used to stay in. As for myself and my mother, we didnae speak a word of English. We never used to go out anywhere by ourselves. My auntie and my father used to take us shoppin'. Our Scottish neighbours had nine in their family. They used to stay in the one room as well, and we were more or less brought up with their kids and we went to school together – they still come to my house sometimes. My auntie used to teach us English in the house after school because she was born here. We just used to sit there like dummies, we didnae ken what people were sayin'. Were they talkin' aboot us or somebody else? And people felt the same when we spoke our language. Then slowly we started speakin' in broken English. It was great! If you were amongst your ain people and you didnae want to say somethin' in your ain language, you'd say it in English. Your parents couldnae understand it properly!

But when we first came, the Scots and us were like strangers to each other: the land and people were different, the culture was different to what I was used to. When I went to school, I didnae find any difficulties. There were four o' us Sikhs in the school an' there were odd times you used to have people making fun and a fool o' you – just for a laugh or joke. We didnae know what they were sayin'. But now within the last ten or fifteen years it's changed 100% – peoples' attitudes, youngsters. People forget all the hard work that the Pakistanis and Indians do here. If they worked as hard, they would be in the same position as we are.

After school, I did the same as my father did, roamed the place goin' roond the doors with a case of clothes. At first, when I started off it was hard. I used to feel embarrassed and shy. When the school kids came out I just used to stop doin' it until they'd gone away, 'cause they'd never seen anybody like me with a turban. They used to follow you roond: didnae say nothin', they just used to follow you and watch what you were doin', an' I felt very embarrassed. I asked my father once or twice if I could remove my turban but he wouldnae allow it. He said, 'Our religion is not to get your hair cut. You were born a Sikh and you will die with long hair'. I did that job for three years, but as time went along I got bored so I stopped and worked on the railways for four years at St Margaret's (where Meadowbank is now). I was there as a fireman but that place shut down an' I started to learn to drive lorries in Brownlie's Timberyard in Easter Road.

I knew a lot of people in Leith then because my school pals were workin' at places I went to during work. I made friends. It's like everythin': if you go to a new place, until they get to know you, they're gonnae ignore you. But once they've found out the way you speak, or the way you work, and you muck about with them, they just take you as one of themselves.

I was working on lorries for seven years. Then I was on the buses, seven years on the Corporation. I got a lot o' bother. On the bad shifts there were a few passengers I used to find very hard. But that wasnae the reason I packed it in in the end. The bad shifts at the weekend were gettin' worse – ken, I used to get threatened or people didnae pay their fares. If four or five came up after the pubs, they started arguin' with you or callin' you all the names, and if you phoned up the control, by the time the control van came they were off. It was bad there so I went on to the SMT. That wasnae bad, ken, I was goin' out o' town, seein' countryside. I used to get a lot o' hassle there and a' but the people were used to you more because every day the same people used to travel the same route. You got to know the people and they used to defend you if trouble came along. But the only physical trouble I ever had was on the Corporation buses, on the last Number 12 bus down Niddrie. When I first started, I was conductin' one night and people werenae paying their fares and were shoutin' and swearin'. I told an Inspector downstairs, 'They're not payin' their fares'. He said, 'That's your job, you'd better go an' do it'. I had to go back up again and one boy started takin' my turban off. I just hit him and ran downstairs because there was too many o' them upstairs. The Inspector was downstairs so he stopped the bus an' got the police, but the police were afraid to go on.

When there's ten or twelve o' them and the top deck's full o' them you wouldnae dare go upstairs and ask them for fares. The last bus always has trouble but bein' a coloured person that gives them more o' an edge to do things. There's always one person starts it off and there are two or three who say, 'Just leave it . . .' I wouldnae say they were all bad but as it goes on they all join in. A' the time your mind's on them in case they try to interfere with anybody on the bus. If they do and the police come, you're the one who's going to be charged if you didnae do anything about it. They'll give you your books.

After workin' on the SMT I went drivin' the private coaches. That was alright, goin' down to London, Dundee, Aberdeen. I done that for four years. After that I got a shop.

As I was sa in', a lot o' people used to mix back then. I had a lot o' friends. But now there's a lot o' changes. In my opinion, people who don't mix with other people, foreigners, don't know what their culture is like, or how they're brought up. The people that understand are those that stay next door or grow up together. They accept it. People that don't, their parents teach them a' this 'Paki-this' or 'Why did they come here?' and the kids pick up these things and keep them in their minds. If there's a group, it seems they start shoutin', but on their own you never get any bother at a'. Sometimes it's skinheads or just loafers, standin' aboot wastin' time at night. It's gettin' worse.

Once or twice my children have had trouble with the police, gettin' picked up. One day my second youngest was playin' with his mates. There's a chemist's place just by where they were playin' aboot, where somebody broke in. And the young white boys that my kid was playin' with were the same age, same height and everythin'. The two police grabbed my laddie and started askin' questions aboot the place. At that time it was aboot 9 o'clock and my oldest laddie was comin' from my brother's. He went up and asked, 'What's the matter, Constable?' and explained to him that it was his brother. And the police started pullin' at him, started swearin' at him. I was bag-shiftin' that night, and when I came home he was upset and he told me about it. The following day I phoned the police station and I explained to them about the swearin' and everythin'. The policeman had said to my son, 'You black bastard, if you ever do that again, or if I see you near that door with any of these boys, I'm goin' to lift you.' I made a complaint to them and I've never seen those policemen again on this beat.

There's still a lot of things goin' on but people just don't want to admit it. The law itself, in Edinburgh – the police – are very bad in my experience. One of my friends is a Pakistani boy. About three weeks ago his shop in the Kirkgate was broken into. The police phoned him at one or two in the mornin' and told him to come down to the shop because the alarm was goin'. He and his brother went down. They went into their shop and twenty minutes later six boys came. They started doin' them in and they stabbed him. I don't know how he managed it but he phoned the police . . . He's still waitin' for them comin'! They just don't bother. You go through the procedure of makin' a complaint, then they tell you if you want to take it further they'll get another town or division to investigate it. Well how do we know that they're investigatin' properly? One man's no' gonnae shop another man. It's a public individual that needs to go in there an' investigate, not the police themselves.

I've worked nearly everywhere and I've met a lot o' people. When they get to know you, as I said, they're different people altogether – once they know what you're like, what your culture's like, how you take people towards you. Only two things I used to say to them: 'Don't make a fool o' anybody,' and 'Don't mix with religion if you know nothin' about it.' And don't think everybody's the same. If five or six Scottish people are standin' there and one's done wrong that doesnae mean they're all wrong.

Mrs Singh Our family's very close-knit. The families help each other, you know. They help with their elderly, whereas here the elderly people, they're worried that they might be put into a home with nobody to look after them. In our community it's the youngest son's wife responsibility. Our community likes to have sons because the daughters, when they get married, go away to their in-law's house, whereas when the sons get married they have to look after the parents in their old age. And the person who's got three or four sons, they've got no worries at all because they can live maybe a few months in each son's house. I mean, the daughters-in-law see that they're fed well and clothed well. For us in Edinburgh, it works exactly the same. The tradition is carried on.

It is unfair in a sense, because right from the beginning, when the daughters are born, they're treated as if they belong to another family. The parents are just bringing 'em up until they come of age to get married and then, before they're sent to their in-law's house, they're told that, 'We've been your parents for so long and now these are your parents.' Here this has not changed at all. In fact it's stricter than what it is in India. Here in Britain the community feels that they don't want to let the traditions die because they've brought them from India to a different country. Here they would get blamed for being Westernised and forgetting all their traditions, so in that sense we've stuck to them, more so than our relatives in India. In India, they're freer in a sense.

Baldev You see, we've got to hand it down to our kids. In India they don't need to as much. They're bein' brought up there in Indian society.

Mrs Singh Things change in India. There's new fashions, whereas we're stuck with the old fashions and we don't know what's happening unless somebody's been there for a visit. Then again, we worry that if we change, what will our neighbours say? We go by that a lot. It's put a lot of pressure on us. I've never seen India; I was born here and yet I was brought up with all the traditions and I have to pass these on. The girls are not allowed to go out – I mean, maybe when we were small, up to the age of about ten years old, we were allowed to go out and play, but we weren't allowed to mix even with boys of our own age. Now, if we have a party, the men will be in one room and the women will be in another. It's because we've been brought up that way we just accept it like that, you know. If my husband was having a party and he had friends in, maybe British men with their wives, I wouldn't be allowed into the room even though his friends' wives were here. And it doesn't bother me. But our children, even though they've been brought up that way, they still say, 'Why do we have to do this?'

Baldev It's been handed down to us an' if we change it, we'll feel it inside ourselves that we're doin' somethin' wrong. The Gurdwara says we should adapt to things, try to change a little. But not too much.

Mrs Singh One argument that comes up, is that our women have to cover their face in front of older menfolk. That's not in the Sikh religion but that came to be hundreds of years ago when the Turks and Moguls invaded India and they were kidnapping all the women. If they saw a woman and she was beautiful they'd just kidnap her. Because of that, they started covering their faces and it's carried on since then. When we go to the temple there's lots of elderly men there whom we've to cover our faces from. If we do that, in a sense, we're covering our face from God as well, which shouldn't be. Because it's been carried on, now no one's got the guts to uncover their face and walk in. Maybe if a few families changed it the rest of the community would talk about them.

Baldev My mother an' father picked my wife for me. She used to live in Glasgow. My uncle started the ball rollin'. It was a weekend, I went down to my wife's house and there must have been 13 or 14 o' them there. I knew some o' her family because I worked with them goin' roond the doors. They asked the questions: 'How old are you? Are you workin'? Will you still have to go roond the doors?' The followin' day I came home and a week later I got engaged. I was quite happy because we are told when we are young that our mother and father pick wives for us and that was that. With my boys, it's the same. My son is engaged. My wife and I have picked a wife for him in Doncaster so they're hopin' to get married.

Now everybody's more Westernised. Divorces – you never used to hear o' a divorce in our community, but now you do sometimes. They're forced to get married and a few years later we hear, 'So-an'-so got divorced.' It's no fair on the lassie, especially in our own community. Once the lassie's married she's degraded if she gets divorced. There's naebody's gonnae marry her unless he's desperate, or he's already been divorced. You see, always the married woman's purity is important. Even if she is still pure after she's been married a month, even if she's never been to bed nor done nothin'. In our community naebody believes that and her life is ruined. After a divorce if she stays with her parents, she can't do the things she would like to do. She can't get dressed well to go to the parties with the women or to the weddin's 'cause people'll talk aboot her. She's as good as dead. Of course, I think that this is wrong. Everythin' doesn't always work out well. Never has, never will. There's a lot o' people make mistakes, there's a lot o' people do bad things as well as good things. I'm no sayin' it's wrong that boys are picked for you, what

I'm sayin's wrong is the way they go about after they get married. They still have the old routines of a single man and it's no fair on the woman. If a woman did the same to the man I wouldnae like it, so why do it to the lassie? Of course, a lassie cannae say nothin' to her husband and he takes advantage sometimes.

But the way a British woman is brought up, the things she does, our women could never even dream of doin'. The things the Scots girls do, they don't even know themselves what they're doin'. The sexual education in school, I think that's bad, awfy bad. What's shown on the television, that's just as bad.

I've grown up here. The education for the kids is good, the livin's good but it is a hard life for us. Our people work very hard to make ends meet, so what we've got we like to belong to us. When we first came to this country we used to stay as lodgers payin' rent. Through time, slow an' steady, we'd buy houses an' become our own kings o' the castle. Our people always like to own their own property. Power amongst yourselves! And that's how we like our kids to be. That's why we help them. When they get married, when they buy their own house, we finance them. Then after that they're on their own until they need help, then we help them again. Here you're a hundred percent different. At 16 or 17, kids are workin', they don't want to know their parents. I think a lot o' the parents are to blame an' a'. If the parents took a grip with their kids instead o' goin' out drinkin' or bingo or gamblin' . . . but they neglect them when they're young. In the schemes, kids are playin' till 12 o'clock, 1 o'clock in the mornin'. As they get older they've got nothin' else to do, that's when they start breakin' things – violence, fightin', killin', stabbin', it's nothin' to them, they're used to these things. If kids never get their parents' love or discipline what can you expect?

I went back to India, two years ago, for the first time since I left and it's a change of life altogether. There's more people, more traffic. Now there's a road to my village and there's bikes, rickshaws, taxis, buses, lorries, bullock-carts, camels, elephants, people are walkin' – everythin'. Madness! An' the law – traffic lights an' the police – naebody pays attention to them! It's all built up now where we used to stay. It's all hotels, factories, big bungalows. There's a lot o' memories came back but I couldnae live there now. I couldnae cope with it, we're so used to the system here. There, as long as you've got plenty money you can get a lot o' things done, there's nae problem. If you're poor you can sit there a' day waitin' for an appointment. You can sit there in a hall an' the clerk isnae gonnae take your file to the gaffer, or whoever it may be – he's just gonnae keep that file an' keep turnin' it over an' over again. That's just to start with. I've experienced it!

People are dyin' there. They cannae afford even to get somethin' to eat, never mind the medicine. But there are good sides to the people. Professionally, especially the lawyers, police, doctors, they're no good – all bribery. If somebody gives them a lot o' money they'll do anything for them. A person can be dying and you can call a doctor and he can see the state the family's in. He'll give medicine for the symptom, say it's gonnae cost a lot, they'll explain they cannae pay, and he'll just walk away. But if people on the streets are hungry the community themselves will help them, they help each other. Every community helps their own.

I've brought my children up with both sides. What I didnae get when I was young, they got. I don't stop them from mixin' with other people – as long as they keep their religion, an' they know everything about their culture an' don't break that, I don't mind at a'. My son's in the ATC, been there for four years now. He's gonnae join the RAF shortly. So he's been everywhere, Germany, Holland an' other places with the camps, so he's used to people. It's like everythin' else, when they first see him it's a wee bit dodgy.

Quite a lot of Sikhs are Westernised down south. Not in Scotland. In the south you find a lot, a helluva lot, and we feel bad aboot that. Some o' the things they do, it's no real. But I never had to get my hair cut. I've been refused a lot o' jobs. They never said it directly, but I took the hint: because o' the turban I'd not got the job. I don't think Leith Sikhs will change too badly, though they will get more Westernised. I can see that now with the youngsters that are growin' up. Of course, there's our community to blame for that. There's not enough youngsters come to the Gurdwara. They should force them to come. The only thing stoppin' us here are the shops, businesses. On Wednesday afternoon, when we have our service, if a person has a shop he should close it and take his family down. Maybe three or four years that person's been in business, and the punters will know whether that shop's open or not. If one man shuts his shop the rest would follow. It'd make a difference to the business but no a helluva lot.

My aim was to get my own business. I've got a shop now, but I've always wanted to get a pub. There are no Sikh pubs in Edinburgh. There's one in Glasgow now, and when I went to Southampton two years ago, my cousin's friend had a big, big club. And I've seen it, and the atmosphere was great, ken, it was just like home!

We were among the first Sikhs here. We've stayed here comin' up for thirty years. We are citizens of this country, we're so British ourselves. We would like the community to feel the same way we feel but this isn't happenin'. It's the hardest thing for other people to accept us.

SOPHIA

Coming to the Dark Land

Sophia Lavranou was born in 1932 in a village in the south of Corfu. She came to work in Edinburgh in 1960 and has lived there ever since.

Chlomos was on a hill so you could see the whole of Corfu. We had property – we grew potatoes and we had a lot of olive trees. We had every kind of animal – two horses, a donkey, cows, sheep. We were well off, not rich but very comfortable. Working very hard. My father was a butcher and he also had a boat going from Corfu to Igoumenitsa on the mainland, exporting and importing from one place to another. We were four sisters, my father and step-mother – my mother died when I was only two and a half years old so I don't remember her.

I went to school at six years old. In 1941, we were under the Italian occupation and later, for one year, under the Germans.[1] I remember every morning when we went to school, we had to salute the Italian flag. An Italian lady called Parini used to come with a doctor and see if the children were all right, and she used to bring a piece of sultana cake. The Italians ran the school but we were allowed Greek teachers and Greek language. It was very simple but I liked school very much.

The Italians took Corfu and seven Ionian islands. Whatever we had, we had to declare to them. For example, they never let us have any wheat for bread. The people used to have these stone wheels and they'd hide in the bushes just to grind oats for a little porridge. They used to give us very little: for every person a pound of flour a week. But we loved the Italians. The soldiers were very nice and when the children were very hungry, they would go to them and the soldiers used to cut a piece from their own bread, *panola*, and give it to the children. They searched my house a thousand times because my father would kill a lamb or a kid for people who were ill, which they didn't allow, and we had to take everything away to the neighbours and hide it. The Italians didn't kill people if they found things they

96

didn't like. They hit them, battered them until the blood was coming out of their mouths, but the Germans would kill – completely different. We were afraid of the Germans. One young boy of my village, he wasn't very bright, he made a little gun by himself and he went to the beach to kill birds to eat, and the Germans caught him. The next day they shot the boy down in front of everybody.

When the Germans came, they let us have our school as long as they could take anything they wanted for themselves from our houses. They took about 800 gallons of olive oil from my house. Somebody had a radio in the village and they went to my godmother, she was half-German, and told her to inform the person who had the radio to take it down to their station. This person refused to hand it over so they just took a cannon and shot it at our village. It was summertime and I had my goat with me. I was picking up the washing and I heard this 'Chiff chiff chiff' – the little pieces of shrapnel. I was hit by one. You see this scar by my eyebrow? That was because I didn't know anything about what was going on. It was very hot and I tried to take it out and I was crying. They killed the sister of the man who had the radio, his first cousin, and his neighbour – three people – and one girl lost her eyes. The Germans stayed for over a year.

At first, the Greeks were fighting to throw the Germans out, but then they were just fighting each other in the civil war. It is disturbing to remember. The ELAS and EDES: the left and the right fighting each other.[2] That destroyed Greece more than the Second World War. It lasted from 1944 to 1949. Corfu didn't have any fighting. We didn't have this hate – but my cousin was killed in the Peloponnese by the Communists. Everybody came and mourned for my cousin. On my mother's side two or three cousins were left-wing, and on my father's side we were all right-wing, but I didn't know very much because I was fourteen when all of this happened and living in a village, we didn't know about politics and what was really happening in other parts of Greece. We were singing songs against each other but we didn't understand the hate.

It wasn't a very exciting life. Living in a village, you had to get up very early in the morning to go to work. We used to work very hard, which I hated. I was always ill you know, I wasn't very much alive. I used to look after my animals, which I loved, and I was with my sisters and all of them loved me very much. I was the apple of my father's eye because of my mother dying when I was very young. From the time I was very young I was helping and I worked every morning before I went to school. Although I liked school very much, from ten years old they stopped me going because it was the

Depression, and if you had a farm you needed to look after the animals every day. The secondary school wasn't in the village. You had to go to Corfu town to study for six years. Nowadays the bus takes every child to the town in the morning and back in the evening. But it wasn't compulsory to send children to school back then, and some people couldn't afford to pay for their children to board in the town. My father and step-mother thought it wasn't a good idea for me to live in the town. It was very difficult for me because Greece wasn't then as it is now where every girl goes to secondary school. It wasn't considered nice for a girl to leave the village. If you went to the town you might lose your mind and start to have a boyfriend, and that wasn't very noble!

Because they didn't allow me to go to school, I had this psychological problem. I always thought I wasn't very well. Nothing worked out for me. I went to Athens to have two operations when I was twenty three and I stayed for ten months. That was the change that made me make the decision to leave. I saw a very different life and I didn't want to stay in the village: I wanted a better and different life.

I went back to the village and there we had a very nice young man working for us and this boy wanted to marry me. My father and sisters found out and they weren't very pleased. They wanted somebody who had more money, a name: not somebody who worked for them. So I thought I had better find a way to leave. My sisters were all married and everything was left in my hands. I couldn't cope! I went to see my godmother who I loved very much and who was very fond of me, and I asked her if she knew anybody abroad for whom I could go and work. She had a friend in Athens who had a daughter in Edinburgh with three children, and we fixed it. And then I told my father. My family tried to get everybody to make me change my mind but, of course, I am very strong-willed like a Scot!

So I left home on 3rd September 1960. I wanted to learn a language and I wanted to go somewhere abroad. I was the first girl in my village to go to Athens, and I was the first girl to go abroad. I came from Athens to London by train, which took three or four days. I couldn't speak English – I knew nothing, and I was afraid that I might lose my seat in the compartment, so I didn't move very much. And it was very rough crossing the English Channel. When you're coming to stay in this country you have to go to the doctor for a check-up, and in Dover they took me into a dark room for this. I didn't know about this, nobody had told me and I was so terrified! Then I got the train to London. At London I came out of the train with my shoes in my hand and my little suitcase. A friend met me and I spent the night in London. I had a bath and it was like a chimney-sweep had been in it.

I spent the night in London and the next day they put me on the train to Edinburgh. I had to stand up because there were a lot of people. When I came to Waverley station, all the children I was to look after were waiting for me. I always remember my room with the nice bedcovers and the chest of drawers, a lovely bouquet of flowers and the dog.

When I was very young, during the war, a lot of people from the town stayed in my house. Because of the bombing in Corfu town they came to the villages: 16 or 17 people in a small house! We kept up a friendship and used to go to the town to visit them. One of them had a friend in Scotland – they called it *Scotia* in Greek. *Scotus* is 'darkness' in Greek, so *Scotia* sounds like the 'dark land'. They told me that there the sky is grey and rainy and cold, and I imagined this and said, 'I might go to Scotland one day'. I never thought I was going to spend my life here. I couldn't imagine the sky to be grey. In Greece, most of the time it is blue. When I came here that's what was in my mind: I would see the darkness – and I did!

I wrote to my godmother, 'Scotland is very nice but the buildings are very black and everywhere there is mess from the dogs'. But I couldn't speak English at all and I made a lot of mistakes. Instead of saying 'burgers' I said 'buggers!' First of all I was living in with the family I worked for and they were very kind, very good. I wasn't sure whether to go back to Greece. I didn't want to go back to the village and I was sure my father wouldn't allow me to live in a town in Greece like Athens, so I thought I'd better stay away and go every second year to visit them. I thought it was better that way. Then I bought the flat, I continued working for that family and I worked for other people, cooking for them. I also teach Greek cooking in the evening.

When I came, I didn't want to stay for very long. If you emigrate and you live in somebody else's country, then you are not yourself: you belong neither here nor there. When I go to Corfu, after four weeks, I miss my flat and all my friends here, and I want to come back. When I am here, I spend a lot of money on the telephone phoning my sisters! And if I hear Greek songs on the radio I just start to cry. It's a very funny feeling. If you leave your home, you become different. You realise that life is different from what you thought it was. There's nowhere it's easy to be yourself. Some people are ambitious to make money or to become a big star. If you're not going back it's not because you find life better somewhere else, it's because you don't want to have failed. I mean, I didn't want my stepmother to say, 'I told you you wouldn't be very happy and you would come back'. You've got to show them that you can do things which they think you can't.

People here are more independent. I've come from one extreme to another. If, for example, I was in Greece, I would have had to be with my father. I couldn't do anything I wanted to because my father was there. Even when I went back on holiday for a month I had to stay and look after him when he was ill. Even now, if I was in Corfu, I couldn't go abroad. First of all, I couldn't work and have money which I have here. Secondly, it's not acceptable for a girl there to take a plane and go because she just wants to see a friend. I think the government helps people here and that is why they are independent. This makes the family split and you don't feel very much for your families. You don't mind what your sister does – she can do whatever she likes – but in Greece the brothers are very close to their sisters and would never allow anybody to take advantage of them. We always have this pride and shame in our families. I don't know whether it is good or bad but every country has its own customs. I think there is too much independence here: the mother and father should be more responsible for the child and now in Greece, because of all the tourists, it's changing there as well.

I know a lot of people who I am still friends with and I've had a very happy time here. Once the window cleaner said, 'Oh you've bought a flat'. I said, 'Yes, it's very nice'. He said, 'You foreigners, you come into this country, you make money and you just buy property'. I said, 'You must know I haven't spent this money in the pub, I just like to have something. I am working for it and I have every right to have property.' Once I was in British Home Stores and a lady said to me 'It's my turn'. I said, 'I'm sorry, it's my turn' – 'Oh I'm not wasting my time with a foreigner!' 'Oh', I said, 'If I am a foreigner to you, you are a foreigner to me, so we are equal!' But I think, in general, people are very kind. It's only the narrow-minded.

There's quite a few Greek people in Edinburgh. Quite a few ladies married during the war when the British were in Greece. And there are a few men – with Scottish girls going across for holidays they meet Greek boys and get married. The Orthodox Church wasn't here when I came. There was a Russian service but I didn't understand any Russian so I used to go to Glasgow. Then the priest from Glasgow used to come here once a month to All Saints'

Church. Now we have a priest, Father John, who does the services in Greek. He can speak English, Greek and Russian.

I haven't got a family here and in the back of my mind is always Corfu. Here is my flat but there is my home. I miss my sisters. I love it here but the people are more reserved. Though I have been away for 26 years my friends in Corfu are as I left them. But it is not the Corfu that I knew – all the tourists. People have become more materialistic: before they were very hospitable and good. But my village is unspoilt! My village is lovely and the people are the same. I'm going back to Corfu when I retire. I have a house in Corfu, my own lovely house, the place where I was born. My father left it to me. All my family is there. My village is the most beautiful village in Corfu.

Pournari

What a pity they felled you, my lovely Pournari
Your leaves and limbs gave rich shade and beauty.
When I hear you are cut down I weep
And far off in a foreign land, the past leaps
Into my mind. Images and thoughts come:
I need time to list them, one by one:
All the village boys you shaded from the sun
Came to show you their first butterfly love
And in the still of night, under the stars,
They sang me a love song and played their guitars.
You were the villagers' pride,
A place of dreams for every boy that spied
On us – girls fetching water from the spring.
You were our friend on the wayside.
If only I could capture the past and bring
Those boys, scattered so far and wide,
I'm sure that down deep in the earth
Your roots would be satisfied.
But I must bid you farewell, Pournari,
For I am far away in Scotia
I still have my memories – Sophia

NOTES

1. In 1941–43 Italy invaded Greece from Albania. However, the German forces had to step in to hold the area for the Italians when they were driven back by the Greeks. Following the Anglo-Italian armistice

in September 1943, Germany took over the military campaign against
Greece. In 1944 Greece was liberated by British forces.

2. EAM-ELAS (the National Liberation Front and the National
Popular Liberation Army) and EDES (the Greek Democratic National
Army) initiated as guerilla forces during the German occupation. When
the Germans withdrew in 1944 both forces were brought together by
the British in a coalition government but due to mistrust and other
complications no agreement was reached. However, following the
election of 1946 further conflict flared up and British forces were
withdrawn. By 1949, when the US-backed Greek army took control,
50,000 Greeks had lost their lives.

MYRIAM

'By the Skin of Our Teeth'

In her twenties Myriam witnessed the rise of Nazism. She
escaped from Germany three months before war broke out.

I was born in a small village near Frankfurt in Germany on 11
November 1910. When I went to school there were only 3,000 people
living there. It is now a town of 10,000. It was a very picturesque
village near where the river Main enters the Rhine. It had a porcelain
factory in the old days and a lot of agriculture with very small farms
– two cows and a horse, that kind of thing.

My parents' families – I mean the previous generation – were big.
Both sides had nine children, but we only had two girls. The graves
of my family were destroyed by the Nazis. If you look for background, our family came from the province of Hesse. We didn't even
step out of our province, you know. They married someone from
Hesse and stayed in Hesse – they didn't move. We were Germans.
Our religion was Jewish but we were Germans. We were rooted but
now I have no feelings at all. There was a small Jewish community
of about ten families, most of whom emigrated when Hitler came.
But I, my sister, my parents, we went to Frankfurt in 1935. We were
Orthodox Jews but we were very integrated, I would say assimilated,
and my father was drafted in the First World War in 1915. He went
in November and in December my little sister was born. There's five
years between us. The war ended in 1918 but Papa didn't come home
until 1919 because he was a prisoner of war in Oswestry in Wales. He
loved England. He always said he should never have come back.

We had the army of occupation from 1918 to 1919.[1] Although we
didn't have a farm, we had a farmhouse. My father was a grainer and
we had a big barn in which twenty negroes were billeted. We had
the French Officers' mess in my father's retail shop and in the yard
they had their big field kitchen. One room was taken by the French
sergeants. One room was occupied by two other Frenchmen and I
remember all that so clearly as if it was yesterday.

My father built up quite a flourishing business again and then the inflation came. My parents lost everything. From one day to another the prices went up and if you had sold something the day before, the next day you would probably only replace it with something for half the value. And so we had to sell the house and move into a flat in the village.

I took a job in Frankfurt and trained as a saleswoman. In Germany that's three years' training. You don't just go behind a desk and sell, you have to learn about it. We had to go to day-release classes twice a week. We even got sales psychology in 1926. I was ten years in that firm. I became a buyer and then changed to a smaller place but then the owners emigrated to America. I got another job as a buyer in a Jewish firm and then of course 1938 finished everything.

The Nazis came to power in 1933 and the first action they took against the Jews was to boycott all the Jewish shops. But they had to stay open and if any non-Jew entered a Jewish shop he would be assaulted when he came out. It was very, very frightening. One of the shop-owners where I was working – it was a Jewish firm – was an old, old man and he was taken out of the shop and paraded throughout Frankfurt with his hands up in the air. Oh it was sad. But 1933 was only the beginning. After that there was one law after another.

My sister, meantime, had gone to what the Germans call a middle school and travelled to Frankfurt daily. She was a superb pupil, a brilliant girl, with a flair for languages. She was a secretary and she got into the same firm I had been in. We were never rich. We had comfortable times in Germany, and then when the inflation took everything away from us it was really the two girls who kept the parents going.

After 1935 there was a law: the Jews and the non-Jews couldn't mix.[2] But we had a lot of good hiking companions and we still went out with them on the quiet. If we were with them we were never assaulted because we didn't look too obviously Jewish which was a blessing. And I always said to my sister, 'Gosh, what it must be like to have a dark skin because you can't hide from them!' But later on, if we went out with Jews, you probably got a stone thrown at you, you know, that kind of thing. But previously no. All our friends were faithful to us to the last minute.

If you were a Jew you could only live in a house that was Jewish-owned. As soon as the Jewish owner emigrated, if they sold the house to a non-Jew, anybody Jewish in the house had to leave. So all the time you were on the lookout for a flat. I think my parents must have moved three or four times after we had gone, and we moved twice actually, whilst we were still there. One flat we had wasn't a Jewish-owned house but the woman was a member of the Freemason's Lodge and that was frowned upon. The landlady had the greatest sympathy for us, but one day she came to us and said, 'I'm terribly sorry, the woman in the top flat creates – I'm sorry you'll have to move'. Hitler was in Frankfurt and of course everybody was high – they were absolutely elated, the Nazis. And there was this SS man – they had to be a certain height and they had to prove they were Nordic. They gave those people instruction in race detection – you would know a Jew by his hooked nose, by his flat feet. You always knew a Jew. I was always a bit daring, and this SS man came down the stairs and I came in and he said, 'Heil Hitler!' I said, 'Good evening'. 'And why didn't you salute with the German salute?' 'Because I am Jewish and I'm not allowed to.' 'Oh,' he said, 'I'm sorry'. Two days later I was cleaning the stairs and the SS man came down and I said, 'Now have a look at me – it will do your racial studies good'. And he said, 'I did say sorry'. I said, 'Yes you did'. And that was all there was to it.

Another time, in a train, a fellow wanted to date me and I looked at him and he was in military uniform and looked Japanese. And I said, 'I'm surprised that you are in uniform' (the cheek of me!), 'you don't look Nordic at all.' I think he said he was of Spanish descent and I said, 'you could get into the army then?' He said, 'Oh yes, we don't belong to the race that we detest'. And then he wanted to date me, and I said, 'I'm sorry, you can't meet me, I belong to the race that you detest!' There were other Nazis in that carriage. They all got up and came over and were as friendly as could be: this had happened to them too. They just didn't know how to treat courage. They were told Jews were cowards and when they came across somebody who stuck their neck out they just didn't know how to treat them. Maybe another Jewess would have been frightened and would not have spoken to him right from the beginning, but I always challenged them. And believe it or not they were all at the windows, waving to me, when I left the carriage [laughs].

My worst experience was when I was visiting in 1938 in the north. I was with my cousins and on the morning of 9th November 1938, at 6 o'clock, my old uncle came into the room where my cousin and myself slept and said, 'Now girls, don't get excited, the SS are outside and we are all to be taken into custody. Get dressed'. So I went to the SS men and said, 'I don't belong here. Do you want me, too?' 'Oh yes, come along, come along.' That was an experience. We were shepherded to an old military barracks – they had collected all the Jewish people in a small room. There was a young boy saying farewell to his parents. The family had permission to go to Holland that day but the parents were held back and made the little boy go. And he had to say goodbye to his parents in that room, crowded with people. A young boy of about 13, that's all he was. Then they separated us – they took the men away and let the women go home. So in that whole Jewish community, which was much bigger than in our village, there were no men. My uncle came back after two days and I by chance got on the same bus. I had a big bunch of flowers and I said, 'Oh uncle, you must have them, I'm so pleased to see you'. and he answered, 'Oh child, you hold them, I haven't got the strength'. That was my uncle, 70 years old. And then we heard a knock at the door. The Gestapo was outside. My cousin had heart trouble so she sent me to open the door. My teeth were rattling. I was so frightened of the Gestapo. He was enquiring why a non-Jewish man visited my uncle the night before. What business had my uncle with him? My uncle said, 'Oh that I can show you – I've got a letter – he wants to buy our house'. And that was all right then. So that was the nastiest experience really that I had.

We were members of the Jewish First Aid Group and we got a phone call to come to the station. 'Bring a thermos flask with hot coffee if you can. We are expecting prisoners from a concentration camp, from Buchenwald, to arrive at the main railway station tonight. They will be very frightened. Comfort them a bit, give them some hot coffee, assure them that their people are alright – that is what they want to know.' And I innocently asked, 'But, how will we know them?' And the man in charge said, 'You will know them alright!' And when they did arrive their hair was shorn off, their clothes were all crumpled looking – they had been through disinfection. They had had those clothes on for months on end. And they were very frightened – really very frightened. We offered them shelter overnight if they didn't want to continue, but they were all very keen to get away to their own families. That was a bad experience too.

Another bad experience was when they moved all the Polish Jews from Frankfurt.[3] They were all rounded up before the Pogrom, I think a year before, and again the First Aid Group was busy helping these people. They all came with just what they could grab at the spur of the moment, probably a pillow or hairbrush or something, you know, with children in their arms. We helped them to carry the children and put them in these trains. Two days later we got another phone call. They were all returned. Poland wouldn't let them in. These poor people had been two days and two nights in the carriage and had come back to Frankfurt. We helped to unload them. I had a white summer coat on, you know, it was black when I had finished carrying those kids.

One of my cousins had asked me to go to Hamburg, where he had application papers lying with the Uruguayan Consulate, and I had to travel by train. But it was eerie. The train was very empty and when I came to Bremen I had to change trains. It was just awful. Every Jewish shop had been smashed and the shutters were down and on them was written, 'This is the revenge for killing Vom Rath in Paris.'[4] That was frightening. That was very frightening.

A cousin of mine came back to Frankfurt in December from concentration camp, because he had a chance to go to Shanghai (at that point if one could prove that one had permission to enter a foreign country one might be released from concentration camp). But he didn't go, because the Jewish community employed him to help with emigration so the Nazis let him be. When he came back my cousin's wife came and said, 'Look, he's coming to see you. You'll get a shock when you see him but don't let on. He came home last night and I had to soak him in the bath – his socks were grown into his feet'. And they charged him 10 marks a week for keeping him in concentration camp. He had to pay for his keep. He came up and he was an old grey man, with a shorn head, grey in the face. My mother offered him a cup of coffee and something to eat. 'No, thank you.' So my mother put out a home-baked loaf. It was the Sabbath and she had baked a lovely poppyseed loaf. God, he couldn't stop eating! He just couldn't stop eating. And they weren't allowed to talk about their experiences. This is how it never leaked out properly, I think. Because they threatened you, 'If you speak about it, next time we'll not only take you – we'll take your whole family'. They took that cousin and his family in 1942 and none returned.

My father, who was at the Front in 1914–18, was sure they wouldn't take him. He had a medal in the war. He'd never done anybody any harm, had never been involved with the law or anything. He was certain nothing would happen to him. And then in 1942 they took him and my mother.

My sister married a German non-Jew in 1958 and every year I visit them. In four weeks' time I will be in Germany again and I always make a point of seeing all my old friends – they're so good and faithful. You have to. They risked their lives for us. I had that bond with my non-Jewish friends. That meant an awful lot. They

E

came to visit up to the last minute. In fact, they helped us to sew
in our names and get packed. They even came to the station which
was dangerous. And after we had left, when our parents had nothing
to live on – nothing – these non-Jewish friends would drop in bread
for them, a ration card, or something like that. They couldn't speak
to them – they were just passing.

I was very lucky. In 1937 I met a group of Irish boys on a train
and I kept in contact with one of them. He returned to Germany in
1938 and he wanted to treat me to an evening out. Well everywhere
you went there was a sign, 'Jews are not wanted here'. And I said,
'I know of a Jewish café but I don't know if you are allowed in'.
And he said, 'Let them stop me – I'm British!' So we went to that
Jewish café where I was known. And after a while he said, 'There's
a funny atmosphere – what's wrong here? There's nobody here and
everything is so subdued'. I said, 'I'll tell you what's wrong. There
was a raid here last night by the Nazis for anyone who was in arrears
with their tax. They lifted them out of here and no one will come to
this café again'. So he said, 'Drink up. Come out. Come out'. And
when we came out he said, 'Well, look, you know, whenever you
need a friend you have a friend in Ireland. If you want to come I will
help you'. And at that time I said that I wouldn't leave my parents.

That was 1938, but at the end of '38 I wrote, 'Help! Help!' after the
Pogrom when they burnt the synagogues. Oh! It was terrible. And
I wouldn't have gone, but my mother said to me, 'We have had our
lives and you have yours in front of you and you must go'. So we
got out by the skin of our teeth at the end of May in 1939.

My friend guaranteed for me and the Refugee Committee in
Frankfurt said, 'That means he has to keep you'. I said, 'Oh no, I
can't have that', so the poor fellow had to start all over again to get
me a domestic permit and he had to find a woman who was prepared
to ask me to work as a domestic. Of course, it was very difficult to
get into other countries. There was a conference in Aviéns and only
Columbia said they would accept Jews.

My sister and I emigrated on the same day. Can you imagine
what it meant for my parents knowing that we were going and could
never return while Hitler ruled? And we didn't know where we were
going. I had two permits actually. I had one to stay in Northern
Ireland and I had one to stay in London – to become a nurse. But
my sister had only the one permit to become a nurse in London, and
the fellow I knew had done so much to get me out that I couldn't
say no and so I went to Ireland. I had a pretty rough time there. It
was hard. I wasn't allowed to do anything in Northern Ireland but

domestic work. In 1939 I was just about 28 and I stayed six months in an awful job as a domestic servant. Then I went to a very nice family as nanny to three children – eventually four children – and I stayed three years.

In Ireland there were many refugees. An awful lot of them were domestics and they hadn't been used to domestic service but they had no choice. Some were domestic servants and some worked in factories. There was one who had her own business in Germany – a very elegant woman – she was a domestic servant. We weren't used to it and it was terribly hard.

My sister came over in 1940 when there was an invasion fear. She came to Ireland because she was thrown out of hospital in London because they couldn't have aliens working in hospitals in case there was an invasion. So she said, 'If I have to be a domestic servant I'd rather we were together'. So she chanced crossing the Irish sea and came over and joined me and became a governess.

In 1940 I was taken to Armagh prison suspected of being a spy! The lady I had first worked for denounced me because she was annoyed that I left her. I found that out, years afterwards, from a police sergeant who was a bit stricken with me. He took me out and told me the full story. You needed an alien's card, you see, an identity card, and you had to go to the Aliens Department. The Inspector there said, 'You speak very good English. Where did you learn it?' and I said, 'Well I took an intensive course for two years before I emigrated'. After I had passed my tribunal and was classified 'Category C, friendly alien', the lady I worked for put the spike in and without another interview they marked me 'Suspicious Character'. You see, I had innocently told her that I was getting letters from my parents. The war had already started and the letters came via a friend in Belgium. They went first to my sister and my sister sent them from London to Ireland. That was what she imparted to the police.

On 8 June 1940, one morning at 6 o'clock, a policeman and policewoman came and took me away and went through my correspondence and all my possessions. They laughed because my sister had written, 'If the Germans come to England I'll dig myself a hole and never come out of it'. You know, it was all in those letters and yet they took me away. I thought I would be going to internment, you know. You have heard of internment camps, they are not like prisons.

There were ten of us and we arrived in Armagh Prison and we had one real Nazi woman with us – that was the worst of it. That woman, you know, she was a really suspicious character and we others were all innocent. You know, it really was quite an experience to be in prison. The first two nights they put us in the cell and locked us up and they would come about 11 o'clock with a torch and look through the peephole to see if we were still there. I saw the funny side of it, you know. But then we complained to the Home Office and things changed. The doors were left open in our wing and we could move about and keep ourselves busy, study English, play games and do gymnastics to keep ourselves fit. As quickly as we got in, just as quickly we were released. We couldn't even take our cases. They came later. 'Come on. Come on. You're going out!' That was it. So that was our experience.

I was nine weeks in Armagh Prison. But the remarkable thing was that every one of us was taken back to the people we had been with before prison. There was not one of them said, 'I don't want her in my house anymore'. On the contrary, we got parcels and we were visited. My friend who had brought me out of Germany was an officer in the Royal Marines and he came to Armagh to visit. He used to say 'Mata Hari – the beautiful spy!' [laughs].

For a while you heard from your parents, and then suddenly you didn't hear anymore and that was that. According to what we have been informed by my cousin, my father died first and my mother died three or four months later in concentration camp. But when we made enquiries in Frankfurt they had different information and theirs is probably right. They were transferred, transported to an unknown destination in the east. But I like to believe what my cousin found out in the first instance because I now have a date and can put a memorial candle out on that date, you see. It gives me something to hold on to. That's what my sister and I do. We go to the synagogue on that memorial day, and light a candle at home. I don't know really what is true, whether they went to the east or not. They might have finished in Auschwitz. I don't know. And what good does it do me if I do know? What good does it do me?

In 1942 I was listening to a broadcast by Archbishop Temple of York. He said that in Poland, Jews were shot into their graves and that upset me terribly. I said to the mother of the children I looked after that I would have to do something towards the war effort and join the Fire Service in Belfast. My sister agreed with me and we both joined. When the air-raids kind of petered out in Belfast we decided we would like to try the ATS. We joined and you won't believe it, we came to York and our first day at camp was on the day after VE day! I was in the ATS for about eighteen months. I could have stayed on but I didn't want to, and went back to Ireland. My sister, meantime, had been posted with the Education Corps to Edinburgh and I started training in Ireland for Hotel Management and did two years.

We're only two sisters and I felt it was downright stupid for us to be apart. My sister sent me glowing reports about Edinburgh and the Festival and the theatres and all that. I was in a seaside hotel by then in Port Stuart and I thought, 'Oh this is silly. I'm going to Edinburgh'.

I came to Edinburgh in December 1948 and took a temporary job as housekeeper in a guest house and then I got into a big city hotel. I wanted a city hotel because I'd only been in a seaside hotel. I was first in reception, book-keeping, and I hated it. I was so unhappy the first three weeks and then they offered me a job helping the head chef in the kitchen. I was the only girl with thirty-five men, so I was thoroughly spoiled. I really was. They were charming to me right to the end. I had a wonderful farewell party when I retired and I'm still in contact with some of my former colleagues. It was a wonderful place to work and it belonged to the railways then.

When I came to Edinburgh it struck me that most of the Jewish refugees here had come from Vienna; the men had joined the Pioneer Corps and were posted here and stayed on.[5] That's how they got to Edinburgh. Most of them were academics. There was a doctor and his wife (the latter was a famous scientist), a famous composer and various professional people. I came in '48 so some of them had already left Edinburgh and gone to America if they had an affidavit and could travel and there were very few German Jews. There was one family who made tartan souvenirs. But there are very few left here now.

I don't keep all our dietary laws but I do belong to the Jewish community and I was brought up Orthodox so I know it all – I can't set a foot wrong in a Rabbi's house! I go to the synagogue. The fast day is next month and I'll keep to that, and the Jewish New Year.

I found the Edinburgh people very pleasant. I can't say anything else. I love living here – it is the most gorgeous city. You couldn't live in a better city than Edinburgh. When I was younger I went out dancing. I was a member of the gramophone society, I used to go once a week. I was a member of the League of Health and Beauty, and I went to gymnastics and we had a dance occasionally, and I took some Italian classes.

I'm a British subject, you know. I got my naturalisation in Northern Ireland. The Head Constable came, brought me my passport and said, 'I want to welcome you into the United Kingdom and I am sure you will be a credit to us.' I feel so British. In fact – I feel so Scottish. I can't help it. I love the Scots people – I think they are wonderful.

NOTES

1. Under the Treaty of Versailles, Allied forces occupied much of the Rhineland after the First World War. In 1936 Hitler's troops regained control of the area.

2. In November 1936 a series of acts (the Nuremburg Laws) withdrew citizenship from German Jews.

3. This refers to the expulsion by Germany of Polish-born Jews. In early October 1938 the Polish Government announced that all Jews who had lived outside Poland for more than five years would have their passports revoked and thereby become stateless. In retaliation, on 18 October 1938 the Nazi Government decreed that all Polish-born Jews leave the country with no more than one suitcase of luggage. Initially, the Polish Government refused to allow them entry.

4. The Kristallnacht or Night of Broken Glass, on 9 November 1938, was a nationally organised attack on synagogues and Jewish institutions. It was sparked off by the assassination of Vom Rath, Third Counsellor in the German Embassy in Paris, by Herschel Grynsban. Grynsban, a 17 year-old German-Jewish emigre, acted in retaliation for the German expulsion of Polish Jews.

5. Formed in 1930, the Pioneer Corps started off as an auxiliary force for overseas soldiers. By 1942 it had over 300 fully combatant companies.

JOSÉ

'We've Lost One Battle but not the War'

Like many others, his support for the Allende government forced José Emilio to become a political refugee from General Pinochet's military regime in Chile. He, his wife and his four children found housing in Scotland with the help of Scottish miners.

I was born in the south of Chile in Puerto Montt – that's my area – 11th January 1938. I didn't know too much because my family moved to Concepcion area – Talcaguano. I arrived there when I was three years old. I grew up in that area. It's a big port and all the navy ships arrive there and prepare all the provisions and ammunition. My father owned a workshop and worked in mechanics, motor repair, plastering and plumbing. He was like a contractor. The house was like a workshop and a house together.

The programme of industry-building started from 1960 when a steel factory was developed which employed 5,000 people, also a lot of fish factories. More people wanted to work and all the companies built houses for the people but there weren't enough so the people took land for themselves to make a house. Many people from the countryside area, you know from the Andes mountains, came to work and there weren't houses for all the people. Sometimes two families lived in one room. There was a big explosion of industry.

My father was not a very rich man, he was middle class. I took the left-wing idea from my family and my father. He was really a self-educated man and he had a lot of problems when he was a child because his father and mother died when he was very small, maybe 4 or 5 years old. And he taught me history, you know. He met very bad people in life and he encouraged me to take the good things. He was a really intelligent guy. He learned very quickly. He was an apprentice in a factory and he learned for himself and was really a very good father. He taught me about the difference between the

113

rich and the poor and also he taught me about the contradiction of religion. He was a religious person himself but he saw a contradiction between what the priests said and what they were doing (although now, of course, with Liberation Theology, many priests help the poor). He was a very honest person and every morning he gave food, money, sometimes clothes. That's when I started to understand the situation of the poor people. He told me we don't need to give charity all the time. He didn't believe in charity; you need to organise yourself and organise other people. If we elect a government we need to elect the right government to benefit the majority of the people. My father taught me that my country is a rich country but that it's in the hands of the multinationals and they exploited our people. That's the reason the people are poor there. Also he was very strict with me because he grew up alone without a family. He tried to do the best for me because I was the one son – I didn't have any brothers or sisters.

In the primary school – from Primary 4 – they start to teach the history of other countries and geography. They know exactly where the five continents are, they know all the histories, the revolutions in the Arabic countries, Greece, Italy and the Roman Empire and also the English Empire as well.

I knew all the history of the kings and queens because they are an example to the Chilean law. The Magna Carta – we know that, and the Round Table people. We know Richard I and we know the Houses of Parliament. We know the difference between the House of Commons and the House of Lords. It's like a picture on the wall – symbolic.

In Chile there is political activity in the secondary school. From 12 or 13 years old they start to participate. In the primary schools there are elections but not in the political way. The children are learning to vote and they elect the president of the course – most of the time because they are a good student. When they grow up, they go to Primary 6 or 7, they tend to have the influence from the father and they start to understand politics. For me it is really important because the children have a more open mind and also they learn from the father. If he has a problem of wage conditions and he stays on strike, they participate with the father in the political rallies as well – all the family. Here, in Britain, the youngsters are not bothered about the situation of the father because they know from 16 or 17 years old they have money from the government, but the young in Chile are different, they worry because when the father doesn't have money from work then they don't have an education. Sometimes in the area, if there is some factory on strike, the secondary school have a meeting and try to organise solidarity with the people in the factory. If it is a long strike the children start to organise a caravan for raising money and food for the people on strike. At some rallies there are children of 16 years and they start to make a speech, a very well organised speech about why the workers go on strike, why they support it, why they call for the youngest to participate – it's a very, very political speech you know. Maybe at 12 or 13 years they finish the primary school and go to the Secondary school. From the second year there are lots of discussions because one of the subjects is philosophy and they have to study politics. And they start to analyse the liberal idea and the Marxist idea and there are lots of discussions. It's the same in Chile as Britain – they educate the rich people to control the country. But the difference was that the common schools started to educate the people for taking power. That is the reason Allende won the election.

When I was in Primary 5 or 6 if I saw a guy punishing a small boy, I tried to make my own justice and fight him and protect the wee boy against the big boy. Sometimes I'd fight two or three times a week. I remember I was elected President in the primary school, you know. I tried to organise a strike of the children in the school because there was a lot of punishment from the teacher. The teachers were very, very strict at that time and they had a stick to punish the children. We had a very strong protest, a one-day strike for the children to stop going to the classroom. We made a queue of the children – like a regiment and that day when the bell sounded nobody would go into the classroom and the teachers didn't know anything. All the children said, 'No – we won't go'. And the teachers said, 'Why don't you go to the classrooms?' and I said 'I am the President of the school and we do not agree to be punished, because during this week a lot of children complained about the punishment'. We asked all the teachers to stop the punishment of the children and the director of the school said 'Well we'll talk about that another time if everyone will go directly to the classroom'. And I said, 'OK'. After that they sent for my father; they asked for all the fathers and all the fathers appeared in the school. My father said, 'I'll punish you!' But, in fact, that protest was really good because not many children complained after that. And the teacher said to me, 'Someday, José, in the future, you will be a good leader of the country but you need to be very careful what you are doing'. And they encouraged me to continue to study.

I left home and went to the navy. I didn't like the regime in the navy and also I saw the difference between the high class and the people belonging to the working class. The privates were cleverer people than the officers but the officers had the chance to go to the academy because they had money. I understood the situation because the officers defend the interests of the high class. And I understood what it meant: the class struggle. The working class is obedient to the high class, disciplined in the interests of the high class. When I worked in the navy I'd finished only my primary school. But during that time, I went to the night school, and took secondary education. When I travelled with the ship, we got only time in the port for study, but I took the books I was studying and I read a lot of things in my spare time. When I was in Puntarena, two years 1956–60, I was in the secondary school final year and my teacher introduced me to Marx's *Capital* and also Nasser's *Philosophy of the Revolution*. One day I was in my barracks and every Saturday they had an inspection and they opened my box and found the books, and they said, 'Why do you read that?' and I said 'Well it is because it is from my teacher at the night class'. They said, 'You don't need to read that'. I said 'Well I need to take the exam.' They said 'If you don't take the exam you don't need to read these books.' And after they said, 'You need to stay in seven-day arrest and don't go to the school. Stay in the barracks,' and they took all the books.

That's when I started to participate in political activities because there were a lot of problems in the navy and the army in 1960, bad relations with the officers and also very bad food. I remember us not having enough good heating and Puntarena is really a very cold area. The winter is really very cold – the snow – 20° below zero. So we organised for a mutiny but people infiltrated the group and denounced us. I left the navy – I had to leave because of the mutiny attempt. They took me to a military trial and we denied all the things. They didn't have enough evidence for proof. We needed to leave the navy because if they got proof they'd condemn us to three or four years in jail.

When I left the navy I went to my father's workshop and I started to work with him and I started participating. And that's how I got to know my wife as well – my wife was involved in political activity in the secondary school. After my father died I needed to take over but a lot of problems were there with the Allende government. There weren't materials for making steel, no pipes. A boycott from America broke many small factories. That's when I sold part of the workshop. I started to work in a factory after that. I worked maybe a year because I was more and more involved in political activity. I was elected to a national position in some particular left-wing party. I was politically involved with the Allende government. I was working in a particular area of adult education: organising a school in the factory. The thing was, the school goes to the factory, not the people in the factory to the school because many people didn't like to go back to school. It was a really good programme because most of the people were learning to read, and the people who didn't finish primary school education, because they left early to go to work, finished their secondary education. The university opened more places for the working classes and the people who went to university had a grant from the government.

I needed to travel practically every day and that morning when the military took over I was waiting for an engineer to give me a lift to the place where I was working. He picked me up and the road was blocked by the navy. They stopped us but I said, 'I'll continue – I'm walking'. I passed by the blockade and I continued walking and a lorry came towards me and I said, 'There isn't any way to Concepcion', and the guy turned round and gave me a lift. We saw a lot of machine guns pointing at the train from Concepcion to Santiago. I got out of the lorry and started talking to some people and they said that nobody could pass from here to Tolma. All the factories had stopped and I saw the army and the police take prisoners – people from the fishing factory. A woman was coming from my factory. She said to me, 'The police and the army are looking for you.' She gave me some address, 'You need to go to that house – that house is protection for you'. Eventually I went back to Concepcion. But they were looking for me in the area. When I arrived in my town I tried to contact my people in Concepcion. Everybody was underground and they recommended me to do the same. I didn't fear anything when I crossed the blockade but when I heard that Allende was killed and the military coup was from the right wing – that's when I knew that it was a dangerous situation.

We tried to organise the people to defend the government but later we received instructions that we didn't have any guns for doing anything, you know. Allende was a very democratic president, the people believed in what they were doing. He won the election in a democratic way but what happened? The right wing didn't respect the decision of the majority because they didn't like to lose. Many people believed the military people would return power to the civilians.

I remember in 1973, I tried to contact my people in my ex-job and I contacted one of them and he said he'd send me all the books and names of the people and the teachers who were on the course.

'Steady on', I said, 'You need to burn everything'. And he did that.
He burned all the books and notes I had in my office.

In October the army searched my house and took me to prison
– concentration camp. They accused me of having a gun, of making
a resistance group, but that was not true. I was in interrogation and
tortured but what happened to me is nothing compared to what happened to people during the first days of the coup in the prison. Many
young girls were raped. We know that. The guy said, 'Why do you
organise the resistance?', but the truth was I was working organising
food for the children and also we organised assistance to the people in
jail. In some ways we orientated the people who needed to organise
the resistance – the passive resistance against the government.

I stayed in solitary confinement and I saw them tie up some people.
They showed me to them, to see if they recognised me but they never
spoke a word. It was ten or twelve days of torture – they punched
me and gave me electric shocks on my head and arms and started
to increase the current. I stayed in solitary confinement maybe two
or three months. One day the guy called me and said, 'You are free
now but you need to sign this paper to say nothing has happened
to you. If you recognise some people from here on the street you
need to be very quiet. If you recognise somebody in the street it is
dangerous for you because something will happen to you'. And after
that I was free.

I was very shocked and stayed in the house all the time at first.
Then I started to contact my people again but the police and the
Secret Army stopped me in the street. They were making a lot of
complaints against me and I disappeared from my house. My wife
knew where I was going. I left my home, my country, for Argentina,
to go where my organisation sent me. We don't like our people to
leave the country but you need to keep people alive. But if you go to
another country you need to participate in all the solidarity activity
and organise the people.

In Argentina it was quite difficult. We were in a refugee hotel and
the police at that time were very strong and they had a very close relationship with the Chilean police. Many Chilean people disappeared
or were sent back to Chile. That is why we needed to be very careful
in what we were doing and who we contacted. That's why I left.

I applied for a visa to different countries – to Canada, New
Zealand, Cuba and the Soviet Union as well, and Great Britain and
Norway. Canada gave a visa only for myself and my children and not
for my wife. The second countries were Great Britain and Norway.
The Soviet Union and Cuba had to analyse my case but they didn't

give an answer very quickly. I came here because the United Nations said, 'You go to Britain.'

We arrived in London. All the Chilean people waited in a refugee hotel for a month. We received an offer from Scotland, from the miners, because my area is a mining area. I never worked in a mine but my Political Contact in Chile was a miner. The Scottish miners were very good for solidarity with Chile. They had a house for my family and myself in Cowdenbeath. It was a real surprise for me and a very emotional moment when the people gave me the keys of my house. They said, 'You open the door'. Then I saw everything furnished, there was everything in the house – it was really very good. The children had to start to go to school because we arrived on 23rd May.

We stayed maybe nine months but we'd started English classes at Stevenson College and we needed to travel early every morning to Edinburgh. The children had to stay alone in the afternoon so we decided to move. We applied to the housing department and we got a house in Broomhouse and then we moved to Wester Hailes. I finished the English class and got a certificate in welding. I went for a six month course but I did it in three months because I knew the job. I got a job in Aberdeen in the shipyards. I got more qualifications and went to work on oil-rig construction – working maybe three or four years, working one time on a platform offshore. In 1984 I was working and after I finished the job – no more jobs. Except I worked for six months from September 1985 to January 1986 in Torness.

In Chile I knew the history of Great Britain but I knew only the history of the high class, not of the working class. Not till when we arrived here. The history of the working class is really exploitation. I saw the War Museum and I saw many people died in this country to maintain the power of the high class. For me, what happened is that the people who worked to occupy countries like India never received the profit. I don't like the different classes – monarchy, oligarchy and so on. I don't like the monarchy, because that kind of people and the capitalists are a sickness in the society – a parasite. These people live in palaces while there are people dying without medical attention. Great Britain exploited all our nitrate and the Chilean working class were working in very poor conditions and didn't even receive money – they received tokens. That was one of the first big working-class movements in Chile – against the exploitation by the British companies. The profits of that exploitation was not of benefit to the working people in Great Britain but to the minority group – the oligarchy.

For me it is more important that the working class have more participation in the rule of the country. For example, nobody goes to the union meetings here. In Chile if they have a union meeting after work everybody goes. During the Allende government when we had an increase in money, more televisions, better conditions in the house for women, the women would go to the meetings as well and participate in the community.

In Britain my impression is that the working-class people are very friendly, very compassionate, but not political enough. They say sometimes that they support Chile solidarity. They say, 'Poor Chile. What happens in your country?' But they don't know what happens in their own country. Sometimes they give money, sometimes they give compassion.

I don't like Social Security. I don't like to take unemployment benefit. I don't like that kind of system because it maintains the conformity of the people. It is good if the state pays benefit, for example, when a woman has a child and I'd like better attention for old people and a lot of benefit for students. But not to maintain young people because those people do nothing. They don't make an impression on the government to give them a job. For example, where are these people when there is some rally? There is a lot of unemployment, why don't people protest every day?

All the time we from Chile say we don't come here for economical reasons – we come from a political problem. I was having a conversation in the factory when I was working and I explained that I don't stay here by my own decision. Also, if they say that I take their job then I say to them, 'Why are there so many British people in other countries?'

Some Chilean people, they feel racist persecution. I know, for example, that I don't have a job because when I apply for some jobs the people decide on a British person and not me. I had a job three years or four years ago but now it is different. It's a political thing to keep the British people happier than the foreign people. Some Chilean people have a problem in London where they say things like 'foreign bastard' you know. Many Chilean people, they have good positions: sometimes a manager or a director in a factory. But those people are not working in solidarity, they don't participate in solidarity. They don't like to take Chilean problems to this society or to denounce the British. For example the government here have a deal with the Chilean government. You see, I denounce that. But they like to keep their job rather than maintain the solidarity.

We try to maintain our culture but we don't push it at the children because they live here. I think the children have had some problems but they never talk to me about these problems. But they have lots of friends. In some ways, sometimes we are not happy with the system for the young because we think there is too much liberty. For example, the law that allows the children to leave the parents at 16 years old. That, for us, is not really good because most of the children don't know what they need to do when they stay alone. Chileans have more contacts with the children, more close relationships with the children. Here children grow up very quickly and leave because they feel more freedom. That is the reason sometimes why the children don't worry what happens within the family. But in Chile, the people say, 'Well we need to fight for the future of our families, we need more good modern education, we need better conditions and we need more money to do these things.' And all the time they say that they're doing it for their family. Here the people are more selfish.

My mother died – without any communication because all the letters were censored – since I have been here. I know my mother died after six or seven months. I don't know when exactly.

I can't go back. I'd like to go back. When I applied three years ago the Chilean government refused. But now there are lots of amnesties for all the people. I would like to go back depending on what happens. The struggle is in Chile, not here.

We need to be liars. They'll say, 'Don't make any trouble and participate in anything against the government'. I'll say, 'OK'. We have our own life. I miss the struggle because I like to do things for my country not for myself.

It's a very sentimental thing when you say, 'Oh I miss the countryside, I miss the seaside or the beach'. That is a very sentimental thing. Only I'd like to go back to my country because I'd like to participate in the liberation. I've learnt that I'm very proud of the Chilean people because the Chilean people like fighting for better conditions. We had them but we lost them. We say, 'We lost one battle but not the war'.

SHAHEEN

'I Wanted to be Something'

Shaheen Unis was born in Pakistan in 1949. She married and came to Britain in the mid-sixties. Now her pakoras, samosas and curries are sold in shops throughout Edinburgh.

Our family was quite well off in Pakistan and we had a big house. I think it was the first house to have electricity in our road. My grandfather had a sports business where they made a lot of things like footballs and cricket bats. Ours was quite an average town. The sports business was the main industry then. I remember seeing whole walls with leather hanging off them, they were drying the leather and colouring it to make the footballs. Now it is an industrial city. They make quite a lot of surgical stuff in Selkot, but they don't put stamps on it which I'm really sad about. They send the stuff to Japan, Germany, Britain and it's stamped there although the stuff actually comes from Pakistan. Maybe people don't try hard enough to keep their own identity and be recognised by the world.

I lost my mother when I was thirteen and my grandmother, my mother's mother, brought me up. There were a lot of poor people in our street and every time they needed something they came to my grandmother for spice or onions or some food to cook. Every time a beggar came to the door they would never return empty handed. And that's a habit I've picked up from her.

All the boys and girls from the street used to come to our house and study because we had all the facilities; we had the big fan running in the hall and we used to sit there and study together. And all the girls and boys used to get together to play cricket or badminton. Our cousins used to come and we'd play cards all night. I remember we used to have a big, big plate of rice and we used to all sit together and eat. And that is a moment I can't forget: all the cousins sitting in the house and having food together.

Another thing I remember is the 1963 war with India. That was a horrific day. We were all sitting scared about the war, sirens everywhere and suddenly everything went so dark. And somebody came in and said that India had invaded Pakistan from Jammu. We were so scared – they said they took the young girls away. But my father said, 'There's nothing to worry about, we will just move away from here tomorrow morning.' Everybody was praying. We slept that night and when we woke up a piece of bombshell had come into the house. And that morning everybody was on top of the buses, trying to empty the city. There was shelling for about a fortnight and then we came back and thanked God our house was OK.

I got married at 16 to my first cousin. My father said, 'Would you like to get married? You've got the choice'. And I said, 'Whatever you think is right'. And that was it. In our culture we do obey our elders and parents, but I think if I had liked somebody else I could have just gone and asked my dad. I used to come home from school and sit beside my father and talk to him about everything. He would just listen and never tell me off. We were, I suppose you could say, advanced because my parents had lived in different countries and they'd met other people. They thought it was better to give more freedom to their children. That's how I had the confidence that I was right because my father would never tell me off. I really loved him and when I got married and came to Britain he really missed me. He lost his business; he was just lost without me. I had five brothers and I was the only sister in the family. My father said I was the wealth there – like they say 'Laxmi' – the girl is a Laxmi (the goddess of wealth) in the house. When I went back after five years to Pakistan I couldn't recognise my father. When I saw him I just said, 'I've seen that person somewhere' – and that was my father. When I left him he was huge, and when I saw him again he was so slim. There was nobody there to really look after him and talk to him.

My husband had come here in 1964, before he was married. They sent his visa to Pakistan because they needed the workforce. He came here as a typist, to Bradford, but he kept on moving because the wages weren't very good in those days.

My husband's brother-in-law, who was in Britain, used to come to me when he came home. Men were usually master of the house in Pakistan, and I asked him, 'Do you have to cook your own meal?' and he said 'Yes'. These kinds of things used to amuse me before I came.

As I was only 16 when I left Pakistan, as I was going to the airport I was shaking with fright because I didn't know what to expect. My father said, 'Calm down, nothing will go wrong'. When my husband decided to get a house here and I was to follow him, I was nervous because I'd heard lots or rumours that when boys came back to Pakistan to get married, they'd just leave their wives in Pakistan and get married in Britain again to other women! But my husband said, 'Look, it's nothing like that!'

When I came to Britain, to London, we had one room and I felt really lonely. We had a landlady who was very strict. When we used to make a meal she used to say, 'Clean the kitchen first, clean the cooker, clean the floor, and then take everything upstairs to eat your meal'. I was so used to having meals with the family and I got really upset about it. We had servants in Pakistan and I wasn't used to this at all. I started burning my hands when I was making chapattis. When I used to do the washing I used to get big holes in my hands because of the soap. My husband said, 'Look, you don't have to do the washing in the house, I'll take it to the launderette'. Once he took it and all the colours ran into each other. I said, 'We have to carry on, you can get me gloves'. I started working in a jewel factory in Twickenham on a chain assembly, making big, long chains. And later I designed earrings for them.

Because we didn't have a house or anything when we came to this country, I always had an ambition: I wanted to be something. When I left Pakistan, I told my father, 'Me and my husband will not come back until we have achieved something'. And that's what we did, we worked really hard. My husband was working in a factory that made heat-regulation systems. He used to cry because he thought I was a spoilt one in Pakistan. He looked at me and started crying and said, 'Why are you working so hard?' I said, 'Look, I'm working for you and for myself now because we have to be something and be recognised by the community and by our family. If I sit in the house idle, it's not going to help'. Even my father, when he heard I'd started the job, was really shocked. My husband never forced me to work but he really appreciated it. He has really given me good encouragement and confidence to make something out of myself.

I was pregnant the minute I came to Britain. We actually didn't want a family right away, but then we had our son, and we were pleased. But when I was going to bring my son home our landlords said, 'Three people cannot live in one room. You have to move out'. My husband said, 'Look, my wife hasn't even come back to the house and you're already giving us notice. Please don't do that. Let us find another room and then we will move out'. That was the most bitter experience I had with Londoners. When I look back I don't have bitter feelings, but whenever I had a bitter experience like that I would just pray and ask my God, 'Please let it pass'. It was a hard life here. After they'd given us notice, I was really sad and I was walking on the street. I used to meet one very old Englishman and he used to wheel his wife, who had cancer, around. We just used to say hello to each other, but this time he said, 'You look sad, Mrs Unis. What's wrong?' 'Yes, I am said. I've got an order from my landlord to leave'. He said, 'You've got nothing to worry about, come and live with me'. We went to live with them and I used to help them, do the dishes or give them a little food or something. And they were very appreciative. I still visit them whenever I go to London. We stayed there for a year and they were really good to us.

I started working again two and a half months after I had my first child. I worked for Timex for about six months then after that I worked in the same factory as my husband. We used to pay about £3.50 for a babysitter each week. I have a strong belief you shouldn't stick with your mother all the time. Mothers always spoil their children! I had to go to work; I couldn't have done that in Pakistan. Anyway, I really enjoyed my work and I liked meeting people, and they were very friendly. That's what I really enjoyed – being wanted. I didn't really want to stay at home because I was learning all the time. My husband stuck beside me. I was wearing sleeveless blouses and trousers, and some of our people did ask, 'Why are you wearing these clothes?' One lady said, 'You come from Pakistan and you're wearing sleeveless blouses already!' She was shocked. My husband said, 'If you want to wear them, just wear them'. But for many Pakistani women in Britain it's hard, yes. Very hard. Because the men are not educated enough. Lots of people have come from the villages and haven't been to school or they've been brought up by strict religious people. If the man of the house wants to have a date with another woman he will just sneak out, but the women cannot take their *dupatis* off their heads, which really irritates me. They have to do what their husbands tell them. All over Britain, it happens quite a lot. And this is very bad. You could say the man and the woman are two wheels: the woman can support the pressure of the house and the man can support the pressure of the job. But here women have jobs, they're doing the cooking, they're looking after the children, and the men are just working outside the house. And I think that the women are carrying more pressure in this country. It's because of the culture clash – there are opportunities for ladies to go out and work here. But in Pakistan you have a grandma in the house, you have your mother-in-law in the house, your children, you have relatives coming in and it's really impossible for a woman to go out and do a job – and also impossible for a man to cheat his wife. This is the problem: because we don't have mothers and mother-in-laws or other elders here, men think they can do whatever they like and they don't want their women to go out and find out what's happening. They will ask them to go out to work, yes, but they will not let them into their own lives.

Maybe I have changed quite a lot because I have been dealing with men most of the time, but even in Pakistan I never hesitated to speak to the opposite sex. There is no religion that says the woman is lower than the man. The woman is equal. There is no such religion that says the woman has to sit in the house all day. The men are oppressing the women. Pakistani and Indian men want their wives to be dependent so they prevent them from learning. If a woman wants to go to a party at night-time at about seven o'clock, a gathering for me and my friends, some say, 'No, I can't come out because my husband will not permit me'. At the back of their husbands' minds is the idea that the woman's place is in the house, and they shouldn't go to parties because people like me will give them advice: 'Get out and do your own thing, don't depend on anybody. If you do your own thing they will think you've got some qualities'. Even though our ladies are so intelligent and so sensible, they've been isolated. But since the ladies have come so far from their own country, I think they should help themselves and not be afraid of anything.

We came to Glasgow because my brother-in-law had a restaurant there. And when he opened a restaurant in Edinburgh in 1973 he offered my husband a job in it. He helped us a lot but we couldn't survive on what my husband earned and I asked him, 'Why don't we open up our own business?' – so we decided to. It was Nadia's in Dalry Road. A friend helped us by lending us money and since then we have never looked back. We ran Nadia's for eight years and then lots of restaurants started opening up and the business went down so my husband suggested that we sell pakoras to the shops and I started making them in the house. All the dear friends I have, they all stood by me. Whenever I needed them they came.

Now, lots of people know me in Edinburgh by name or face, because we've been in business here for 15 years. Scottish people have helped me and, because of what I've achieved, my own people really praise me; they respect me.

I love living in Edinburgh. I'm actually proud of living in Edinburgh. The Scottish people are very friendly and helpful. But I would love to go back to live in Pakistan. We have built a very nice house there, with the same luxury as we have here. But the problem is that my husband is a very straightforward person; he likes things easy. We have a business here and a very good income and he doesn't want to start all over again. I usually tell my friends here that I'm going to open up a home for our ladies to be together! But I would really like to go back and retire in Pakistan. I miss my relatives because they give me so much love and importance; when I go back it's just like the queen has arrived. They're all around me.

And you miss the culture, the children going out of your hands. My sons are grown up now. They say things in front of us which we would never have said in front of our parents. The older one has got a girlfriend, which I don't like because we people wouldn't have dared bring boyfriends or girlfriends in front of our parents. I will not stop it because I don't mind them having friends as long as they're not sexual partners. I think he's sensible enough in this way. We do tell them they are not to have sex because the girls are very young: 'You mustn't have sex until you are married'. They are not religious, I have to admit. Basically, I am religious and I know quite a lot about religion. I speak Punjabi to them and they answer me back in English! They want to be Scottish, that's what they're proud to be. I don't mind because I don't want to clash with them. If you saw my sons you'd be surprised because they've both had their hair coloured and their ears pierced. My husband says, 'You can't help it, my dear, they will come back eventually'. I think when they get older they will learn. There comes a time when you want your own identity.

If I went back to Pakistan, as a woman I would have to sit in the house and maybe just enjoy the company of my friends. I couldn't have an active life like I do here. I would find it very hard because I like having a business and being powerful.

'Ukraine Isn't Dead Yet'

Jaroslav Bobak was born in 1920 in Western Ukraine, in a town called Peremyshl (Przemysl) which is now in Poland near the Russian border. He lives with his wife and family in a flat in Wester Hailes, Edinburgh.[1]

Shortly after the First World War, when the Austro-Hungarian Empire broke up and the western part of Ukraine was absorbed into Poland, my father who had reached the rank of sergeant in the Austrian army, joined the Polish army in which he served until 1930. At the beginning of the Polish rule they were desperate for professional soldiers but after ten years they decided that they didn't want Ukrainian NCOs in the army and my father was retired in spite of being quite healthy. Out of 22 million in Poland at that time, there were seven million of us Ukrainians living in Galacia in the south-east of Poland.[1] When my father retired we left the barracks in Peremyshl (Przemysl) and we moved some thirteen kilometres to where mother was born in Nyzankovychi and settled there.

Quite a lot of our relations were living there. That's why we went. Actually, we were related to at least a quarter of the population in one way or another. My grandfather was still alive and it was nice to be beside him. It was a small town, a population of 3,000 people with the usual main buildings and along the main street there were a few shops.

We started school at seven years old. When I started there wasn't so much discrimination in school. Both Poles and Ukrainians are Catholic but we had different priests: every morning we started classes with a prayer and on alternate days there was a Polish and a Ukrainian 'Our Father'.

In 1934 I had the opportunity to enter the secondary school in Peremyshl and it was quite expensive. Being the son of a Polish non-commissioned officer my fees for education were cut by half, so myself and my brother as well as my older sister all took advantage of it. And my sister eventually went to a university in Cracow. At the school all subjects were taught in Ukrainian.

I had to travel by train every morning, thirteen kilometres, and the station must have been about a mile and a half from the house. There was no public transportation so we had to walk regardless of rain or snow, and roads weren't asphalted: they were muddy during the winter. Also, we were working, in a way, helping the family. If we had a crop of grain to cut, we all went together. There was no machinery, you had to use the ordinary hand sickle. We had to dig potatoes with a hand implement, you know, help father to chop the logs, bring the water from the well. There was no water in the houses and there must have been at least seven wells along the street. It was usually mother who went for water but whenever I was there I went. It was very dangerous in winter because the spilled water beside the well formed ice, and it was on a hill. You tried to walk down, carrying water, with ice underneath your feet!

We had rather a small bit of land. The land at the front of each house was probably 35 square metres and there was about 50 square metres at the back where there was usually a shed or barn where you stocked your grain. The rest of the ground was used for gardening. Grain was stocked on both sides of the barn and in the middle there was a threshing area, smoothly made of clay. The wagon drew in, emptied the sheaves of corn, and when it was time to do the threshing usually two people did it. Then you lifted up the new straw and the corn was sieved and swept and taken out of the back door where the shells of corn were separated and the grain was taken to the mill. There were two water mills to make flour to your requisition: whether you wanted white flour, darker flour or wholemeal flour. We kept chickens and rabbits for meat. Some people had cows and pigs. You had to go and buy most of your meat, you know, usually you bought half a pig and it was dealt with by my father. He'd separate the hind leg and so on and then it was smoked and hung up in a loft where it was kept for a long time. Sausages were also made and smoked and hung in the loft.

There were better off people and poorer people. You would notice people who were lacking proper clothing but it wasn't really drastic. No matter how poor you were, you always tried to be clean. There was no welfare of any type at all, but nobody was left to starve. The well-to-do probably had four horses to plough the fields – no machinery you must remember. My uncle was a blacksmith and I was always fascinated by the work he did: shoeing the horses, making the wagons, putting the metal rims round the wheels – and so busy always because everybody was using horses and wagons.

We were living at the foot of the Carpathian mountains and at the end of the harvest season there was a festival. The population from hundreds of kilometres around came to the churches there. To get to the churches you actually had to climb. There were no roads so you had to crawl on all fours to get there. People brought goods and food. They couldn't bring enough with them! And it lasted a week. The place was called Calvaria, which is Calvary. And they had there at least six different Polish and Ukrainian churches. Religious processions walked along different routes to get there. I remember people passing our place and they were from a hundred kilometres away. They walked, carrying banners and singing.

In the village we often had dances outside and played guitars, sitting by a pile of logs. There was singing going on, late, late into the night. We would go for a swim in the river, play handball, play a game similar to cricket called *kitchki*. At least I could understand that, but I still can't understand what is happening in cricket! [laughs]. Football – we played the Polish team – lots of excitement! We did a lot of plays on the stage and I took part in three of them. One was called *Uncle from America* and this was how I learned my first few words of English – they were used in the play. In the *Prosvita*, the community centre, you could play table-tennis, chess, read the paper. There was a library available there and we also had silent films with a piano playing. The American films had subtitles in Polish, but later most of the films were Polish. Quite often, we had a festival in the open which included games like climbing a pole rubbed with soap with a bottle of vodka on the top. And I remember a pole across the river with men sliding themselves towards each other using bags to knock each other into the water. And a lottery took place at the same time so money was collected from the community.

In Nyzankovychi, probably 80 per cent of the population were Ukrainian and the remainder were Poles and Jews. There weren't any drastic situations but there always was that difference. On one occasion I remember I was at secondary school and there were some parades during a Polish national festival. They played the Polish national anthem and, as you know, you have to take your cap off. I didn't, so a policeman came along and hit me on the head and the cap fell off! This is how we felt about it, you see. There were many reasons. For example, the *Prosvita* was a Ukrainian cultural establishment and on any occasion we had a gathering, the Polish policemen were outside. And on top of that they had young civilian Poles who were always ready to don the uniforms and get their rifles out if there was a necessity. Being a young man, I was interested in girls, and very often we talked to the Polish girls and they were quite nice, but among the older generation there was resentment. Quite often our houses were built side by side, with a Ukrainian on one side of the fence and a Polish farmer (often a newcomer from Northern Poland brought in to boost up the Polish population) on the other. And they would come to some exchanging of words – quite often not very pleasant.

I remember my father coming home when he was in the Polish army and telling my mother that his commanding officer had said to him, 'Don't talk to your family in Ukrainian'. Certain jobs were restricted to Poles only. At that time we used the description of our religion as Greek-Catholic (Eastern Rite), and once this was put on the application it usually resulted in a refusal. Of course, our names themselves indicated immediately that we weren't Polish but Ukrainian.

In 1939 I passed exams to enter the pedagogical lyceum in Sambir where I was going to train for three years to become a teacher – but Germany invaded Poland, so that was the end of my plans. First of all we read in the papers of incidents on the border between Poland and Germany. Some Germans penetrated across the border and made raids on neighbouring villages. Mobilisation was proclaimed and more restrictions were imposed.

Then we heard the news on the wireless. There was a lot of shouting going on – 'Heil Hitler' and so on, on the transmission for everybody to hear. And then came the third of September. . .

The Ukrainian population's attitudes towards the situation was that it was something we had been looking forward to. Not because of the political attitude of the Germans – this wasn't very clear to us at the time – but because we were hoping that our existing situation in Poland would change for the better. We didn't know exactly how, but at least some change would take place. And the Germans actually, when they reached our part of the world, treated us differently. If you were a Ukrainian you were slightly better than a Pole. I met some Germans at that time, and I went to a party with two of them. It was late at night and I was going home and I'd got really drunk. I knew that in a field beside the river there were Germans camping, on the move; I knew there would be a guard and I was scared. But when I was stopped – 'Halt, who goes there?' – I explained, 'I've left two of your colleagues after a few drinks, and I'm going home, and I'm Ukrainian'. And that was fine.

Well, the war was going on and eventually Poland was occupied from the west, by Germany, and then the Russians started the invasion from the east. It wasn't far from our place where the two of them met. Peremyshl was split in two by the River San and the northern part of Peremyshl was under German rule and the southern part was under Soviet occupation. My gymnasium was in the south of Peremyshl. It took at least two months before they reorganised school and I went back – under a Russian system, of course. I was accepted as a ninth-year student.

Our encounter with the Germans had been very brief because soon after the Germans, the Russians came and settled down.[2] We heard on the wireless that the First Ukrainian Army was coming to free us from the 'Polish yoke'. My sister and I were awaiting the arrival of the first troops. Most of the faces were Asiatic, narrow eyes, dark complexion: Mongols, Uzbekistanis, Azerbaijanians – this was supposed to be the First Ukrainian Army freeing us from the Polish yoke! They had long coats without vents, and they were such a pitiful looking lot. My sister looked at them with enthusiasm, and she burst into tears with disappointment . . . and shortly afterwards everyone was talking about how Great Stalin was sending his troops here to free us. Every soldier was carrying Stalin's constitution, beautifully bound books, beautiful, red, soft, well-made with good quality paper – 'Here, read the constitution! . . . "He who doesn't work, doesn't eat." "Religion is the opium of the people." "We must get rid of the Polish landlords." "Private property won't exist any more." '

We soon discovered that we'd got to be very quiet about what we said because shortly afterwards, actual Ukrainians in the Red Army started mixing with the young people asking us questions – did we know the Ukrainian national anthem? There were lots of Party members – *politruks* – political advisers. They were dressed as soldiers but they immediately started to spy, to learn what the feeling of the population was. So the people soon learned that they'd got to watch themselves. It soon started too: in the course of the night, a knock on the door – they were asked to take what they could carry and no one saw them again. We heard eventually that they were sent to Siberia and that some of them landed in prisons, but it was not until after the war was finished that communal graves were found. Some were shot and thrown into the graves. The people that were taking a leading part in the social and political community, they disappeared first. But most people played their game, you know, they were 'enthusiastic' about them. My father and sister were secretaries in the *Prosvita* and in the eyes of the Russians, if you were a secretary in certain organisations, you were responsible for a lot of things with which they didn't agree politically.[3] They were both questioned and, of course, they were both innocent. It was a cultural association, you know. (Of course, it was political to a certain extent because, I mean, we didn't praise Stalin. We talked about our lost independence – our short-lived independence which Ukrainians regained in 1918.)[1] And we didn't play 'Workers of the World Unite': we sang 'Shche Ne Vmerla Ukraina' – (Ukraine isn't dead yet). They weren't really charged with anything, but they weren't exactly in the clear.

Meantime, in 1939, I met a Jewish girl who I was very fond of. She was attending the gymnasium as well, but all of a sudden she decided to go to a place called Drohobych (Drogobych) and enter the pedagogical institute there. I wanted to be near her, so I left and went to the same school. They paid us 40 roubles a week for accommodation, so we survived. My landlady was a Jewess, and there we were until 1941. Both of us were going to a place where posts as teachers were available – these were our plans. And then the Russians joined the Allies. One night there was a lot of noise, aeroplanes – Germany had started war against the Soviet Union.[4] I was 120 kilometres from home and Germans had crossed the border and were advancing fast.

Eventually, one night, everything was quiet in town, you couldn't see any Russian troops. Well, we saw some on a horse-drawn wagon with a wounded soldier with a bandage. They actually pointed a gun at us but nothing happened. There was a shortage of food, so later on I went outside and it was very quiet. I came across a group of people who were looting a store, and I went in and got rice and sugar which I gave to my landlady. The people were gathering on the main street and suddenly, out of the quiet and darkness, the first troops of Germans appeared, riding bicycles. They had a terrific welcome from the population in Drohobych. The next day there were reprisals against Jews in the town. I went down to the old Russian secret police headquarters and people had found a big grave in the back yard and they were digging bodies out as I arrived there. I didn't see who did it, but there were six or seven Jews lying on the pile, some of them still moving. When I went back to the house I was grey. The first grey hairs appeared.

We stayed in Drohobych a while and then left with a friend, who took me, my girlfriend and another Ukrainian. A wagon with two horses arrived. We had some Ukrainian ladies' shirts, they're usually embroidered, and a scarf, and we dressed my girlfriend in this and set off home. Halfway we met Slovak troops travelling east to the front. And being Slovaks, they had no difficulty in understanding us. We asked them if they could give us a lift, and they agreed, so we managed to get home.

I found work as a translator in a POW camp where the Germans were bringing Soviet prisoners. They used the old Polish artillery camps. Most of the Soviet prisoners just lived in the open without any sort of shelter or bedding. That job finished and things were very hard at that time, but there was another job available, for a loaf of bread a day, working on the reconstruction of bridges that had been blown up.

It wasn't so long after that Jews were asked to return to their place of origin, so my girlfriend had to leave her auntie and go back to her parents. I was working on a bridge and my girlfriend sent a note asking me to see her off, but I couldn't so I sent my brother to say farewell on my behalf. What happened to her? I've been asking myself that question ever since. I had a letter from her telling me that she'd arrived and she explained to me, 'I told my father about us and my father doesn't mind'. And she said, 'If you can, come and see me'. But with restrictions and distance I never went to see her and I never heard from her again. I mean the answer is obvious. We well know what happened.

Then my sister's husband, who was working in a firm collecting poultry and eggs, found me a job in his office. You see, the people had to contribute – like taxes – eggs, hens, ducks, geese. The Jewish population were involved in killing them, stripping the feathers and packing them in cases. Everything was going to the troops in the East. After that, I got a job as a clerk in the control office of an agricultural co-operative in Peremyshl. My father knew the director. The farmers had to bring their corn there for so much payment – and payment was in vodka, or cigarettes for that matter, because they couldn't buy cigarettes on the market. In the evenings I went to an emergency matriculation course because 1939 – boom! And in 1941 my plans had had to be scrapped. The course was for six months and I passed the examination in March 1944.

I had met a Ukrainian girl who worked in the shop down below as a salesgirl. We were attracted to each other and we were going steady. And on Saturday, 17th June 1944, we got married at rather short notice, because I got the call-up papers from the German army. After Stalingrad, Germany had started to run short of manpower. At that time the Ukrainian Committee, who had no particular power or anything, agreed to the German proposition that a Ukrainian division would be formed, called after our part of the Ukraine: the Fourteenth Galician. The Ukrainian Committee made the point that our unit was only to be used on the eastern front against the Russians. We would fight only against them, so that eventually we could free the Ukraine. So on 18th June, after spending one night with my wife, I boarded a train to take me to Germany, to the camp in Kirshbaum.

For a while I still heard from my wife and I was writing to her and writing to my parents, sister and brother. And then, all of a sudden, no more letters. At that time we had no idea what was going on outside, how the front was moving. We were completely isolated. Before I had reached the German training camp and met up with my division, they had been sent to the front, to a place called Brody.[5] Within five days our Ukrainian division, plus three German divisions, were encircled by Russians who broke through with their heavy armoury. Most of them perished. Hitler was very much interested in happenings in that part of the front and he was told that we actually betrayed him. So I didn't get a uniform until five months later because they weren't quite sure what to do with us. Besides this, about 70 per cent of the original division had been in the underground army in the Ukraine, actually fighting both Germany and Russia.

After four months, about 3,000 of the First Ukrainian Division actually returned to Germany with the commanding officer, informing Hitler that they did a very good job but had no chance. Only 3,000 out of 14,000 returned to Germany. Then I was put into uniform, had initial training, and shortly afterwards we were sent to Czechoslovakia – well, Slovakia, actually – because some Slovak partisans were fighting against the Germans. I believe there was already some penetration by the Russian troops and as I'd already lost contact with my parents and my wife, the Russians must have been pretty close to Czechoslovakia. The Slovaks treated us differently. Though we were wearing German uniforms, we were Ukrainians, we were Slavs.

When we first went there we guarded tunnels in a mountain area near Zilina in a place called Varin. There was a tunnel and at the end of the tunnel was a bridge, which had been blown up, and the Germans were afraid they might blow up the whole tunnel, so this was why we were guarding it on both sides. I didn't stay there long because they requested men to be dog-handlers, so I went to Berlin and spent three months there. Then we were into winter, and our division was ordered to Yugoslavia to chase the Tito partisans.[6] Fifty of us were split up and distributed to different units. The dogs were trained to find people hiding in the trees and bushes, locate mines buried in the ground. After giving the order the dog started making a zigzag, always going forward, searching the area. My dog was called Mali, which in Polish means 'small'.

One day the real thing was on. 150 men were collected and when we arrived we were told to stand five metres from one another. It was a beautiful day and when you looked along you saw nothing but shining helmets. It was something impressive. As far as you could see it was an unbroken line. We were ordered to go forward and I don't know how many villages we saw. There were slogans on the walls, 'Zivo Tito!' – 'Long Live Tito!' As far as we were concerned, the partisans had always been there the day before we came. After that we were transferred to an Austrian village, St Martin. We were staying with this nice, young Austrian woman and we were very idle; there weren't even any duties involved. But I insulted an Austrian officer so I was punished and they brought me to a mountain of potatoes to peel. We received the news that Hitler was dead. And then 8th May came along.

That particular morning a terrific bombardment was going on. It was non-stop. Suddenly there were shells flying over towards the front. We were told that the war was over but the Russian Armistice Day was to be a day later. What we were doing was actually putting a barrage on the Russians as all our units were withdrawing.

We started marching west. We were told to dispose of all the heavy equipment but I still carried my dog's bucket, and an extra blanket for him, and we still kept our arms because it was still very near Tito's territory. Up to that day we always got our daily ration, but from that day onwards there was nothing. Thousands and thousands of troops were marching, some still using their motor-cars or horses, and the artillery still actually pulling their guns with them as well. I started finding friends I knew from home, so we joined together.

In one place, a girl was interested in my dog so I said, 'Well, can you give me two loaves of bread for it?' and she was willing. She went to her house and brought the two loaves and I gave her the dog and told the dog to stay with her. Unfortunately, my command wasn't sufficient. As she was walking away, trying to pull the dog with her, he turned round and bit her and she fainted. Each of us had a bandage in a little pocket inside our jackets, so I put this bandage on her leg and told her to see the doctor. I was left with a dog and two loaves of bread! Then we caught a young sheep to eat and dug up some potatoes that had just been planted, to make a stew. I really don't know how we lived, because we didn't have any food, you see.

I still had my dog, but there was no point in carrying him along with me as I couldn't feed him anything. We were approaching the Alps and there was this village with a church spire and an abandoned cart with some straw on it. I told Mali to jump up and stay there. It was really a climb up the mountain. We went right to the top and I looked back and I saw this village below and this little cart and a yellow spot which was the straw in the centre, and a black spot where my dog was lying. It was heartrending to leave Mali, as I had to.

We crossed the Alps on foot. There were some marvellous sights and beautiful nights in the open, on the slopes. In one place we were sleeping at an Austrian farm, and during the night we all got up quietly. The boys went to the stable, tied rugs over the horses' hooves, carried the wagon out of the farmer's shed, put the two horses into the harness and set off. We'd got the cart as transport – great! We were sitting on the wagon and we must have gone five, maybe six miles, when the farmer arrived on a horse [laughs]. Well, we gave him the whole thing back and that was it.

Eventually we met the first British soldiers on the other side of the Alps and we laid down our arms. There was a big stack of them. We were staying in the open and the British Army were supplying us with tanks of water. We stayed there for a while, and then we were issued with tents and from there we went to a place called Udine, in Italy, where they had concrete army barracks. But our group of five or six decided not to go to the barracks. There was a cemetery and at the back there was a little hut and a tap for water. We thought we could survive there. One day we went to have a wash and who were there but British soldiers having a wash as well, so . . . 'Right you, with us!' So we finished up in the barracks. We were issued rations of five biscuits a day, corned beef between so many men, one third of a white loaf per man. And then lorries arrived and we were taken to a place called Belaria and tents were issued.

One day we were told that the Russian Repatriation Commission would be talking to us. There were 14,000 of us in this camp, and after two days of their visit, only eight men – silly – volunteered to go home. The following day they arrived in these beautiful clean uniforms, shoes and everything. But hardly anybody wanted to go back to the Soviet Union because we knew our fate. We would be traitors because we were fighting against them. And during Stalin's regime, there weren't trials, people were just shot. We knew well what they were like. In Ukraine it had been terror, fear all the time, the secret police listening, spying. On the slightest suspicion you were arrested. Some Cossack units were handed over to Russians without being asked if they wanted to be or not. And I read that they were sent by train to Odessa and machine-gunned.

Before the winter came we were transferred to an ex-airfield near Rimini. This was a purely Ukrainian camp and we'd all been on the Eastern Front at the time the Russians pushed to Hungary, to Austria and Yugoslavia. There, life changed completely. We had a theatre – built by ourselves actually – with corrugated iron, concrete, and seats made out of barrels and canvas fittings. We had film shows, educational visits from abroad: from Canada, from Rome. In the camp they provided facilities for learning a trade. We were getting better rations once we settled there and each unit had its own field kitchen. The British treated us very well. We made a lot of friends among the guards and one of them, his name was Nicholas, actually started to talk Ukrainian. There was a very high fence and watch-towers. I think one man was shot dead trying to crawl under the fence because on the other side the Italians were growing tobacco and he was going to get some.

And then the future – 'What's going to happen?'

During those two years we still didn't know where we were going to go, what they were going to do with us. Eventually, at the beginning of 1947, we were told that we were going to Great Britain and teach-yourself books were distributed to the men to learn English. From Rimini, we went by train to Venice and from there were sailed over the Adriatic, round the bottom of Italy, and turned towards Algiers where we took fresh water. When we arrived at Algiers the ship was anchored a mile away from the shore and soon we had native boats trying to sell us fruit and so on. The men had been busy dismantling some armaments, brass fittings and so on, and they were converting them to rings – 'golden' rings – and on that occasion they became quite useful. I remember sending them on a string to the boats and there were melons and grapefruits coming on to the ship in return. We called that ship a hunger ship because the rations changed entirely from what we were getting in camp. The men were really starving. Everybody wanted to go to the galleys where the food was cooked, because they were able to get some extra rations there. One night there was a commotion on the ship. A group of our boys broke into the bread store and stole some loaves of bread, and from that day there were guards with bayonets and rifles standing there all the time.

Overall it took us twelve days to reach Port Glasgow. New uniforms had been issued which were the same as British uniforms, except that on the back of your jacket and your trousers there was a patch like a brown diamond sewn on. When we arrived, quite a number of people congregated on the quay there and they were waving to us. Because of our khaki uniforms they thought that British soldiers were returning home – which was still happening, of course, two years after the war.

We disembarked and our group of 300 men went by train to Thankerton, near Lanark. This was a transit camp. It was May, and I remember the wooden nissen huts and the British soldiers on guard. A search took place of our belongings and I lost a razor given to me by my father when I left home, which I was sorry to part with. I suppose it could have been treated as a weapon. Then we were directed to different huts. By then it was quite late in the evening but the night wasn't coming! This was something unusual for us to see, daylight up to eleven o'clock. I think we were there for less than a week and then our group was divided into two parties. One of them went to Lockerbie and the other went to Annan. Both camps were used prior to our arrival by German prisoners of war, and there were still some Germans staffing labour offices in the camps.

Our men were engaged by neighbouring farmers to help them on the farms. We had to get up at six o'clock in the morning; within an hour you had to wash, have breakfast, and the labour officer's job was to get the order from the farmers. Things weren't so bad in the camps. I was in both of them actually: first in Lockerbie, and maybe three months afterwards I was transferred to Annan. I was working in Lockerbie, in the office, allocating men for the work and then when I was transferred to Annan, I became storeman and a kitchen clerk. Things were rationed and it was up to me to order meat, eggs, butter and to see that they were properly used. At that time I also had to prepare the pieces for the men going to work. Most of the time it was jam; there wasn't anything better. In Annan I also ran a canteen where the men could buy cigarettes, fruits, soft drinks and once a week, beer. After a while we actually got passes to go out to the towns, to the cinema. Still dressed in POW uniforms, we went to dances, and fairs when they were on in town. Every second week we used to get token money and the following week real British money – less than a pound. Token money you could use only in the canteen. Most of the things we required, like soap, razor-blades and so on were available there. We had a show once a week. The camps were run by the Department of Agriculture and we were paid by them and the YMCA took care of the food and the entertainment. Our camps were always kept nice and clean and flowerbeds appeared in front of huts. A miniature castle was made with a moat and drawbridge. The whole thing is overgrown now and amongst the trees that castle is still there – cement, a little hill and the winding road on to the castle. I always promise my daughter to take her there and show her my 'roots' [laughs].

Our men soon proved themselves to be good workers. Some of the farmers asked if they could have certain men only, they got used to them. Eventually people from the camp were billeted with the farmers so they didn't have to travel back and forth every day.

In 1949 we became civilians. Each of us was given £20 to have a new civilian suit bought and when we were working a certain amount of money was saved for us and when we became civilians that was paid. This was in Annan, and the tailors in Glasgow got to hear about it. There was a terrific rush of tailors to the camps. They called themselves fifty-shilling tailors. They were not fifty shillings, they were dearer! We bought suits and we were paid a bigger wage – something like £3 a week. On the day we were released, we had to celebrate and, of course, we went further away. We knew Annan as the town was only a couple of miles away, so we went over the border to Carlisle and celebrated in pubs there.

In Annan our warden was a Pole. He was later appointed a warden in Mauchline, Ayrshire, and shortly afterwards he made arrangements for me to be transferred to his camp as assistant warden. This was a mixed camp with Poles, Ukrainians, Yugoslavians, Latvians and Lithuanians. The life there was similar to the other two camps. The people were still going to work, and by then quite a number worked in potteries. At that time there were quite a few of them in Ayrshire. We were civilians and some did manage to leave the camp providing they had a job. Quite a number emigrated to the United States or Australia, where they had relatives. In 1952 I remember a moment that moved us deeply was when King George died. We all felt a loss.

It was not until 1954 that the camps closed completely. I was very loth to leave Mauchline and I got a caretaker's job there. I had a dog called Maxie with me, left by German prisoners. He was my only companion and we used to go fishing and for walks. But the job was very boring and eventually the word came that the camp was to be demolished. My services wouldn't be required any longer. Actually, I think there's still one of our chaps at the old camp at Lockerbie. I think he still lives in a hut there and works with the Forestry Commission.

I had made friends with a man from Prestwick and after I left Mauchline I moved to his place. I applied for jobs but the weeks were passing and my money was draining away. I wrote to the Ministry of Agriculture and Fisheries and got another job as caretaker in a camp which was kept open for potato harvesting. After a short spell working in a pub I managed to get lodgings in Edinburgh, in the same house as some Ukrainian friends. The next day I went to the Labour Exchange and I got a note to go to the Caledonian Hotel. I was quite excited: I didn't think I would get anything so soon. There was a night-porter's job available, which I took. And for fifteen years I worked as a night-porter at the Caledonian Hotel. I met some worldwide known personalities, served them, sang Russian songs with Dana Andrews.

At first, our Ukrainian Club was in Windsor Street and then we got the bigger place in Royal Terrace. We hold commemorative concerts on the anniversaries of our poets, writers and national leaders. On festive occasions like Easter and Christmas, we have a communal dinner. On Saturdays we have Ukrainian national dances. We organise schools for the children to learn Ukrainian; my daughter went there for a while. We also have our church in Dalmeny Street – the top was converted to a slightly Ukrainian style.

Going back is simply impossible because each of us is aware of what will happen to us, even after forty years. We haven't been forgiven. Sons of some parents, of the same age as me, went to the Ukraine to see their fathers' roots. They walked through the village and verbal abuse was thrown at them – 'Son of a traitor' and so on.

I think among our people there is more warmth. The Slavonic people are the most hospitable in the world. They will deprive themselves of the best to give it to the guest. People here are probably more selfish. I think they try to be independent. It is difficult to say what I miss most now, but I remember my youth, the things we used to do, and I always say that if it wasn't for the last war, if it wasn't for Hitler and Stalin, things could have been different.

I obviously miss the place where I was born, but there wouldn't be any point going there because I wouldn't meet anybody that I knew before. My brother is now in Poland. At the end of the war he was working as a railwayman travelling over the existing border between Poland and the Soviet Union. My father kept a souvenir from the army, a revolver, and someone reported this to the Soviet police and there was a search. They found the revolver, and my sister and father both spent some time in prison. After they came out, they were told to go to another town. My sister had a problem getting any employment and my father was retired. He applied for a pension, but the Soviet government refused him, pointing out that he was a retired non-commissioned officer in the bourgeois Polish army and he'd got two sons – one in Great Britain and one in Poland – who could help him, which we did. But father was just looking for his rights. He never got them.

When I was in Italy, I received a letter from a Polish solicitor, a friend of our family. I learnt from that letter that my wife died in March 1945, two weeks after my son was born, due to lack of medicine and hospital facilities, and my son was left in the care of my wife's mother. Eventually, my parents got my son to their house and they looked after him. In the end my sister adopted him. He used to write letters to me. He sent me a photograph and told me when he got married – I have a granddaughter by him. Unfortunately, it wasn't possible for us to meet. They have no understanding of our situation.

NOTES

1. After the First World War, Eastern Galacia was absorbed by Poland while the rest of Ukraine enjoyed brief independence in 1918–1920 before falling under both Russian and Polish control.

2. Russian intervention occurred as a result of the Molotov–Ribbentrop agreement between Hitler and Stalin on 28 September 1939. Poland was divided between the two powers along the Narew, Bug and San rivers.

3. This was a pro-Ukrainian educational society. *Prosvita* means 'enlightenment'.

4. 22 June 1941.

5. At the battle of Brody-Lvov (13 July 1944) 40,000 Axis troops were trapped in a two-pronged attack and had to be evacuated.

6. The German Army invaded Yugoslavia after its pro-Axis government was overthrown. Resistance was led by the Communist Tito and the opposing royalist, General Mihajlovic. Tito gained the upper hand and in 1944 the Germans were driven from Yugoslavia.

LAI

'Oh Gosh, This is Another World!'

At 16 years old, Lai Mau was the youngest person to be interviewed for this book. She was born the second of five children in North Vietnam in 1970. Her family fled to Hong Kong in 1980 and a year later they came to Britain.

My ancestors were from China. They came to live in Vietnam two generations ago. I can't even speak Vietnamese now because I was staying in this small village and it was mainly Cantonese people. My parents speak both languages because they needed to make friends with the Vietnamese. At the Chinese school I went to in the village I wrote only Chinese, but I sometimes spoke Vietnamese with other folk there. Some of the Chinese were richer than the Vietnamese. The Vietnamese didn't like the Cantonese – sometimes the Vietnamese kids made faces at us, we'd slap each other, you know, just a wee war. My parents used to tell us not to go near them.

But I liked living there because it was very peaceful. The war didn't affect us because we were near China. They wouldn't touch us because we were so near the border. So they wouldn't dare go near us. There's just a bridge; if you crossed the bridge, there was China. That near. It was just about three miles to the bridge. We were very safe.

It was mainly agricultural. You had to go by boat or by road to reach the cities. It took ages because they were bumpy roads – and you wouldn't even have a bicycle there because you'd be too poor, you know, so you usually went by foot. Some people, if they were farmers, had mules. My family was quite well off but even we didn't have bicycles until just before we left.

In my street there were mainly buildings of brick and concrete. My home was quite big compared to the others because, I remember, we had an upstairs. That's where we dried things: rice and other stuff that my mum sold. She worked in the market and at about five in

143

the morning she used to take food up to sell, and come back about six. My father did a lot of different jobs like Chinese doctor, dancing teacher, basketball player. He was quite famous in the wee village. He treated some of the Cantonese free, but he usually charged Vietnamese. There was a big hospital near us mostly for the Vietnamese working people, but if it was really serious we had to go there. If it was a wee cut or something like that my father could help, but if not he'd send them to the big hospital. We Cantonese were very close to each other. We helped each other a lot.

We had lots of fish. Every two or three weeks my father went with some friends to the harbour, where he bought fresh fish and shrimps. He was a friend of the fisherman – because he was a doctor everyone knew him! And I had this big tank for the fish; they were enormous, the fish, alive: really fresh. I remember my father went and got some fresh fish and crabs – big, red crabs with big pincers – and I was playing with them. My father told me not to play, but I ignored him and got my thumb caught by one! I've still got the scar. It wouldn't let go, you know, and my father was saying he wished it was raining 'cause the crab's most scared of thunder. It hung on for about three minutes and then it started to rain and there was thunder. Luckily, it stopped, otherwise I wouldn't have a thumb left!

Well, my granny's a very nice woman. Sometimes she went to the city and bought lots of tobacco and cigarettes. We used to trade with another community, a tribe. We called them *Banye*. They put vegetable oil on their hair to make it real shiny, and they dressed very different; they had beads and they had big earrings and they pinned their noses and they had thousands of bangles up their arms. They lived away up in the mountains and we called them 'wild people' – they were quite wild anyway. But every week they used to come to get oil and peanuts, and sometimes they needed meat and stuff like that. They were Vietnamese and didn't speak Cantonese. I don't quite understand about their culture – at that time I just thought of playing. In Vietnam there was more room to play and more things to play with. There was land and flowers and trees and fruits that you don't have here: starfruit, lychee. . . . And there's other fruits as well but I can't say them in English. And they're free. You know, at school we'd just pick them and off we'd go. It was so much fun, we'd go picking these small, wild fruits and vegetables in the mountains and I loved eating them. But now we have to run to the shop. We didn't have crisps and things like that in Vietnam, unless you went to the cities.

One of the grannies in my village didn't like my family. And I used to go there and take all her sugar cane. In Vietnam we have a lot of sugar cane. I used to go there and steal it and I usually got caught! [laughs]. I was quite greedy, you know. I used to go up to where my Mum worked and steal with my friend! [laughs]

I wasn't very good at school. I was in nursery for two years because in Chinese school, right, you have to be good at Chinese as we have exams every half year. And if you pass you're allowed to go up to another class, like first year, Primary 1. But if you don't, you stay in the nursery. And I was in the nursery a long time! 'Cause I have quite a lot of sisters, I helped in the house. Everywhere I went I had to put them on my back and hold their hands. I did some washing – nappies and all that. I went to the mountains with my brother and neighbours to get wood, because we didn't have gas or electricity. So when I was six years old I had to fetch wood from the mountains. I fell; I wasn't good at it.

Our back street was quite dirty. The front was all right but at the back we had this big ditch. It was quite a wide ditch and that's where we dumped all the rubbish, like from the toilet. And once when I was five years old, I'd seen my friends jumping across and I though, 'Wow! How can they do that? I want to try it!' I ran across and I slipped and fell into the ditch where all the waste was. I was crying and my father grabbed me up – oh, so smelly! My mother took about ten buckets of water to wash me off. Quite crazy!

We didn't need to wear anything, it was that hot, you know. It's only summer and spring, summer and spring, nowhere near winter. God, the ground was hot: when you touched it, it burned you! 'Cause I was so young, I didn't know anything about wearing clothes until I came over here. I thought, 'Oh God! It must be horrible for kids, babies, to wear clothes'. I didn't wear anything but knickers. We swam all the time because it was so hot. The sea was warm – that's where the bridge was.

Every year someone from the village always died, because we were quite near the sea and there was this bridge across the river there. It's quite a modern bridge, and I don't know why, but our village believed that every year somebody would die on the bridge. Horrible. Every year, sometimes twice in a year, the waters would flood; I thought it was beautiful. But, you see, a lot of people died because sometimes they didn't know, and they walked across. And they'd be in the middle, right, and the waters would be coming. We believed there was some kind of evil spirit: every year somebody's got to die. We believed that the water spirits had to take somebody. It's horrible.

My granny is Buddhist, and so I must have been Buddhist, I suppose but I don't really believe in any gods of any kind. At school we were taught about Buddhism as part of history. But mostly we were told by the older generation, grannies and neighbours, adults. In a year I think we celebrated about four times. We had Chinese New Year, the Moon festival, and another one was the dragon boat race, where we celebrated Our Father of the Land who saved the Chinese. We had boat races: big dragon boats and people rowing. It was very crowded and exciting. And we made little things like boats and sent them away, like sailing debt away. We celebrated by having lots of vegetables, fruits and chicken, duck, pork and incense. We prayed; we prayed for good luck. Buddhism has a lot of forms and it depends which one you believe. There's one, where if you're good you're allowed to go up to heaven when you die, but if you're bad in this world, then – it depends how bad you are – if you're really, really bad you'll be in the eighteenth or nineteenth underground world. That's where evil is. And Buddha is somewhere up there. He blesses you and all that if you do good in this world.

I think people work harder in Vietnam than here. My mother was really skinny with it all. She's getting fat now here, maybe with the butter and cheese. In Vietnam, because it's a communist country, you had to have tickets for food. And sometimes if there was not enough you got less: you felt starved. In each household in a week you got just a few things. Even if you had money, you couldn't buy, you see. You could buy some things from other villages but not much because of rules. You could buy the essentials, but sometimes you couldn't buy more than that. They checked on you. We used to put things away when they came to check. A lot of people did that.

Leaving Vietnam is all mixed up and I can't remember much because I was very young. I don't think about it. It was my father's decision and I had to follow. We went to Hong Kong and stayed there for nearly a year. That's where the refugee camp was. That was when I was ten.

The camp used to be a prison camp – Victoria Prison Camp – and it was built on an island. You couldn't actually go out without going through this gate and you needed to have ID cards. There was this wire, and on the other side were other people from Vietnam but we were not allowed to go over there because on that side you didn't have to go out past the police.

It was very crowded 'cause in a room about this size (10′ × 12′) there were usually about 16 to 20 people. And you had to share the toilet of course. There were about five toilets per block and about three families in one room. They hadn't anything as soft as this bed, just a flat thing, just wood planks, and you didn't get a mattress. It hurt your back a lot.

There were about three different levels and every time you cooked you had to go downstairs. That's where all the sockets were. Lunchtime was very busy, and in the evening people went up and down with their cooking pots. Because we lived on the first floor we were quite lucky 'cause we didn't have to go that far.

My parents worked, and I worked for pocket money. I went out to work in a factory with my auntie. And sometimes people sent work into the camp, so we didn't have to go out: things like flowers, fake flowers. And I used to help my gran make beads and earrings and all that.

In each room we had a telly. But if you didn't pay for the telly you didn't get to watch it. We used to put it on one of the beds, right, and we had blankets around it. The people who paid went inside. This is how it was. But then we got it taken away because someone died of an electric shock and they wouldn't let us watch it. It was silly, they just blamed it on all of us.

I don't know how others there felt, because we were all different and I didn't speak to them, you see, but I think they were quite glad that they'd made it through to the free world. I was there nearly a year, then we came over to Britain. First we went to another camp, in Colinton Road, Edinburgh. It's all away now, finished. It was a big building, a church. When I first came in it wasn't crowded and I thought, 'Wow!' this is fairy-tale like. 'Gosh there's a big castle here!' It was a really big place. And the room was nice. There were lots of beds there and cupboards for things, not as in Hong Kong where you just shoved everything under the bed. And I hadn't had anything soft for sleeping on before, and I would jump on the mattress and play on it. And these pillows – Oh God, these pillows! I'd never seen anything like that. Oh God, your own cupboard – and there were lights to switch on and off and doors – wow! We didn't have doors in Hong Kong, we had these sheets or blankets. And there was a big playground with swings there, and a huge park. If you walked for five minutes there were Scottish kids around and we used to play, muck about with them. Later, before we all moved out to different areas of Edinburgh, it got crowded. Then I thought it was very small. I didn't like it at that time. We lived there for one and a half years.

At first I didn't like Britain very much because I felt I was odd, and everybody was funny here. I thought, 'Oh gosh, this is another world!' In the Hong Kong camp these Americans had taught us the alphabet, 'cat' and 'dog' and the very easy words, but I hardly spoke any English and I felt I was the odd one out in the class. I was quite shy at the time, because I thought if I spoke English: 'Oh no, my pronunciation, they won't understand what I'm saying.' My sisters and friends who stayed in the camp with us were in the school as well. It was OK and my teacher was nice. She treated me the same as the Scottish kids. But more than that, she taught me pronunciation and the easy things. When I first came into the school I'm at now, and at primary school as well, I had fights and all that, because of race. But now I know more English I usually get them back because I can, you know, if my English is good. But then I couldn't say anything.

We have two Pakistanis and there's about twelve Chinese in the whole school. It's quite a big school. We usually play with friends, Scottish friends. I think they know more about the Chinese community now. A few years ago they really didn't know anything about the Chinese here. But I think now they realise there are quite a lot of Chinese around and they see more of us, so they get used to us. Now they usually make friends with us which is good: 'Oh well, I've seen you around lots, what's the point of being prejudiced?' They're nice now, kids that used to fight with me. I think they're making friends.

About three years ago there were a lot of Vietnamese living in this area, and in Wester Hailes and Oxgangs, Sighthill, Burdiehouse and all over, but now they're all going down to London because they couldn't find work here. Although you have social security and unemployment benefit here, when you don't know English it's hard for you to learn if you're old and you find it difficult. And in London there's a Chinatown, a community where Chinese people gather together and help each other.

When I first came out here from the Colinton Road camp, I thought, 'Oh no, I don't like it here. It's not fair, there's no Chinese people around, no Chinese kids. Oh, the Scots – I hate them!' I thought 'Oh no, my English is bad'. But now I like it, because I like Scottish kids. Now I consider myself as part British. I've got Chinese school every Saturday at Morningside and it's OK mucking around with the older kids but I think I can learn more from Scottish kids. If I'm with Chinese, I think, 'Oh, I know that! Oh no, don't tell me that. I've seen that! I know all that'. But with Scottish kids, they say to you, 'Do you know about the Highland Show?' And no, I don't.

I think my father likes it here, and so does my mother, better than Vietnam: because in Vietnam we didn't have television or radio. We didn't have that kind of stuff and we didn't know anything about the world. Now we usually watch the telly and so we know more. And my father didn't have a car – and all that he couldn't have in Vietnam he has now. And he doesn't have to work as hard here. He used to work in a hotel, but he doesn't work now because his English is not very good so he couldn't find a good job.

Vietnam is not a modern country, you know. If I was still in Vietnam now I wouldn't have a radio, I would never see a car, I would never even have seen an aeroplane before. But I think if Vietnam was not a communist country, but a free country, an industrial country, I think I would like it. I would go back. But nothing can change it now.

My brother and I have to help our parents with all sorts of forms – school forms, dinner forms, council forms, insurance forms, dentist forms. (Now my father has learnt English as well, from television, so he speaks a lot.) And when I watch television, films like Frankenstein or something like that, I have to explain them to my granny. She's the most troublesome thing in this house. She doesn't understand English, so I have to tell her what they're saying on the television and explain the story. Sometimes she guesses things and it's all wrong, you know! You have to argue with her! It's terrible!

My granny feels shocked by the waste here. Even the old clothes, like if they're torn, she picks them up and she says, 'Look at this! If you were in Vietnam you wouldn't get stuff like this'. When I first came here I thought, 'Wow, what a big waste!' We didn't pour anything away; we used to keep all the leftovers, right. We thought, 'God, we can't throw that away. We don't have that in Vietnam'. That was about five years ago. But now, the more we watch television and realise the British way of life, we think, 'Yeah, it's OK, there's plenty. We don't need to keep all this rubbish around the house'. But granny still does that. She thinks we're still wasting. She can't get used to it.

'My Goodness, it's Supposed to be a Heavenly Place!'

Sunil Chatterjee was born in Jamshedpur, Bihar, in 1937. He came to Britain in 1962. Now a Scottish distributor for a worldwide company, he lives in the West End of Edinburgh.

I remember it was the war time. We used to go to school and see all the trains full of military people and soldiers – all the British and Americans. They used to come and get ice from the ice factory. I was six or seven years old, and when it was playtime, tiffin, we used to run to the railway station and see the trains passing full of soldiers and they'd give us American and British chocolate and biscuits.

My father used to work for a British company called the Indian Cable Company as an engineer. His general managers were British, one was Scottish and the other was English. My father was a body-builder and a keen sportsman. The British like people who take up physical culture and all that, they appreciated my father's game and they were good friends. At your Christmas time, we used to go to the company and get all the toys. We met a lot of British people there and at that time the impression we got from them, the opinion we had, was that Britain was like a heavenly place, like a dreamworld. There was no stealing, no vandalism, no corruption. All the British we met were highly qualified people and they hid all the weaknesses and showed all the greatness – that's why they called it Great Britain. So that's the influence we had. It was always my dream to come here. When I grew older I used to do body-building, and at that time I used to wish that I could come to this country and become Mr Universe.

When I was ten, my father got a better job in Delhi with a private company, so he transferred there and suddenly India got Independence. The country was divided and we went through all these rough times. I saw people killing each other. My father used to work in the

Moslem quarter, that's where the factory was. When it got pretty bad with all the rioting and killing then he couldn't go. The factory was closed. You could see Moslems going through the bazaar and the street, getting killed. I could see all these bodies lying there, the smell of blood, and I could hear the bullets and the guns. There was a doctor below our house and from time to time we would see Hindus bringing their badly wounded people. I saw him taking the bullets out, I saw this with my own eyes. At that time there was no value for life. I saw a huge, big Moslem, an innocent man, he thought everything was all right, but suddenly these Hindus came and attacked him. While he was running, one man came out of the mill with a tin of wheat flour and he saw this man running – he was a huge, big Pathan, a very healthy man and nobody could stop him. This man threw the tin of flour onto him, it hit his face, and he fell down and then everybody came and stabbed him.

It lasted quite a few months, this violence and killing, and after it stopped all the refugees started coming from Pakistan, all the Hindus coming to Delhi. They put up stalls on the roadside to make their living – little, little stalls with vegetables and groceries. They didn't like to beg for money and they worked hard to make a living. It showed me the positive side of life. I saw that life had no value, with people killing people, and then I also saw, through this process, how the people survived. You know, that's what I learned. They had nothing when they came as refugees and they fought for their survival. The same thing happened to me when I arrived in this country with £5.10/– in my pocket – that's all the Indian government would allow me to take out.

As I said, I had a dream about this country. And as I said, the British people gave this impression; I wanted to see how true it was. My friend came here first to London in 1959 and then he invited me in 1962. When I came, my dream shattered the moment I got off the plane, you know. I saw the buildings – black, everywhere. I came in March and it was still wintry and it was so dark. You could see the pigeon droppings everywhere. I said, 'My goodness, it's supposed to be a heavenly place!' And when I came I found out that everything was just the same as you find in India – mugging, cheating, telling lies. I thought that people here would be very honest, nobody would touch anything, there would be no beggars. I was very depressed. I thought I'd see wonderful things. Even the Christmas cards we used to get from Britain were so beautiful. Of course, now I know that the natural beauty of Scotland is fantastic, but at that time I was very disappointed.

First I came to London to my friend there. It stated on my passport that I was in business, (I had done a course in architecture and we had our own architects business in India; I used to do all the drawing). So I registered my name in London as a draughtsman. I got nothing there. My other friend was in Glasgow so I went there. And still my name is registered there as a draughtsman, but they never offered me any sort of job, never mind one as a draughtsman. So after that my friend said, 'Look, forget it. The best thing is to save a little money, buy property, and let rooms'. I was in Glasgow for three months and helped my friend in business. I saved some money and came to Edinburgh. I bought a house in Union Street with seven rooms. Doctors and their families from India and Pakistan stayed there. I gave them cheaper shelter with a lot of facilities – and they used to cook my meal for me when I came home and we had a lot of fun together. I made money from that and I bought land in India and two more houses here. Through business I raised myself up.

In 1962 Edinburgh was neater and cleaner. At that time, especially in the winter time, after 6 o'clock you couldn't find anybody on Princes Street. But now twelve months in the year you find congestion everywhere. We were about 30 or 40 Asians in Edinburgh, and there weren't many Pakistani shops. There was Khushi's Indian restaurant, and that's still here, and maybe one other. Now you see how many Indian, Pakistani, Bengali restaurants there are.

I believe that there are good and bad in every country. If you meet the right person your life becomes heavenly and if you meet the wrong person, it doesn't matter if they're from your own community or not, it makes life hell. Actually, I never had any plan to get married, but I saw all my friends going back to India, getting married, and coming here again. Every other year they were going home because their wives were homesick of her mother or father was ill. Then I thought that if I married some Indian and brought her here, most probably I'd ruin her life. I knew I was going to stay here for a long time and eventually I decided to marry a Scottish girl. There's no problem if she needs to go home.

Indian culture is not the same as here; the combined family – they like to live together, they like to see each other. Here, an Indian wife will have feelings for her relations and if she doesn't see them, and hears that one by one they are dying, it breaks her heart because she is not there. Now I travel a lot, I meet three or four families every day in different parts of Scotland. I've found that especially the elderly people, the majority of them are very lonely, because their sons and daughters are away from home. They are very busy and they don't have time to see their old parents. That's where I find the difference. In India, they don't leave their old parents living alone. You can't blame anybody because in India it's different. There, unless you are a government employee you don't get any pension. When I was brought up as a child, I saw how my father worked hard and now we are grown up, father doesn't get any pension. He is 86. First it is their duty to give us a proper education, food, clothes. Now it is our duty to look after them. We never forget that. We are close and we cannot imagine our parents living somewhere else and not living properly.

Today I saw a programme about mixed marriages. When there is a child, some families say they have problems: if they have grand-children, which religion are they going to follow? But, see, we're all human beings. If we believe in the human race then nothing can be better than mixed marriages. Because that gives a different outlook on life. When I go to India and take my wife, they all respect her because she is respectable through her deeds. There is no problem about language because all my family speak English and there is no problem about eating because you get all the food here that you get over there nowadays.

However, my wife's side were not very happy. Most probably if I had got married to a Christian girl in India my parents would have been the same, so I understand the difficulties. After our marriage there was a choice for my wife; if she married me that meant that there would be no contact with her parents. That's what her father said. For five years we didn't have any contact with her father. They didn't come to our wedding, nothing. Then I went to India and when I came back I got an invitation to go to their house. We went out for a meal, came back and had a few drinks, right up to 2 o'clock, you know. We were talking about different things. This was the first time I had met them! My father-in-law said, 'I'm not colour-prejudiced or anything like that'. I said, 'Hold on. How long have we been married?' He said, 'Er . . . five years'. I said, 'Did you enjoy my company?' He said, 'Yes, of course'. I said, 'Well why, for five years, have we missed having all this fun? What was the reason?' I said, 'I understand because my father would probably do the same'. But we lost a lot of fun. And now I am the best son-in-law. I had a convention in Monte Carlo and it was their Golden Wedding Anniversary. I worked hard and I qualified to take an extra two people. It was the first time they'd gone abroad, they'd been so busy working. They enjoyed it. At one time, most probably, he thought I was just a pedlar, selling door-to-door, but he never tried to meet me, talk to me, and find out what kind of person I was.

First time I came to Glasgow, I was staying in Renfrew Street. The first weekend I was there my friend was working so I thought, 'Well I'll go and have a little drink'. I went to a bar. There were a lot of sailors coming in and I had a few drinks with them, and then I came out. As I was walking, three boys came in front of me on the footpath. One of them said, 'You black bastard. Get out of the way!' I never said anything, I just kept quiet and walked on but they were in front of me and they stood there. So I stopped and they swore at me. The only answer to this situation was to become more violent, act violent, not necessarily do any bodily harm, but make a posture, 'Arghhhh!' like this, then they'd get scared. Attack is the best form of defence. And I not only did that, I held the boy who swore by the hair, and another boy came behind and I kicked him – I think in the wrong place. They ran away, most probably to get some more people. I put this boy down on the road and in the meantime the sailors came up and said, 'Come on, forget it. Let's go!' A man walked with me towards my home. He said, 'You don't know, but these are Teddy boys and you should avoid them'. But what could I do? They came in front of me in an attacking move so the only thing I could do was to show them that I was more violent than they were, so that they'd get scared. And they got scared all right.

But don't get me wrong. I found out when I came, especially in Glasgow, that people are very friendly. And there wasn't much difference in Edinburgh. I've never really found any problem because my nature is, if somebody is good to me about this much, I will be good to them about that much. If someone is bad to me about this much, I'll be worse to them about that much – both extremes. But here the people are so nice.

I think as you grow older your ideas change. Your attitude to life changes. When I was young I used to do body-building and I never had any lack of strength. I replied to violence with violence. But now I feel different. I try to assess the situation because you don't involve yourself in a situation like that. But what do you want to know from us? Do you want to hear the negative side of life or the positive side? You'll find both, but I think that it depends on the person. In our company I'm the only Indian, but when we call people to try our product there's no 'I don't want the black man, I want the white one . . .'

For the last 15 years I have visited four or five homes every day. Some maybe give a rough welcome when they open the door but the majority treat you like a human being. I've never had any negative thoughts in my mind that I'm inferior. So if I'm not inferior why should I worry if somebody says something? It makes no difference to me. People know what I am; I know what I am, so why should I worry if somebody is a bit rude and swears? So what? That's the way I feel now, but 20 years ago it could be different. I'd have broken his neck maybe. As I said, your thoughts change. We are learning all the time. Now I'm in the selling business and in selling you need to be positive. So by practising that, the positiveness in selling, it becomes a habit in life. Any decision I make, I try to make it in a positive way. Sometimes my bank manager wonders because I always talk big, I think big. But he saw me acting big too, so he has confidence now and lends me money, no problem.

I went all over the country, England, Scotland, Ireland. I was six months in Ireland working in Belfast and Londonderry and across the border. At that time they were all scared of the bombing and killing but I never had any problem. You know the barriers across the road where they check before they let you go through in your car? They never checked me – whenever they saw me they thought I was a doctor so they let me go first! I had the advantage over there! I had a wonderful time.

We are used to luxury and comfort in this country. As far as facilities are concerned, to have a comfortable life, Britain is a lot better than India. For example, if you have a car there, you can't drive on the road because nobody follows the rules. They do have rules and regulations about traffic but nobody follows them. I'd be scared to death to drive in Delhi. If anything goes wrong it's difficult to get parts for repairs. Now if you have a phone, half of the time it doesn't work. If you need calor gas for cooking and phone the people, they say, 'Yes, we're coming'. They promise you the earth. They never come. If you want to pay the electric bill there's always some mistake. And anything you'd like to solve, you've got to go there and stand and wait and wait and wait. If you are lucky, you will get a chance that day or you'll have to come back some other time. And here, if we want to get any information, we pick up the phone, speak to the people and sort it out; that's it, finished in a few seconds. In India, the majority of people don't know what organised business is. Put it this way: when I arrived in this country, my friend couldn't come to meet me, so a girl from a travel agency came with a message from my friend. I signed a form and got £10, a train ticket and directions. It made me realise how organised this country is.

The thing is, in India they don't have any system. There is no discipline, no rules and regulations. Business-wise there is no fixed price, you have to bargain all the time and they always put on a high price if they see you are a foreigner. It is a different price for different people. But I'm a Hindu and religion-wise, only our country can satisfy that side of life. It's very difficult to do that here. Like, people go to the River Ganges and they take a bath and worship and it is not possible to do that here. My father, grandfather and all the generations, they lived there, our blood is from there so we can't forget that.

I'll tell you something, as far as violence is concerned, this country is nothing compared to America. It is the safest country for us. I always feel this is my home. I mean, India is my home, that's where I was born, that's where I'll go back, but this is my home too. I gave this country the most important part of my life from 24 to 50 – 25 years I have given to this country, I've served this country. The job I do, it's selling equipment for people who are suffering with arthritis and backache. That's what I've been doing for the past 15 years. There must be some feeling I have for the people and the country otherwise I wouldn't have done that.

When we first came here our main aim was to do some kind of business, make quick money and then go back home. But for some reason or other it's not always possible. We involve ourselves with having children and getting them educated. You can't just jump and go back. In a way, I was lucky. My wife is Scottish, we have been married for 19 years, we don't have any children and we are free that way. Now I've taken my wife four times to India. She liked India. I've built a house in Delhi. Now, what I plan is that in four years' time she'll retire from her job and then we'll stay six months in India and six months here. And when we get older we'll decide where we're going to stay permanently.

When I used to go into pubs here, people would come up to me quite often and say, 'Why don't you go home?' I'd say, 'No I'm not going home. You sucked us dry for 300 years, now I'm going to stay here and suck you dry!' [mimics vampire].

Now I work with a worldwide company. You know, I've been to five continents and I've seen many countries through my business. I've attended many conventions in Europe and America. People come from all over the world to participate twice a year and we greet each other like brother and sister. We may or may not understand each others' language but we have the family feeling because we belong to the same company. That's what I think, that if people from all over the world had the same feeling, it doesn't matter what colour or creed we are, that will create peace and harmony and make a better world.

PARVIN

'There was no Time to be Emotional'

Parvin was born in Mashad in the north-east of Iran in 1958. She and her British husband were evacuated by the British Embassy at the height of the Iranian revolution. She now has two children.

The first house we lived in was my grandparents'. Everything then seemed to be so big; the streets looked wider and now they just look like narrow footpaths! It seemed to be a very large house with plum trees and cherry trees growing in the middle of what I thought at that time was a huge garden. We had a servant who lived in her own quarters and the family used to share the main building. And I remember in Iran the basements are used quite a lot in the hot season because they remain cooler (there was no air-conditioning or any-thing like that). And there was a little pool there. It's quite common to have ponds and fountains in the basement. That's the first thing I can remember out of my childhood. That house and my uncle. He used to come and visit when he had work in Mashad.

My father at that time was a merchant, selling goods like saffron and spices, and he was also in charge of the accounts of a big store. My grandfather was in the army but he retired very, very early when he was quite young. Most of all I remember my grandfather because he was a prominent figure in the family with his long sheepskin coat, which Afghan and Pakistani men wear too – while the women run around and serve them!

Women's work consisted mainly of domestic jobs – cooking, cleaning – and since we had no electrical goods then it was a matter of sweeping with brooms. My grandmother used to get up at sunrise and by the time we'd all got up, almost all the work would be done! She used to sweep the yard, sprinkle water because it was so hot most of the year, and spread the kelims, as we called them. Then my grandfather used to wake up and she would bring the breakfast. The servant used to do heavy jobs like washing.

We had very simple lives. We had electricity but no electrical goods – hoovers, washing machines, televisions – anything like that. There were hardly any activities at all really, except in the home. No recreation whatsoever – no parks, no swimming pools. The main occupation was visiting relatives. Your relatives would just come and land on you; they don't warn you they are coming. Because of this Middle-Eastern hospitality, when they came, huge meals had to be cooked. It just seemed to be a feast throughout. And when we didn't have visitors, I remember my grandmother was mainly serving my grandfather. Every time you'd look round, my grandmother was serving him a basket of fruit – or, in Iran, we just eat lettuce leaves, dipped in a syrup made with rhubarb, and that she made quite often for him. We didn't have a very good diet mainly because of shortages of food. Like any other Middle-Eastern country, the quality of meat is awful and the main diet was just rice and some Iranian casseroles.

Our houses don't have a gable roof because we don't have a problem with rain so they're flat roofs, and we sleep on them at night in summer – just marvellous! Every house has its own garden (the idea of flats just didn't exist in Iran until later on in the Shah's regime). The gardens are all surrounded by walls of at least six feet, so really when you walk in the streets, you have no idea what goes on behind these walls. So families are very separated from each other in a sense. It's a very strange environment really. There's no society in the sense that you have here. No, people have always been very suspicious of each other, for political reasons, and I think it's really left a deep mark: they live behind tall walls and they have nothing to do with each other. People don't do things collectively at all. You very much rely on family.

My town is very green. Iranians have always planted a lot of trees. Once you leave the city there's this green belt but when you go beyond that it's dry and desert-like compared to the countryside here. The streets weren't tarmacked for a long time and I remember the dust coming into the air every time the occasional car went by. We used to have horse-carriages instead of cars. I loved that; we called it the *doroshkeh*. I remember we used to see the odd *doroshkeh* when I was at primary school and after that we never saw one again. They just vanished, replaced by cars.

The town was quite busy – no big stores, all small local shops. Consumer goods and food were limited; it was mainly just the local products, nothing processed. My city is a very holy city because of a shrine where one of Mohammed's disciples is buried. It used to attract at least a million pilgrims every year so we had this big market in the centre of the city until it was demolished, replaced with a ghastly modern market by the Shah. The men sold various things like cucumbers or rock salt. They just piled up a little barrow and they used to push this through the streets and shout whatever they were selling and women would come out of the house to buy.

One festival I very much looked forward to was our New Year. It's not religious, it's a traditional ceremony. The mullahs would like to get rid of the whole idea but they can't because of its deep roots: it's 3,000 years old. I used to look forward to the family gathering and to preparing the table. We set the table with the *Qu'ran* and seven things whose names begin with the letter 'S' in Farsi – vinegar, fresh green herbs, a bowl of goldfish, a mirror, a paste called *samanu*, which is only made at New Year, a piece of cheese very much like the feta cheese one buys here, and painted eggs. The oldest member of the family, which was my grandfather, used to hand out, not presents, but new notes taken from the bank. So it's not a commercial ceremony at all, like Christmas here. People put no emphasis on that at all, so it's really very pleasant. It was very much a family affair. Once television came in, the Shah's and the Prime Minister's speeches contaminated the whole thing.

When we were young, boys and girls mixed in the streets – unlike later on in life when sexes would be socially segregated. I would say they were segregated from 13 up. The youths' social life revolved around that of their parents from that age. Some families simply wouldn't allow their daughters to come out to play because they would have to wear the *chador* and that isn't practical to play in. I remember when I was a very young girl, a very large number of people forced their women to wear the *chador*, yes. It was unusual for a girl not to wear it, you really stood out in the street. I only wore it when I was forced to go to the shrine by my grandmother! When my grandmother was quite a young woman the Shah's father banned women from wearing the *chador*. It was a false Westernisation in a way. He forced everyone to wear hats. I have a photograph somewhere of my grandmother as a very young woman having to wear a hat and pose in front of this camera, and she said she found it extremely difficult to do that because given the choice she would wear the *chador*. And she reverted to that when the restriction was lifted after the Second World War.

I went to school at seven. There were six years of primary and then six years of secondary. It was segregated and because there weren't enough school buildings available for a few months, at first I used to go only in the mornings from 8 till 12 and then for a few months in the afternoons only. So we had this shift system which is characteristic of poor countries where there aren't enough schools or teachers. We had overcrowded classes and very uncomfortable, horrid, wooden benches. We were three, or sometimes four hours sat on a bench. It was very strict from a discipline point of view, so everyone was trained to behave well. I remember one awful thing – there was this little coal room where there were no windows, and any child who was really naughty would be sent there for half an hour or an hour. It was absolutely pitch dark. We children were very frightened of that. Although I went to the best high school in the town, we had a very dingy library which you could obtain nothing from. We had no clubs and sport was non-existent. At the end of the year we had to sit exams. So a lot of people worked just for the sake of the exam instead of true study. We learnt everything by heart, and as long as we could recite it word for word that was fine. There was no in-depth study of anything. Our history was a joke – all rewritten – and all we studied was dates, chronological events. There was no analysis whatsoever. History was never critically examined. There was no use of extra-curricular books. I finished a year later than the others because I failed my final exam. So I was 19 when I finished. Education was very grim.

Because of the Shah's use of political censorship, writing wasn't encouraged at all, so really as a country we had no books. That's the case even now, unfortunately. They've taken their toll, the years of the Shah.

The first books I got to read were the books my father brought me, from a very popular Iranian writer who actually won an international award. He was a teacher, living and working in a village in a north-western province, and when he was in his twenties he was reported to have drowned in the river there. But everybody knew he'd been murdered by the secret police. Most of his books were banned for a period of time. But I remember, one day when I was eight or nine, my father just bought them. After that I was quite desperate to find books but it was very difficult to get hold of any.

My parents certainly wanted me to do well academically, but they were quite aware that I wasn't keen. They would have liked me to have done better, but the fact that I was a girl and would inevitably marry, probably made a difference. They didn't persist as they did in the case of my brother. They went to great lengths to send him out of Iran for a university education.

Marriage really was the only way of survival for women. If they went to school, after they finished it was virtually out of the question for a woman to move out of her parents' house into a property of her own. So you either lived with your parents for the rest of your life, and at the same time tried to get a job or, the option was to marry. Prejudice was particularly noticeable in marriage, so who you married was very important – what sort of status he had, what sort of education, how much money he had. And the wedding ceremony was very important. The dowry had to be huge, you had to wear the best dress and give the best wedding party. So in that sense, yes, class distinctions were there because you could tell which social class people belonged to by the quality of their wedding party.

There were a lot of land-owning people who owned acres and acres of land and many, many big houses. And also there were those who owned the bazaars, the merchants, and actually they're very influential, politically and economically. But if you didn't belong to the land-owning class or to the bazaaris, there wasn't much difference in wealth between people. But of course, there was a very, very poor and deprived class as well. When I studied my nursing I got to know a lot of them. I used to go to their houses. Their living conditions were just appalling. When I look around here, some pets have better lives than the poor did in my country. I remember one house I went to visit, the daughter had been a patient in the hospital. She lived in a little mud hut in a part of the town in which no addresses could be given, because there were no houses, just mud huts. There was this mud hut, no windows, no carpets, just newspapers spread on the floor. There was a mother and daughter and the daughter was very ill, and all they had was an oil-burning stove and a big pan of water boiling. No possessions whatsoever and no hope either. Later those areas became breeding grounds for opposition to the Shah.

After I finished high school I started nursing college. I finished one year and then I was unable to continue because of the revolution. I found the course most inadequate. There were no readily available text books and instead of trying to understand, we had to spend the time writing everything down. The practical work there was an eye-opener. I worked in the biggest hospital in the city and it attracted people from all over the province, so I got into contact with all kinds of people. It just revealed how inadequate our health services were. There was an acute shortage of all equipment, poorly trained nurses, indifferent and disinterested doctors, so it was a right sham really.

I remember we had very bad cases of bed sores, which is an indication of poor nursing. There were some horrific cases of people who had been lying on beds without ever being moved, and their bones were actually exposed. It was absolutely terrible. It just shows what the quality of nursing was like. The patients who came to that hospital didn't pay. They were all very poor villagers. Being in hospital, they often lost their jobs and because of the lack of a social security system and a national insurance scheme their families were completely exposed. Some of them had to pay for treatment, which was very high, considering the poverty they came from. I remember one man had cancer of some sort. He had six children and because he was in hospital there was no one to carry on his business. He wasn't covered by insurance, and that meant that his family had no income. And we told him that he was going to die, and we told his family. His wife got some help from the mosque, I think, from these on-the-surface benevolent Moslems. But that was the usual plight for a lot of people. So really it was agony and despair. And the women would have to go out and earn a living. Because they weren't educated, all they could do was work as a home-help where they could take their children with them. People were most exploited at that level. For the majority of people that was Iran.

University students have always been politically active. They had a long history of political strikes behind them and they were more prepared than anyone else to do something against the Shah's regime. There was growing tension in high schools also. Generally, parents tried to forget about the whole thing, because they knew the price they would have to pay would be very high. If the slightest opposition was detected, one would just vanish, arrested by the secret police. Gruesome prisons they had, and all methods of torture were applied. I remember once, I was in the third year of my secondary school, we were going to sit a physics exam and my best friend didn't arrive, so she missed it. Afterwards I went to her house and her mother said she didn't know where she was. She reappeared after a month and a half. She'd been taken to prison. She told me that just before the exam, four plain-clothes men knocked on the door, went into her room, woke her up and told her mother to get her ready, and in front of her parents they took her away. I think she had been tortured. She would have been fifteen then. That sort of thing went on quite often.

Yes, there was an awareness of how strong the secret police were and everybody feared them. There was no sense of community because the secret police had penetrated all levels, and people just couldn't trust each other. Even from primary one we had at least one child in the class who was an informer. Anything we said could be immediately reported, and most likely the headmaster or headmistress of the school would be working for the secret police too. They would be forced to, they had no choice. If they approached you and asked you to collaborate, you had no choice but to accept because if you turned them down the consequences would be too great. This would be interpreted as opposition.

The problem with the Shah was that he tried, brutally, to westernise the country, regardless of its history and religion, by means of television, fashion, music, education, and also by growing class distinction. A number of people who managed to go to university, particularly those who did medicine, earned huge sums of money. It was the same thing with engineers. And the poor felt that nothing was being done to help their living conditions. We'd always had a rich, wealthy class and a majority of poor people, but once this westernisation came about, particularly with the advent of television, it was really revealed how a minority of people lived and how the majority were suffering.

There is a definite sense of inferiority felt by Asians in relation to the West. And that was very much reinforced by the Shah. It seemed the whole country was for sale, for Americans to come and take. And that caused resentment among a lot of religious people. That's where religion came into it, that was the element they could fight the Shah with. I'm not religious at all and my family have never been. Religion was never discussed in our house, nobody ever went to the mosque to pray; nobody ever prayed except my grandmother and I remember I was very unwilling to learn to pray when we had to at school. The girls have to start praying at the age of nine and one is meant to be taught at home. Most people were more religious than us, but in a hypocritical way. That's what put me off religion. You have to be an Iranian to appreciate that. Every Moslem has a duty to go to Mecca once in his lifetime, and that had become a ceremony during which you could distinguish the classes from each other by the wealth, by the amount of money they had spent on their trip to Mecca. And they used to go to Mecca and take thousands and thousands of *rials* with them. When they got back they'd have suitcases full of watches and clothes, so it really became a commercial trip and it lost all its religious importance. They used to sacrifice a sheep on their arrival home, and of course the rich sacrificed more sheep than the poor did. I would have nothing to do with it. But then again, my family is very unusual because in a way we were not only uninterested in religion but we didn't hide it either. A lot of people were probably not interested but they would keep up the appearance by going to the mosque sometimes, and having mullahs at home, reciting religious songs and giving religious speeches. That was called *roseh*, and it was very common. There would be separate rooms for women and men and one mullah would preach to the women and one mullah to the men. *Roseh* was held regularly by some families; they did it every month no matter how they led the rest of their lives. It was just to keep up the appearance.

But I think the way religion helped people was to relieve the pain a little, by actually offering a sanctuary like a mosque, where the secret police couldn't touch you – or where you thought they couldn't touch you. In fact, religion is a very binding force in Iran, it always has been. In comparison, I find Britain very fragmented – you have one group of people who are definitely religious and a majority who just aren't.

The revolution began in the mosques. They were the only places where people could gather and hear revolutionary speeches and play Ayatollah Khomeini's cassettes quite freely. They knew that the soldiers weren't prepared to shoot people in mosques. And one mistake the government did make was when they shot people in the shrine in my home town – you can see the bullet holes in the walls. People just couldn't forgive that sort of thing.

I met my husband in my home town where he was my teacher for six months. We had no relationship during that time at all; to me he was Mr So-and-so and to him I was Miss So-and-so. And I used to get invited to his house with the whole class. It was tactical, because he couldn't invite me on my own! At the end, at a party he asked me to marry him. I told my family. My parents said, 'It's up to you. It's your life. You decide'. I don't think any of us at that time could actually envisage what would happen: that if such a marriage took place, I would have to leave Iran at some point – it just didn't seem possible at that time.

My husband was going to leave for his summer holiday and we only had ten days in which to marry. A civil marriage was out of the question because it would take too long – we would have to get permission from the secret police which would have taken five or six months. So we had to go for a religious ceremony which meant that my husband would have to convert to Islam, there was no other way. So we went with my family to the house of an Ayatollah, a house in one of the oldest parts of the city. It was the beginning of the revolution just that very day in Mashad! And I remember as we were walking towards the house, suddenly trucks full of soldiers pulled in, surrounding it, because the Ayatollah's advisor had died suddenly.

The government was claiming that he was killed in a car accident, but the people thought he had been killed by the secret police. There was tension in the air and the government anticipated some sort of unrest, focussing around that house. They surrounded it so we couldn't get in at first. The soldiers stopped us and then my grandfather talked to them and said, 'It's a marriage going to take place. You can't stop a marriage for any reason, political or non-political'. And the soldiers let us in. We went into this house and sat in a room and the Ayatollah came in. My husband had to convert before the marriage ceremony took place. It's very straightforward: he was given a little speech on Islam, a formality really, then he repeated three times the verses from the Qu'ran which are part of the prayer which takes place five times a day. After that he wed us, and that was it, we were married. There was no paperwork, nothing. It just shows the strength of religion – it would be accepted by absolutely everyone.

My husband left Iran ten days later and I joined him as soon as I got a passport. We had a few months' break in Britain; I met his family and we went through a civil marriage here, then we went back to Iran. By that time I was pregnant and we still hadn't got permission for a civil marriage in Iran. They demanded tens and tens of photographs and forms to be filled in, visits to my local police station, visits to my husband's local police station. And at each police station they had a detailed history of all our relatives: names, occupations, where they lived, everything – the intelligence network obviously. Anyway, we just endured all that, and once we got the written permission to carry out a civil marriage we only had twenty-four hours left! Otherwise it wouldn't have any effect. There was a nationwide strike and it was virtually impossible to get from one part of the city to the other. All the taxi drivers and bus drivers had gone on strike and there were barricades, tanks, soldiers, everywhere. Once we got to a registry office we had to persuade somebody to open up to wed us. Anyway in the last half hour we managed to get through it! The civil marriage was necessary because if I was not legally married to my husband, then travelling to Iran from abroad would be very difficult for me. The authorities wouldn't recognise him as my legal husband, or my children as my legal children.

One of the main tools the nation had against the Shah was nationwide strikes to bring the country to a halt. Absolutely everybody went on strike, including the nursing college. That affected me personally because I never started my second year. It never reopened while I was there.

When we used to go out shopping, suddenly we'd see this wall of two or three million people walking towards us – a mass demonstration. And then we'd look on the other side and there'd be Chieftain tanks pulling near. It was like this all the time. It was not an armed revolution at all. People had no arms whatsoever until the later stages of the revolution when they invaded military barracks and confiscated a lot of guns, and so on. They just counted on the soldiers' inability and unwillingness to shoot them. On some occasions Chieftain tanks actually did run over people, and later those responsible for those incidents were lynched. I remember one incident clearly: we were coming home when we saw this wall of people coming towards us across the street, and in front of them were hundreds and hundreds of motor-cyclists shielding the people on foot. We looked the other way and there were tanks coming from the other end of the street. We just stood there and we could see the demonstrators were moving forward, and the tanks were moving forward inch by inch and they were coming together. In that incident tanks overran people after we got away. One time a car was overrun by a tank outside our house. We went out and it was flat! The other thing I remember is non-stop helicopter flights over the city to monitor what was going on. Whenever I hear a helicopter flying I think it just sounds like Mashad during the revolution.

We didn't leave Iran of our own free will, we were told to leave by the British Embassy. There was a very, very large number of Westerners working in Iran and the British Embassy over-reacted. They felt the expatriates would be in some danger if they didn't leave because anti-foreign feelings would be high. They gave us one week in which to leave. It came as such a sudden shock that we had no time to discuss how we felt about it. At the airport, my mother was very upset because she knew that I was leaving for good, and I was upset for a long time after. But it happened in such circumstances that we didn't have time for personal feelings really. We had to run around and organise our luggage and see as many friends as we could to say goodbye. Really there was no time to be emotional about it all.

We left in December 1978 and the Shah went in February 1979. I remember hearing of his departure in England when I was listening to the radio.

We went to Northamptonshire to stay with my husband's parents. My husband had lost his job, we didn't have that much money and I was three months' pregnant. I remember when I arrived in Britain, I found the houses, built of red brick, very interesting, and it had obviously rained very heavily and then the sun was shining and it looked so beautiful . . . the air was fresh and the buildings were so different from Iran. It was so green. I couldn't get over how green this country was. My first impression of Britain was a physical impression, not its people or the way they live.

I'd seen a lot of films in Iran in which the image of the West portrayed was one of decadence: family values don't mean anything, tradition means nothing, religion doesn't exist, and it's all night-clubs and alcohol and all the rest of it. I think it is a very false picture. I remember my uncle said to me before I left, 'Don't go there with a preconceived idea, just go and see and absorb. Don't talk, just listen and after a while, when you've taken all this in, judge what you've seen and then very gently come out of yourself'. I remember that was his advice and I think I did just that, actually!

But I was very unhappy about being forced to leave at such a critical time when my family were really in danger – people were being shot at, it was a state of revolution. I was very worried about my family back home. The entire communications system had broken down so there was no way I could phone them. Letters did not reach them. Their letters didn't reach me. That meant that the only news I got was through the TV. I used to see news films about my home town and the fighting between the military and the people. I remember the children's ward in the hospital where I had practised had been attacked by the soldiers and they had shot a few doctors, nurses and children. That was very sad because I had a lot of friends working in that hospital. I got very depressed.

After nine months we went to Saudi Arabia. My husband got a job there and I followed him about three months later with my child. It was very difficult to get a visa to go to Saudi Arabia at the time because I was Iranian and they were afraid of the revolutionary Iranians! So I had to get a British passport and then apply. We lived in Riyadh in Saudi Arabia until we had to leave in 1983. During that time we'd had a little bungalow built somewhere near Dumfries. We'd decided we weren't going to live in a city in Britain because my husband didn't like city life and I was quite open at that time, mainly because I didn't know what the difference was. It was in the middle of the countryside and a very beautiful part of the country too.

I found it extremely hard in Dumfries because all the time in Riyadh we had lived in a compound with eleven other families so we led a very communal life there and one was never lonely. And suddenly we left that to live in the countryside in southern Scotland where I didn't know anybody. I even had difficulty understanding their accents. My husband had to go to London for a six-month course, so there I was, left with two children in Dumfries. The nearest shops were twenty minutes' drive and it was a very cold winter. I was snowed in for a few days, I couldn't even open the front door! We had twelve-hour powercuts that winter. It wasn't a very nice start to life in Britain.

I found people didn't know how to handle me, how to approach me. There wasn't a community, just individual families living in their houses having nothing to do with each other. We lived there exactly a year before we came to Edinburgh.

In Edinburgh there are a large number of foreigners and I'm not in such a minority. I find it easier to relate to the local population than I did in Dumfries. I like the city, I like the buildings in Edinburgh, I think it is a very beautiful city and it's full of character.

I would like to preserve my own culture but it is virtually impossible to do so. I think my way of life would have been different had I stayed in Iran. I would probably have been quite religious but now I'm not because the pressure isn't there. Had I lived in Iran under the present regime it would have been inescapable!

My children can't be Iranians. They know there are links with Iran but they consider themselves Scottish really, particularly my son. Living here, it's very difficult to maintain my Iranian standards as far as my children are concerned, because they go to a British school, their friends are all British, they read English books, they watch British TV. I'm particularly unhappy about my daughter, as I feel I don't want to have a teenage daughter in Britain because of the life young British girls lead. I don't like the extent of freedom they have. I don't like the social pressures here, like early pre-marital sex, and alcohol. But I don't think she should be protected as I was in my teenage years. I won't approve of her going to a pub with her friends when she's 16, staying out till midnight. I don't think I could possibly allow her to do that. But then, there are so many social pressures that I will have to compromise. . . .

I talk to the children a lot about my own childhood. I try to take them to Iran as often as I can, which is not easy now. They find my childhood quite interesting but it's like reading them a book, it isn't real to them. I tried to teach my son Farsi, and the few times we've been to Iran he's spoken it perfectly well. But recently he's been resisting it a lot and I think I've just lost courage . . . he pretends that he doesn't understand. I try to speak to them but they never answer me back in Farsi, even if they know the answer.

There are 25,000 Iranians living here but they haven't formed a solid community in any part of Britain. They're very dispersed and not in contact with each other simply because they don't trust each other politically. They're not seen as a threat for that reason probably, and the majority of them are educated people who have found it quite easy to find good jobs. They're not poor at all, they've managed to integrate very well into British society, and the only reason it hasn't been publicised is because it hasn't really been noticed.

There's great apathy in Britain. The majority of people don't usually think about ethnic minorities and they don't want to establish any contact, not if they can help it! And I find generally, despite having such large numbers of minority groups in Britain, there is very little coverage in the media. I've never had any unpleasant encounters myself but I've come across a lot of people who have clearly tried to avoid me. I try to account for it by believing that they didn't know how to approach me, but I think there is also an element of racism – not very strong, but it is there. But what I find difficult is the apathy in this country. I'm not racially abused because I don't look that different from the rest of the population. Had I darker skin, yes, I would probably have experienced more racism.

I remember two years ago I was travelling home from Istanbul with my Iranian passport. Although I had a valid re-entry visa and my husband was travelling with me, customs officials would not allow me to enter, because this official said, 'Although you are allowed to enter the country, there's no proof that you're allowed to live here'. Like everybody else, I don't necessarily carry my naturalisation documents with me all the time. After about half an hour the man gave up and let me through. But I found that pretty humiliating and unpleasant. I don't know what it is like to enter Heathrow coming from Africa, Bangladesh or India. We've encountered that kind of racism when my family have applied for visas to come to Britain. The visa application process is most humiliating both in Tehran and even when they get to Heathrow, so I've decided I don't want them to come to Britain because I don't want them to have to go through that. When it comes to visa applications in particular, they seem to have no respect whatsoever for the human being who is applying for the visa: that he or she has limited time and resources; that he or she can't travel forwards and backwards between cities too often; that not everyone always lies, and not everyone is dying to come and settle in Britain.

Since we left in '78 we've returned a few times and every time Iran has changed beyond recognition. It's not the Iran I knew and grew up in at all. Even the street names have all been changed. They've all got revolutionary names now, so I have difficulty directing the taxi drivers. People seem worn out, disillusioned, very depressed, because the revolution didn't take the course they had hoped it would. Somebody said that Iranians were effectively betrayed and I think that is very true. It was a genuine revolution, the kind of revolution which doesn't occur very often, but the course it took afterwards wasn't anticipated at all. It went badly wrong simply because of its leadership, because of fanaticism.

When I go back I find a lot of people who I knew are dead – executed, disappeared, killed at war – or escaped. Relationships have changed, people seem to have become distant from each other. There is a certain bitterness and resentment in everyone.

Immediately after the revolution everyone was very high and optimistic and believed in the revolution. There were hard discussions going on everywhere; there was total freedom of the press, total freedom of speech. For the first time in centuries, Iranians really experienced democracy, and for that very reason they didn't know how to react to it. Various political parties just erupted. Iran was very pleasant after the revolution, but the regime could only cope with about 18 months of democracy and after that everything tightened up. Total censorship of the press was implemented; political parties were eliminated; freedom of speech vanished.

It has got worse every time I have gone back. Iran has become a very suppressed country. Now people don't even feel safe in their own homes. Alcohol is banned, but people still drink in their homes, and the revolutionary guards, without any authority, feel free to burst into any house and arrest people if they find alcohol. Consequences can be a minimum of eighty lashes. All those thugs – I call them thugs because that's what they really are – who worked for the Shah, are now in disguise working for the new regime. All those who took part in the revolution and captured military barracks and seized a lot of arms never handed them back. A lot of people were armed who weren't quite sure how to cope with being armed. So Iran is a very dangerous place just now. There has been no development either, from what I could see.

This revolution has meant a lot of restrictions for women. Women have to be covered – all parts of the body except just hands and face. The regime is very fanatical about it. I remember the last time I was in Tehran, in the streets there were revolutionary guardswomen, who wore the traditional black *chador*. It was a very frightening sight actually; they looked very aggressive, hostile people. And they all carried machine-guns under their *chadors*. If they saw one piece of hair uncovered by scarf they would really leap on you and it could be quite a frightening experience to be told how to dress by one of them. I remember people were clearly annoyed that at the age of two my daughter wasn't wearing a scarf to cover her hair. She couldn't wear a sundress outside although it was 100 degrees Fahrenheit.

It's important to know that the sort of liberty Iranian women enjoyed was very short-lived, because it didn't start until the post-world-war period. So perhaps there are only two generations of women who have had access to higher education or who could go into certain professions. As for the present young generation, there'll be no question of them being able to attempt to enter any of these professions. The women's workforce is gradually being pushed back into the home, to breed children. Women find it particularly claustrophobic in Iran – well I do when I go back.

For what they call ideological reasons, there is no entertainment in Iran. None whatsoever. So life is very grim and it's compounded by the cost of basic foods and other materials. I think I could cope with the war and the casualties and the depression, but not with the repression and the lack of entertainment. That, nobody has got used to yet. There's no music, for example, except the revolutionary drum-beating or religious songs. The radio and television are totally dominated by religious programmes. But I think there is a limit to how much one can absorb religion, and beyond that, it not only loses its effect, but it causes a lot of anger – if not apathy.

TREVOR

Being Less Personal

In 1955, when he was 14, Trevor Larmond left Jamaica to
join his mother who had come to Britain six years earlier. He
now lives in Scotland and is a university lecturer.

I was born in Kingston Jamaica in 1940. Although some people from
Jamaica went to the war, I didn't have the same impressions of the
war as a child in Britain would have done, you know, rationing and
all this sort of thing. But what we did notice was that there were a lot
of warships in Kingston. Jamaica was a colony at the time and what
you had was a large expatriate population of white British who lived
in Kingston but were not a part of it.

They lived outside the centre of the city, so you had a large suburban population of expatriates whom the native population almost
ignored. They were not a part of the social fabric, they were not a
threat, they were just there. The white sailors and soldiers were more
part of the social fabric of the city than were the expatriate population
who were working for banks, the university, and the government.
So when I came to London I didn't think there was a great difference
other than that you saw a lot more white people in your daily life. I
didn't find it a great social change. And although there is a difference
between standard English and Jamaican patois English, the difference
is something which the white person stresses, which the white social
system has pointed out. So it's really a white problem – it's a white
observation. That's where a lot of the problem started: where people
have said to Jamaicans, 'Well, you don't speak English'. You then
immediately start attacking their long established connection with
the British system.

To Jamaicans or to foreigners who were part of the British
Empire, their associations and affiliations with Great Britain are not
in doubt. And therefore, it was not surprising to us that people were
asked in the West Indies to come and work here. It's only surprising
to the people here. Again it was not a great trauma for West Indians

to come and work here, it's the reaction of the native population that's the trauma. The problem is trying to convince the white British here (whose knowledge of their history is probably not very good or completely non-existent) about the historical relationship between the West Indies and Great Britain. It's more of a white British problem. Although it hurts black people – it's like somebody telling a Scottish person that they're not Scottish. I mean that's what the reaction has done.

I think people always have this misconception that the blacks had a lot of trouble settling in. It's not true. You don't get Jamaicans bellyaching about settling in. I came over when I was nearly 15, on my own. That wasn't extraordinary, probably a lot of other children did the same. My mother was one of the first Jamaicans to come over, she had come here in 1948 so I was eight when she left. The next time I saw her I was 14 years and about ten months. My mother wanted me to work in a shop, I think, but I had to go to Shelbourne Road Secondary School, in the middle of London till the end of the summer term. I played cricket for the school and apparently I was very good at it. The local headmaster of the grammar school saw in the *Islington Gazette* that there was a secondary-modern schoolboy playing for London, so I got transferred to the local grammar school, Highbury County. I stayed there until '57 and then I left (after playing cricket for the school) and worked as a technician at London University till 1960. The professor at London University got me to complete O levels and A levels. At the time it wasn't easy to get into university if you were an immigrant. You could get a grant but the universities wouldn't take immigrants. There were facilities for students from overseas to come into the system because you could apply through your government or your High Commission, and they'd sanction you. But there were no facilities for an immigrant who had emigrated from a country that was not independent. So I had to go to the Jamaican High Commission and say, 'Well would you sanction me as an overseas student?' And they said, 'No, because you're not,' because I didn't fulfil the criteria as an overseas student. But I was one of the first immigrants to get into university because the professor phoned up Leicester and got me in. I stayed at Leicester for three years, got an honours degree in Botany, went back to London, worked in a restaurant for about six months, and then saw an advertisement, and came to Edinburgh. I started my PhD in 1965, finished in 1967, stayed on in 1968 as a post-doctoral fellow and went to work in a research institute until the late seventies. I then came back to Scotland as a university lecturer.

I'm on committees of the Church which deal with racism. It's difficult, it's very difficult to identify racism. What you have to watch is that it is superimposed upon the natural prejudices which people have against people as a whole: where you come from, the way you speak, the way you dress. And what is dangerous I think, in the country as a whole, is that blacks are trapped into fulfilling stereotypes. If you're white and you've got your hair cut in a particular way or sprayed with paint, and you are seen sitting on the side of the road rolling a cigarette – the police are more likely to think that you are rolling a joint. But if you are dressed in a three-piece suit with a nice blue and white shirt, with city-type shoes and a bowler hat and are rolling a cigarette on the bench, it could be a joint but you won't get picked up. I think if you were rolling a joint in a three-piece suit and you were *black* you probably wouldn't be picked up. This is what I'm trying to say: a lot of whites have got the choice of being many things but a lot of blacks are limited in their choice of stereotypes. They have not got either the educational facilities or the housing conditions. So to me it's self-evident they're going to remain on the edge of society. If people want to do any good about these things, they'll ensure socially that blacks do not fulfil the stereotypes of poorly-educated people living in poor conditions. I know in the ideal world people shouldn't be arrested because they're poorly educated, poorly dressed and whatever, but we're not living in an ideal situation, and in any modern civilised society, in inverted commas, you will get into trouble if you live on the edge of society and fulfil stereotypes of what a criminal looks like. The abnormally high figures of blacks and poor whites in jail confirm this.

So let's not just say it's racism, let's say that in fact the social conditions are such that blacks are fulfilling historical stereotypes of inferiority, which we must try and get rid of. You've done it for the whites. You're a long way from the 1850 stereotype of the poor working-class white being almost just a little bit above an animal vis à vis the white middle and upper class. You've moved away because what you've done is created a better educational climate.

So I'm trying to be less personal. What I don't want to say is, that, OK, somebody spat on me on the train or somebody threw a bottle at my uncle's house as happened in London, or my brother got arrested and stuff like that. I wouldn't get paranoid about it because that tends to hold you back in terms of how you relate to society. I could tell you that my mother who's been here since 1948 didn't get British citizenship when she applied because she'd overstayed her visit to America by weeks. Now a lot of people would cite that as basic racial prejudice. I think that it could be, but I think that it is more important that we do something about the education system to ensure that a West Indian, if he gets into a situation like my mother, or my brother, is in a position to defend himself. Just changing the system to ensure that these people are protected by some sort of white institution, the local legal aid, some well-intentioned solicitor, I don't think that's important. The individual must be educated and socially aware enough to protect himself. That's what I've been able to do myself, I've been able to go through the system more effectively because I know the limitations of the system. I know my limitations as somebody from abroad and therefore I am able to co-exist with the system. I believe in education. I wouldn't have the social mobility I have if I weren't educated. I'd still be in the slums of London. You know, black kids were being put in ESN classes, I myself was put in an ESN class when I first came. They gave you a set of questions like 'Where is the House of Lords?' you know. What the hell did I know about it! [laughs] But because I played cricket and went to Highbury County! One could call it prejudice or one could say it's just complete ignorance on the part of the system. What we've got to do is not just criticise the system but try and change it.

So you can see my view on these things. The people that want to help must be aware that the first thing they must do is not change individuals, they've got to change aspects of how the system operates. The system was designed to operate for whites, and it will exclude all sorts of people because it wasn't designed for them. Now we must try and make sure that the system works for everybody. Providing the institutions in the system as a whole don't discriminate, then I think everybody has to take their chances. You shouldn't get lost in the personal, individual thing. Then it becomes difficult because you're wondering what experience the person's been through. Is this somebody who has done badly in the society, or somebody the society has treated badly? And how are we going to apply what they say to solving the problem? I'm saying forget what has happened to me and my brother and my mother and my cousins, let's try and do something for the kids two or three generations away.

And don't worry about the blacks not being able defend themselves personally against individuals. Where the blacks are vulnerable is against the institution wherein they've got to read and they've got to verbally defend themselves, and that's where the middle class is in its element. So, where the blacks are weak is against the institution. That's where they need defending.

But what the hell do you expect the average British person to do as far as reacting to a black immigrant is concerned when, from the taking of our countries in the colonial period, your father and his father's father were told, through their textbooks and the way they lived, that the people from these countries were animals? In fact, I asked a white friend of mine – I've known her for 21 years and we're very close friends – I said, 'You tell me honestly what you really thought of black people 30 years ago. Honestly, I don't want any emotional, social thing, or you extrapolating back. I want you to tell me'. And you know what she said? She said to me, 'Honestly, when I was a child my textbook had animals in it from the jungle, and in the same book there was a black man standing with a spear in front of a hut, and as far as I was concerned he was just like an animal because he was in the same book. There was no black man wearing a suit, or going to work.' 'So,' she said, 'my image, my imagery, was that the black man was just slightly above the animals. I never thought I'd ever meet one, much less be friendly with one. And that,' she said, 'probably underlies all the attitudes of the people in this country who are over 25 (even those who are under 25 may have been influenced by their parents)'. Therefore the stereotype of the black is going to be hellishly difficult to get rid of. It was part of your education, part of that system. So try to get rid of that by telling people that, 'The blacks are really good guys and they're human beings like ourselves', or whatever! You've had hundreds of years telling them that they're not! But what I'm saying is, if you have a social situation where you go into a bank and you see blacks, and you go into the labour exchange and you see blacks working, giving out the dole, or you go into the hospital and you see blacks, not just cleaning the floor, but being doctors, it doesn't make you like the blacks but it gets rid of the stereotype. That's what I call equality. That's what all people should be working for so that this multiracial society can use the energies of all its citizens to the full.

SHREEN

'We are Here for a Reason'

Shreen Barwary was born in 1950 in a small village in Kurdish
Iraq. She came to Britain to join her husband in 1976.

I grew up in a big family. We used to live in a great big house with all
our relatives; uncles and cousins all together. My immediate family
consisted of 3 brothers and myself. The family was religious and my
father was the head of the community, responsible for solving problems like water distribution, lease of land and how the harvest was
worked out. Besides this, the family looked after a boarding centre
where students from Turkey as well as Iraq came to study Islam.
Every evening, a hot meal was provided for the poor and needy and
the centre was also used for settling tribal disputes. As leaders of the
centre my family were highly respected.

The village was very beautiful and there was a little airport so it
was accessible. It wasn't a very big village, I think about a thousand
people, and most of them were farmers. The buildings were made
of stone and mud. We have severe winters and deep snow. And in
summer it is very warm so mud is ideal for the buildings. In the
winter it gives warmth and in the summer it keeps the buildings
cool. There were very, very high mountains and it was very hard to
climb them. For drinking water we had spring water that ran all the
year round.

As a community we were very close. If a neighbour was in
hardship and too poor to afford food or clothes, usually we would
send some food, and if we had extra clothing we'd give that too. In
all these matters we were all very helpful. It was so peaceful, it was
so nice, you could go out at any time of day or night. When we were
very young children, we used to go into the mountains and no one
ever threatened us. The only thing we were afraid of was wildlife
– wolves, and we also have a lot of bears, big brown bears and
sometimes they would attack people. People were so nice. If they

saw you walking on your own they would pick you up on their ponies or mules and look after you, and feed you, until you were back home again.

It's very green, very peaceful. I remember when we were little we'd go and hunt for these little birds. It sounds very barbaric [laughs]. We used to make a trap. There was a kind of plant, if you cut its seeds and boiled them it turned to a very elastic gum, and you'd spread it over long sticks and put them near water so that when birds came to drink they'd stand on the sticks and get caught. You'd make a barbecue in the wild. They were delicious, I tell you – sizzling! [laughs]. Very fragile, you know, you could eat them with their bones.

My other joy was when my mother used to boil eggs and then paint them different colours – like Easter here – and then you'd go and play. You'd hold them in your hand and bet with other children, and you'd crack them together. If mine broke my friend would take it and if I broke her egg I would take hers, so sometimes you got a lot of eggs which you couldn't always eat! Another thing we used to do was play with walnuts, like playing marbles here. Sometimes you came back with a sackful of nuts.

Henna was another event. I remember my mother used to make some pastry into the shape of an apple or heart, paint it with henna and she would press this on the tips of your fingers so you would have coloured, patterned hands.

Eid was usually a very big event. We have two religious occasions, one after Ramadan and one after the people go on pilgrimage to Mecca. Ramadan is three days' celebration and *Eid* lasts four days. I suppose it's like Christmas here, people buy lots of new clothes, make lots of special dishes and sweets and visit each other. They usually give children sweets, or money, or little presents.

Also, we have *Nowroz*. It's a very big festival celebrated by Kurds and Persians, and it has a great story behind it. They say there used to be a king who was very ruthless, violent and uncaring. He had an incurable disease and his doctor advised him that the only cure would be to eat the brain of a human. So every day he would send his soldiers to kill a young boy and boil his brain, and he would eat it. The villagers started getting worried. They said, 'This is not fair, in the end we will have no sons left. We'll have to do something about it'. But they were terrified that the king would kill all the people. Then one of the men, his name was Kawar, he was a blacksmith and so he was a brave man. He said, 'If we get together and unite we can win'. Then decided on the 21st March that everybody, whatever weapon they had, would get ready, and for the starting signal, Kawar would go to the top of the mountain and light a fire. So that's what they did; the whole region got together and attacked the king and killed him. So it's a celebration of freedom and also the 21st March is the beginning of spring in Kurdistan. And on this occasion you see big fires on the top of each mountain. They dance the Kurdish dance and play Kurdish music and again everyone is always welcome to stay with you for a couple of days. We would have a big picnic together. That would be a group of about 150 people and each of them would make a very special dish and we'd sit in a very big circle and eat together, play music and dance out in the open.

The freedom of women depends on the level of education and on the family itself. Some families are very flexible. The women who are very restricted are usually very religious. I can't speak for all, but from my own experience, my father, although he was a very religious person, was especially nice to me. In our society they prefer boys to girls, but my father made me feel very special, very lovable, very comfortable with him. Even now, when I remember home, it is my father who comes first to my mind.

I think that Kurdish women have more freedom than Arab women. They've always been in fields with men, working together and building. They don't wear *hijab* or *aba* but long, very efficient and practical clothes and a scarf on their heads. These clothes serve two purposes, that of being a Moslem and also for protection because the weather can be harsh.

Kurdistan is a nation and Islam is a religion so we are Kurds and we are Moslems. Although our language is Kurdish we have to learn Arabic. Right from the beginning they teach you Arabic in schools because it is the official language, and when you reach secondary school you start learning English. The Kurds cover a very big area. The population is about 20 million spread through Iraq, Iran, Turkey, a bit of Syria and a bit of Russia. Unfortunately, Kurdistan was divided between these countries after the First World War.[1] These countries are, I think, very racist, very anti-Kurdish.

The Kurdish part of Iraq has the oil wells, so I suppose what they claim, is that if the Kurds had their independence we wouldn't give them any oil. We always say we will share according to their population, but they don't agree. Kurdistan is a very beautiful country. It is great for agriculture and livestock. But unfortunately, instead of building it up the Iraqi government always destroys it.[2] I mean, they buy all these tanks and they send aeroplanes to destroy villages and kill people. If they had used Kurdistan as a tourist attraction,

I suppose they could have made millions out of that, let alone the oil.

Until 1958, Kurdish people lived peacefully, but in 1959 Arab nationalism grew and some of the government officials began to discriminate against Kurds. This led to the Kurds demanding their basic rights – education in Kurdish language, equal opportunities and self government.

Over the years the government have tried to impose a policy of Arabisation to force Kurds out of their land and bring Arabs in to settle, so that they could say, 'There are no Kurds here, so how can you claim it is your land?' Now there are no Kurds in Kirkuk, the centre of the oil wells. Kurds are accustomed to cold weather, but they were sent to the middle and south of Iraq. It is too hot for them there, the land is level, and they are used to mountain farming and looking after their livestock. We have our own language, traditions and behaviour, so to go and cope with all that, we don't find it easy.

The government put lots of our people in camps where they were watched all the time and they brought lots of Arabs to Kurdistan. They bribed them with money, they built houses for them, they supplied them with electricity and water – everything they needed. Some Arabs couldn't resist the temptation but some refused as a matter of principle saying, 'It is not our land, we are not used to this climate.' Some were frightened and left. They didn't know how to look after their sheep in Kurdistan. They were terrified of the cold. The government and the police supported them but actually the life was not pleasant for them so they left. When they took Kurds to the south they bribed Arabs: 'If you marry a Kurdish woman you'll get a thousand dollars'. This was a way of making Kurds lose their identity.

Despite several changes in government, attitudes towards Kurds did not change although Kurdish leaders were more than willing to make an agreement. In 1968, the Ba'athist Arabic Socialist Party came to power with the intention of crushing the Kurdish movement by force. Fortunately, they didn't succeed so they looked for an alternative solution. In 1970 they made a treaty where the Kurds would be free to practise their celebrations, wear their costumes, use their language and have a voice in the government. But this was another trick. The government sent a delegate to see the Kurdish leader General Barzani and present him with the Qu'ran in which they had hidden a bomb that exploded prematurely killing the delegate and injuring the leader and others. The Kurds began to find themselves completely ruled by Arabs. All the mayors, the heads of police, the university lecturers – all the big positions with big money or power were in the hands of Arabs.[3] The government did not recognise the Kurdish leaders anymore and fighting broke out between the Iraqi army and the Kurdish forces. People fled because the planes were bombing the villages. In 1971 our old house, our great big house, was bombed and destroyed.

You see, there were Kurdish doctors, engineers, students, clerks, and they all fled – left their beautiful houses and possessions and went to join the revolution. It was very, very close to gaining victory. The strength of the Iraqi army forced the Kurds to be more dependent on Iran and the USA for food and other equipment but they didn't realise that Iran was using the Kurds for its own benefit. Then there was a treaty between Saddam, the Shah and Kissinger – that's how the revolution failed.[4] In the treaty Iraq gave away part of the Shatt-al-Arab waterway to Iran and in return the Shah withdrew his support for the Kurds. The Kurds found themselves surrounded by three powerful armies. The Kurds were helpless and didn't see much point in continuing. Al-Barzani had no chance. If you have a big revolution and you don't have support, what can you do nowadays – just fight with a stick? So the revolution failed and a lot of people committed suicide. They just couldn't take it.

Our family was not involved in fighting, but we were all involved whether we liked it or not. Like I said, my family were mostly religious people and they didn't want to interfere with politics, but we lost a lot of land, we lost our house, we lost our livestock, we lost our villages, we lost everything really. Kurdistan has always been unsettled and now it's getting even worse. The Iraqi and Turkish armies are pursuing Kurds on both sides.

We had left our village in 1959 because the situation started getting very unsettled and unsafe. Schools were closed and people were afraid to go out. After we left the village we were never able to go back again, and anyway our house was destroyed. When I left the village I was seven years old. I think the best part of my life was there. We went to Mosul, a big city in the north, which they now claim is basically an Arab city. I wasn't unhappy there, I was very young at the time, but I always regretted leaving the village.

I was 18 when I left school. When I got married I was supposed to go and finish my education, but I got pregnant and the government said married women weren't allowed to go to school. I regretted leaving school and when I wanted to go back I couldn't.

My husband was very unhappy in his work. The people there dis-
criminated against him because he was a Kurd. During the Kurdish
revolution there were casualties every day and the staff would sit and
make fun of this. But at the time he couldn't sit and argue with them
because they wouldn't appreciate or understand. It was a waste of
time. Sometimes he would speak back because he couldn't listen to
their humiliation of him. If he said things about the government, of
course, there were informers everywhere. Also his work was affect-
ing his health. He was an engineer in a cement factory and the dust
was getting to him. He had like a cold twelve months of the year and
his eyes were very red. He asked to be moved to somewhere better
or even to resign. But he wasn't able to resign because at the time,
the government said anyone who resigned would be prosecuted and
jailed for between five and fifteen years. He said, 'I don't want your
position. I don't want your money. I want nothing from you. Just
let me resign. I will do something on my own'. They wouldn't let
him do that either.

He made a lot of useful and practical work devices for the factory
that made the work safer for the workers, as he was concerned about
their safety and welfare. But they didn't like that. His boss was upset.
And later two people were killed in the factory because they were
doing a job they weren't trained for, and two workers were crippled.
He was very upset, so he had to leave.

He thought the easy way out was to go and study. It was possible
to go and study abroad, so he went to do his MSc in Birmingham
and then returned to Iraq. He worked, and hoped and prayed that the
government would change, that things would get better. In Iraq, you
know, since 1958, no government had lasted more than four or five
years. He thought it would be the same with this one. But unfortunately, it is still there and going from bad to worse every day.

I was 26 when I came over here in 1976 to join my husband
in Birmingham. Moving here didn't really bother me, or frighten
me, I was just happy to be with my husband and to be as a family
together.

In Britain the buildings disappointed me. We had much nicer
houses in Iraq, some of them looked like palaces. When I first came
here they all looked alike. I was looking from the aeroplane, I saw
all these little houses, little blocks, and I thought, 'These must be the
villages. When I get to London it will be different'. But when I was
in London it was the same.

People are here, ethnic minorities, for various reasons. They don't
all come because they are starving, and I think this is the general idea:

that you come here because you are starving. If we could be at home I'm sure that we'd be living a much better life than here, much more comfortable financially and socially. Now me and my husband are working but we are just surviving really. We can just make it up to the end of the month and pay all the bills. But we are here for a reason and we always look forward to going back. Some people were very kind, very concerned, very understanding. But the society here is quite different. I mean, in our society it is the extended family, it is very close – the family itself and the community. For me, it's hard to find that all these old ladies are living on their own with nobody, nobody. Maybe at Christmas, once a year, their children come to see them. In Iraq, they come at least once a day to see how their old parents are, and if they're sick they will go and look after them, will take them to their houses. I was surprised to find this lack of kindness here. I find it very upsetting.

The other thing that shocked me here is the way they label people by their colour. I wasn't aware of it at all. They say, 'This is a black man, white man, yellow man, brown man'. Why should they label you by your colour? I have found here that the whites – well they call themselves white – spend a fortune to go to Spain or Portugal to get a suntan. Why should they discriminate against a person's colour if they like suntans so much? I couldn't understand that. You don't look at the colour of a person, you look at their personality, at their manner, at the work they're producing. It's not the colour. I found it really unbelievable and I really hate it. My children are not very dark, or very fair. Sometimes children in the school will say, 'Why don't you go home?' Or they call them 'Black' and this, I think, upsets the children too.

It's funny: lots of my friends are foreign – not necessarily Arab, but American, Dutch, Indian, Pakistani. I think the British tend always to keep their distance. I don't know why. I found them a bit formal. I mean, in our country, when you meet each other, you have a meal together, you are friends. Your friends phone you regularly, visit you, and it is not necessary all the time to make an appointment. Here you have to phone to make an appointment. You have to indicate whether you're coming for lunch or tea [laughs].

In our country you don't smile at a person if you don't know them. If you smile, especially if a woman smiles at a man she has never met, it's suspicious, you know. But here, you find a man or a woman passing will often smile at you. At first I couldn't understand what they smiled for! But now I just smile back and go on and it doesn't bother me [laughs]. In Kurdistan when you go past someone they will always greet you, they say, 'Salaam', but they don't smile for no reason. There must be something funny for you to smile! Here, in some ways, I find life is much easier. I mean, you go to the supermarkets and you find all the meat cut and nicely presented, vegetables are available. I found it interesting to find all kinds of fruits and vegetables all the year round. In our country we have seasons with their own weather, fruits and vegetables. And you tend to look forward to the next season to find something different. Here you don't have the joy of going and cutting your own vegetables or finding your own fruits. In Iraq we have big gardens with orange trees, grapes, pomegranates, figs, you name it, all kinds of fruit. Vegetables you don't grow very often unless you are a farmer, because they are very cheap. They put them on carts and deliver them right to your house. But here, life is easier. It shortens the time we spend on cooking, especially our type of cooking. It always takes a long time to peel and cut the vegetables into small pieces, cut the meat, and cook it. I mean, women could spend from 8 o'clock in the morning until 12 or 1 o'clock just making one or two dishes, it's incredible!

In Kurdistan when it's winter, you lay all the carpets and you wear warmer clothes and close all the doors and windows. When it's summer, you have to remove all the carpets and put away all the woollen jumpers and get summer clothes out. When I came here, the first sunny day, I packed away all the warm clothes. Two days later I started getting really cold and my friend said, 'I was telling you!' and I said, 'Oh, you must be joking!' – 'No, this country has no winter or summer. It's cold all year round!'

In Britain education is good, the Health Service is good. But I found the freedom more fascinating than anything else – freedom to talk, express yourself, say what you want. In Iraq, you don't dare say anything about the president: you'd be killed. But with Britain having been a colonial power and having a big empire, you didn't create all this freedom by yourself. I mean, you have gone to far away countries, and you have learnt from their civilisation, from their freedom and from their rules. You saw and experienced a lot and fortunately you used it. Iraq had a very great civilisation. We were very powerful in science, architecture, and Britain learnt things from Islamic civilisations.

Unfortunately, what my children know about Kurds and Kurdistan and our traditions is limited to what they hear from us. They are always proud to be Kurds and proud to be Iraqi and they always look forward to going back home, although they look on Edinburgh as their second home. I think it is because when I came here they were very little and they have been educated here. I would like them to remember that they have a country to go back to and we have certain beliefs and certain traditions I would like them to practise, but I don't force them to do anything they don't believe in. I would like them to form their own ideas and beliefs.

We celebrate *Norwoz* in London, where there's a big celebration every year which we usually go to. But here in Edinburgh we don't have a very big Kurdish community, there are just a few students and we don't see much of them. There is a problem actually, because most of the Iraqi students here are with the government and could be used as informers. I mean, my husband and myself don't keep our feelings to ourselves. And I am sure our names are on their list. So you avoid trouble. Why have a headache for nothing? And it's not just us, we have to think about our families at home, so we don't feel comfortable being in touch with these students.

I went back in 1980, just before the war with Iran. People were depressed. There was plenty of money around but people were unhappy and things hadn't changed really and there was a lot of pressure. Nowadays, you see people of 30 having heart attacks. Cancer and high blood-pressure have increased because people are not allowed to speak their minds. Even in their houses they are frightened that maybe the children will hear, go outside and say something. The government have people working for them everywhere, so you can't trust anybody.

In our country the problem is the leaders. If you are a good leader you won't necessarily lose your power. If you are kind the people will like you, but if you boss them around, kill people or put them in prison, what will you gain? But our country is not fully free. We are still under Western influence and I suppose our leaders always have to be agreeable to the West. So they work more to satisfy them rather than their own people.

We want to go back, of course, but the situation isn't safe. If you don't support what the government do, you are against them, you are an enemy already to them. I think they would like to think that my husband is an enemy because he is frank and open. I mean, you can't say, 'Great, you are doing well' when they are persecuting people and thousands of people are in prison for nothing.

No, I can't see any way that there is going to be a settlement or that things are going to be any better. If you look at the Middle East it is boiling over. There is no peace anywhere. Look at Iraq, Iran, Lebanon, Palestine, Jordan, Egypt, everywhere. And unfortunately

I think the Western powers are very happy about it. They are selling their weapons, they are making huge profits and we are paying the price. I think that as long as we have the oil the problem will stay there. When it runs out maybe things will change, I don't know. No way could we go back now. I wouldn't like to go and see my children in prison because they'd spoken their minds and said what they felt about the government.

NOTES

1. The Kurdish population was divided after the First World War when national boundaries were enforced. This impeded seasonal migrations and let to detribalisation and associated problems.

2. In 1920 the Treaty of Sèvres provided for the autonomy of the Kurdish region of Iraq but this was never ratified. The Kurds have never forgotten this and there were armed risings in 1931 and 1944. After the overthrow of the monarchy in 1958 there was renewed hope for Kurdish autonomy but this was never fulfilled.

3. Due to Kurdish pressure, the new Ba'athist government, who are still in power under Saddam Hussein, agreed that Kurds would be granted autonomous status over a period of four years. In 1974 the government announced plans for very limited autonomy. The Kurds rejected this and began an uprising under Mustafa-al-Barzani.

4. In 1975 there was a dispute over the common border in the Gulf region between Iraq and Iran and this led to Iran giving substantial material support to the Iraqi Kurds. Iranian aid was curtailed with the temporary settlement of the dispute.

'The Trouble Was We Were Behind Barbed Wire'

Toni Capaldi was born in 1912, in a tiny hamlet near Picinisco in the south of Italy. He came to Edinburgh when he was three years old. His wife Lidia was born in Edinburgh of a Scottish mother and an Italian father. They have three children.

Toni There was poverty in Italy, specially in our parts, and in the summertime the men used to go out playing their little flutes to earn some money. My father's brother travelled from Picinisco right up to Russia and played before one of the Tsars and was given a gold coin. Sometimes the men used to make quite a nice little packet, other times they were robbed on the way and things like this. It was very hard in Italy – that's why we came over here.

My father came to Edinburgh because his four brothers were already here. The oldest one was Orazio, then there were Uncle Louis, Uncle Albert, Uncle Joe, then my father Serafino, but which of them came here first I don't know. We all came to Leith or Portobello. My father went into my uncle's business – an ice-cream shop. At that time they also had a fish and chip shop. He was with my uncle for about a year and then he got a shop of his own down in Great Junction Street, Leith. There were quite a few Italians already here when my mother and I arrived.

Our lives were different from those of the Scottish people – eating habits, for instance. My mother used to cook in the shop, and we'd have our dinner in the back shop or sometimes out in the front. On weekdays, but specially on Sundays, we'd have wine on the table, that was one thing. People used to make their own macaroni with flour and eggs, water, then roll it out and cut it. And a lot of them used to even make their own Italian sausages. There were one or two Italian shops that just sold pasta and Italian sausages, cheese and butter. Even before the war there was Marshalls here that used to make spaghetti and cut macaroni and it was very good too! But _ who taught them how to make it, I don't know: most likely some Italian, because you must remember we were here for years and years, long before anybody that I knew came. Take old Rizzio, for instance!

Lidia There's a cemetery down the Canongate, and there's tomb-stones there of two brothers – Italians – who were married to two sisters, and it's from about 1700 odd.

Toni On top of that, in Edinburgh, the Grassmarket was full of Italian immigrants. It was called 'Little Italy'. One woman used to go about with a hurdy-gurdy with a little monkey, and one with a little bird – a sparrow or something – that used to pick out a card for telling people's fortunes. One of these daft things, but it used to collect money and that's how they lived a lot of them, by playing accordians and that.

My mother's uncle for instance, he walked from Picinisco to Portsmouth playing the flute and dancing around. Now, he was in Portsmouth for quite a little while, and while he was there he was in digs with this Jewish family. Well, my mother's uncle always used to tell me that this Jewish man always used to try and get him to learn to make Fry's chocolate cream – you know, the Fry's chocolate cream? Well like that. And he used to say, 'Why don't you learn, Simon?' (My uncle's name was Simon Pelosi.) But he was only young and he said he had a head like stone – it just wouldn't go in you see. He came up to Glasgow for a little while, but he was only here for a month at the most and then went back to Italy.

Lidia My father came here in about 1913. He went to Glasgow to stay with his sister who had a barber's shop, and then he came to Edinburgh and opened a barber's shop in the Arcade – you know the Arcade up the Bridges? Then in 1920 he opened a business in Elm Row – Notarianni's.

He was the first ladies' hairdresser in Edinburgh. For years he was the president of the Edinburgh hairdressers; he won an awful lot of cups and medals and things like that.

Most of the Italians in Edinburgh couldn't read or write. For instance, when the travellers used to come to the shops, maybe to get an order paid or something like that, the traveller would write the cheque and the Italian just used to sign it. But my father was from Vallerotonda in Italy. He wasn't a peasant, to let you under-stand, he was educated, so the Italians asked him to be president of the Edinburgh Ice-Cream Alliance.

Likes of pre-war, the Italians never mixed with the Scottish people. They were very clannish. Anybody going out of the Italian circle was banned. My father did, he married a Scottish woman, so we didn't mix much with the Italians.

Toni She's right there, because the Italians, unfortunately, couldn't speak English. One thing they used to do, and I always remember this, they used to play cards once a week in the back shop – this was the men's enjoyment. Not for money, they didn't have any money to spend. Kelly's, a lemonade firm, used to supply them with beer. And how the men knew who was holding the card game was they'd ask the man delivering the soft drinks to the shops, 'Where's the Bass bein' delivered to?' And it'd be, 'Go to Crolla's, he's doin' it' or 'Capaldi's doin' it'. And they used to get drunk and enjoy themselves.

And while I was a boy, I remember, they'd have a dinner. My mother would cook something, Mrs Crolla would cook something, somebody else would cook something and they'd bring it together and have a meal, maybe in my parents' place, maybe at the Crolla's.

My uncle's fish and chip shop was about 50 yards from our shop, and as we were in the ice-cream trade, come the winter time my father used to say, 'Go down and help your uncle'. So I would go down and help him in his shop. And at night-time we used to always get a fish supper and a glass of Vimto. Now I hate the stuff! [laughs] I've tried it often since! But he was a wonderful cook – this is the one that went to Russia. The shop's away now, it was in the Kirkgate – Albert's. But this used to go on all the time with a lot of other people that had children: 'Go help your uncle'. And you wouldn't get any money in your pocket. Money – they didn't have it, and they expected their children to work very hard.

Lidia When Toni was young he wasn't allowed to go to school. Until he was about twelve he had to work in the shop.

Toni Well, where they came from there was a school, but very few people went to it. People wanted their children to work. My mother was at school for a week and my father maybe a little longer. Well his own father, Raphael, was a very wise man; he was really one of those men that could tell you things, but not through education.

When I was twelve years old, I wasn't well and my mother's father took me back to Picinisco – well not even to Picinisco, we didn't come from Picinisco, but from a place outside, just three or four houses away in the hills. You could say 80% of the old Edinburgh Italians were from these wee places around Picinisco. And you'll hear many stories about who was the first one of them to come over here – could be Crolla, could be a Demarco, could be a Capaldi, but I don't know who it was and we're too far gone to find out. Anyway, I stayed with my father's sister and my grandmother for about nine months. The way of life was hard. There was food, but it was just plain, what they'd dug out of the earth sort of idea. And they made their own bread and killed their sheep and chickens. There was no running water in any of the houses, you had to go to the well; no electricity, just paraffin lamps and candles; no toilets, you had to go down to the stable.

The Italian woman had a lot to do in the house, and she was the boss of the house. And when they used to go out in the fields workin', the women used to help, but they used to always go back to the house to get the food ready. And during the summertime they'd bring the food down to wherever the men were working. As I said, there were about half a dozen houses and they all used to help each other. One day they would work on my grandfather's place, and next week they'd be workin' on Mr Crolla's or Mr Boni's land and very rarely was there money transferred from hand to hand. But the one whose place was being worked, well, they supplied the food for them to eat that day.

The Edinburgh Italians used to have a picnic on the 15th of August every year. It was more or less a sports day and we would compete against Glasgow, Dundee. After the war we used always to go to Alva because it was halfway between Edinburgh and Glasgow, and also it was nice for the Aberdeen people to come down. We used to go over in buses, and bring picnics. And we used to put a table cloth down in the park and it wasn't 'yours' and 'mine', everybody's was the same. That's when the wine was flowin'. We used to have a tug o' war, and there was this cup that we used to play for – in fact my father donated a cup which was played for every year: The Serafino Capaldi Cup.

We weren't rich but – what shall I say – we had to work for our money and we didn't spend it. But when it was a wedding or an outing, then the money came out. But the Scots, unfortunately, they spend weekly. I've noticed that. Now, I used to have a lot of Scots friends and their idea of enjoyment was goin' out on a Friday night and gettin' drunk. Every week. You used to have to carry them home at nights. Not that I'm a teetotaller; I used to drink, but not as much as they did.

If I was ever late home at night my father would never let me in, but my mother or my sister used to get up and let me in. And one night I was through in Glasgow at a dance and I came home late – in the mornin'. And I'm in the kitchen goin' to make myself a cup of tea and my father came through, 'Oh, you're up early, Toni'. I says, 'Yes, I couldn't sleep last night and I'm just goin' to have a cup of tea then go down and open the shop'. So I went down and opened the shop. A few years later, he says, 'Oh, not goin' down to open the shop early these days?' I says, 'No, I can sleep now'. He says, 'You think I'm daft, eh?'

My father's English was poor – and his Italian, because he spoke a dialect, more or less the dialect that I've developed today.

Lidia – Toni's brother used to say that when his father spoke they needed an interpreter. That was right up until the day he died.

Toni So my father used to speak to me in Italian and I used to reply in English; even to this day, if somebody speaks to me in Italian, I've got to think first in English and translate it into Italian to reply. But I never did speak proper Italian anyway, I spoke a dialect. Sometimes I try to speak to some of the Italian tourists that come over here and they know right away that I'm not a proper Italian.

Lidia My father hardly ever spoke to us in Italian, he said he felt very foolish when nobody answered him. But I can understand pure Italian, though I can't understand what Toni says. You see, if my father did speak to me in Italian, he spoke pure Italian. Then I met Toni. Well, the word for match is *fiamiferro*, but Toni taught me it was called a *piceril*. So this night I was showing off about me knowing what a match was – my father took a cigarette and I says, 'Oh, you want a *piceril*'. 'Who taught you that word!' I says, 'Oh, I heard it . . .' You see, he didn't know I was going around with Toni. He says, 'Don't ever let me hear you using that word again. The word is *fiamiferro*'.

When I got engaged to Toni I was doing an Italian woman's hair – she came from a place near where my father was from – and she said, 'I don't mind who you marry as long as it's not somebody from Picinisco!' And I remember after we were married, we were staying in Italy at my aunt's house and Toni said, 'Now I'm taking you to see my aunt'. So I was all dressed in white – white shoes, white bag, white dress – and we had to drive away up this mountain. Eventually we got up to this place. And this woman came out with a cloth round her head, and one tooth, you see. And of course Toni spoke to her in Italian. And what she did was she pinched all up my arm to see if I had enough flesh on me! [laughs] So then she must have said to Toni, 'Come into the house', so we went into the house – but she had to chase all the chickens and pigs out. And I had my white dress – where could I sit, you know, because the chickens and that were everywhere. That's the type of place the Italians came from.

Toni But that was what they knew – and my aunts always made me welcome. Of course the new Italians are different altogether, and my wife's relations in Vallerotonda were different from my people. There were in a town and more educated than my father's people.

Lidia But Italy was so poor pre-war that when my father took my mother to Italy he just took her to Milan, Florence, Rome, Capri and all these places. Not to where he came from – and yet where he came from was quite respectable. He never went back to his home until 1951.

Toni They were ashamed because they didn't have much and when they came over here they saw what was here – poverty here was nothing like it was in Italy.

Lidia Toni's parents were very old-fashioned. I remember once going to see him when he was ill. We were sitting playing cards and my skirt must have gone up to my knees, and his mum came and pulled it down! And there used to be a lot of arranged marriages. They lived the same in the olden days as the Pakistanis do now, you know, with arranged marriages and what not. And with me being half-Scottish, when I got engaged to Toni there was pandemonium. From my family and his – in fact, we eloped [laughs]. That's because, first of all my father didn't have an ice-cream shop or a fish and chip shop, and secondly, I was half-Scottish. That was another objection likes of his parents had, because my father didn't come from the same village as them.

Toni Of course, that was at the beginning – but as the years went by, I and my brother and sisters mixed with the Scottish people. We sort of got away from the apron strings.

Lidia It started to change after the Second World War.

Toni I was interned for exactly three years, from the 10th of June 1940 until the 10th June 1943.

Lidia We had been to the pictures and when we came out his father's shop in Antigua Street was closed – so Toni says, 'Must go and see what's happening'. They stayed above the shop you see. So we went upstairs to see why the shop was closed, and the detectives were in the house and grabbed him! Och, well, I was a wee bit weepy at the time.

Toni As they said, they took us in for our own protection, because most of the Italian shops had been smashed. People were rioting and also trying to pinch things. But to me, the authorities seemed over-zealous because I didn't know anything about Italy. You must remember, my education was here: this was our home. Over and above that, I used to get on very well with the police, 'cos we were just around the corner from the police station. Well, the policeman said to my father, 'It's not us, Mr Capaldi, it's the law. I've got to take you in, and you'll be better off in anyway, in case the trouble starts'. So I was taken in at exactly the same time as my mother and my father.

Lidia I went home and my father says, 'Och, it'll be all right, he'll be out tomorrow'. Toni had given me the keys to the shop and, the next day, detectives came up to my mother and father's house and said, 'We believe you've got the keys to Mr Capaldi's shop'. I says, 'Yes'. They took me down to Leith in the police car – my father came with me – and when we got there there were people all round the shop so I had to walk with the detectives round about me. And when I went into the shop, the sweets and everything were all on the floor. I've never been very tall, but I was about six feet by the time I came out with all the sweets stuck on my shoes. Everything had been smashed.

And I'll tell you what happened just after that: my father got our shop in Elm Row boarded up. And people used to walk in (as I said it was a hairdresser's shop) just to see what the damage was. So I phoned Gayfield Square and they sent down a policeman to stand outside the shop. My father had taken out British nationality and that's why he wasn't interned.

Toni Quite a lot of them in the community were interned. We were taken to the police station up the High Street, and from there I was taken out to Donaldson's School which was a prisoner of war camp at that time – well, not so much prisoners of war, but merchant sailors, German sailors. Truth was, I thought we were goin' to remain there the way things looked, that we'd be all right, we'd be near our loved ones. But, eventually, after about a month, we were taken to Bury down in England.

Lidia When Toni was moved from Donaldson's he wrote a note and on the outside he wrote, 'Please take this to 7 Atholl Place and you'll get a reward'. And he threw it out of the window of the railway carriage and one of the railmen found it and brought it to me. He was just telling me that he was being moved.

Toni We didn't know where we were going, but what if I had been a spy? You know these things could . . . well, never mind. While we were at Bury some people were taken away to the Isle of Man (at that time my mother was in Saughton Prison, and from Saughton she went to the Isle o' Man – I didn't see her at all till much later). All the older men were called, and my father tried to get me to go with them. He went to the command there and said, 'Can't my son come with me?' They said, 'No, it's all right, he'll follow after you'. So I automatically took it that I was goin' to Isle o' Man because that's where I thought he was goin'. But he was on the Andorra Star and I was on the third batch to Canada.

Lidia To let you understand, this Andorra Star was an ambulance ship and it was taking an awful lot of injured Canadian soldiers back to Canada. But they were also taking internees. Of course, the ship was torpedoed and the soldiers who were below in the infirmary all went down because they couldn't escape. And I would say half the population of the Edinburgh Italians – the old Italians – also went down with the Andorra Star.

Toni It was while we were on the high sea that one of the soldiers came down and said, 'Have you heard that the Italian internees on the Andorra Star have been sunk by the Germans?' But you see, I was under the impression, like many others, that my father had already gone to the Isle o' Man. We didn't know until we were in Canada and the letters started arriving: 'Your father's lost at sea'. Eventually we just pieced everything together. A lot of my friends' fathers were on that ship, and a lot of them were lost. I got a letter from my fiancee telling me about my father being injured, and I was – how shall I say – relieved, and tears came from my eyes. And one or two o' the boys came round me, internees like myself, 'Don't tell me you've lost your father too, Toni?' I says, 'No, it's all right, my father's been saved'. But, you know . . .

Lidia When you heard about the ship, you had to go to the Swiss consulate and they had a list of people who'd been aboard. And Toni's sister had gone up there and discovered that their father was on it, but that he had been saved. He was taken to Maryhill, Glasgow, and I chummed her through to see him. And I wrote and told Toni.

Toni After a while in Canada, I was brought back to the Isle of Man. Conditions were all right there. We had the King's sweet chef cooking for us – he was interned because he was Italian. And all the other chefs in all the hotels – the Savoy, the Ritz and these places – were all Italians. And they were great characters.

My brother was British and he was interned under 18B – with Tiny Rowland. A lot of Jews were interned, Italian Jews and also German and Russian Jews but gradually they were released.

Lidia They were real artists in the camps. I have a picture, taken from a photograph of me, that was done for a packet of cigarettes. That's the sort of thing they did. And I used to get glass-blown figurines. I had about a dozen of them.

Toni Oh, we had a Venetian glass-blower, he was wonderful!

Lidia Crinolined ladies with their lace skirts and the men with their monocles and their high sticks and top hats. All in glass. Every time I went to see Toni I came home with bundles of stuff made in the camp. And, to let you understand, they learnt trades. And you could take a university degree while you were interned. And an awful lot of men came out with degrees and made names for themselves that wouldn't have if they hadn't been interned.

Toni Correspondence courses and, oh, we had teachers there, they were professors; there was even one who developed colour film while he was there . . . Even a lot of priests' novices had been taken in with us. All the priests used to say the mass for us in the Isle of Man.

Over and above that, I was well treated. The soldiers realised that we weren't fifth columnists as they'd thought at the beginning. We'd about 30 or 40 to a guest house and we'd have a house captain. At the beginning there were four of us in one room, but one by one they left and eventually I had a room to myself.

Lidia They had for free what people now pay for. I had to write to the Home Office for permission to visit. But it was great going there because there was no rationing and you could buy clothes. Maybe, in the week, we got about three visits. I'd visit Toni, and I'd go and see his mother down at Port St Mary, his brother in Peel. I was over there once, and Toni was to visit his mother and one of the soldiers said to me that they were taking such and such a train and if I caught it I'd be able to share a compartment with him. So there was him, the soldier and me all there! [laughs]

Toni Now and again you could get a transfer to another house. And we could mix with the other groups 'cos we were all behind the barbed wire along the prom. You could go from house to house, but not to the German camp, nor to the Polish Jews' camp.

We had roll call in the morning and then we used to go back inside and have our breakfast. But it was our own chefs that used to do the cooking. And some of us used to go out working on the farms and so we used to bring in chickens and maybe eggs.

Truth is I was never ill-treated, but some of them were pushed around. 'Hurry up!' 'Get moving!' Naturally some people resented bein' pushed about. But you just have to go with it. But the trouble was we were behind barbed wire and we couldn't walk out. We didn't have any freedom. The only freedom we did have was when we went to work on the farms. And some of the farmers were really rough; they wanted their shilling out of you – that's what we got

paid. I can assure you some of the Italians put their blood into it – well
the Italian boys liked to work and they were glad to get away from
the camps. Some of the guards were really rough.

   We used to have football, do a lot of sports, you know. But nothing like your freedom. The comradeship there was good though. I
mean, unfortunately some of the friends I made were English boys
or boys from way up north and I have never seen them since. Now
and again I hear of them but one by one we're disappearing.
Lidia I had a shop in Leith Street that I got from my father in 1954
and we started selling souvenirs. But then of course, Leith Street was
knocked down so he went back to his ice-cream shop down Leith.
Toni Coming back to the fold . . . But the Italian community
in Edinburgh has come out of the ice-cream trade altogether, and
the fish and chips. Some of them have become tailors, wholesale
confectioners or hairdressers like my wife and daughter.
Lidia He chased me so he could get free hair cuts for the rest of his life!
Toni They've gone out of the business altogether, maybe into
the professions. Some of them are doctors, lawyers, accountants,
engineers, nurses. Then, after the war, these new Italians came in.
Quite a big majority of the Italians in Edinburgh today came after the
Second World War. We call them the new Italians. We had it hard,
my parents had it hard, but they didn't. They already knew how to
speak English.
Lidia There's none of the original Italians left. The only one that's
alive is Toni's mother. She's 90 odd. The rest are all dead. It's a funny
thing, there was always a stigma about the Italians, the old Italians,
and then it was sort of lived down. But then the new Italians coming
over here put a stigma on us again. They saw us as sticking very
close, not having a broad outlook. They've come because there's
poverty still in Italy, but they're going back very young – in their
forties – and retiring because they've made so much money here.
Toni But as I've said already, I'm more of a foreigner over there than
I am over here.
Lidia You were very anti-Scottish when you came back from
internment. You didn't want to know the Scots. When I married
Toni after he came home I had to drop all my Scottish friends 'cos
he didn't like them.
Toni Well I was afraid. I wasn't afraid of injury but I was afraid.
Don't forget, when I came out, the war was still going on and I was
afraid for them because I was an Italian; I was an alien and if they sort
of got too friendly with me: 'Oh what's he doin' with him?' You get
narrow-minded people no matter where you go – they think things,

you know, which aren't true. But I got over it. I was more sorry for them because some of them, they just – what shall I say – missed the friendship that I had for them, because of their narrow-mindedness. But, no, no, I got on well with my Scottish friends. As I said, my three children all married Scottish people, and I still have a lot of good Scottish friends. You'll get this not only from me. We've come together. We've respected them, they've respected us.